T0358462

QUANTITY AND QUALITY IN ECONOMIC RESEARCH

Quantity and Quality in Economic Research

Studies in Applied Business Research

Volume IV

Edited by
THEOLOGOS HOMER BONITSIS
School of Management
New Jersey Institute of Technology
and The Graduate Faculty of Rutgers University

ROY CHAMBERLAIN BROWN
School of Business
Allentown College

Routledge
Taylor & Francis Group

LONDON AND NEW YORK

First published 1997 by Ashgate Publishing

Reissued 2018 by Routledge
2 Park Square, Milton Park, Abingdon, Oxon, OX14 4RN
711 Third Avenue, New York, NY 10017, USA

Routledge is an imprint of the Taylor & Francis Group, an informa business

Copyright © International Society of Statistical Science in Economics 1997

All rights reserved. No part of this book may be reprinted or reproduced or utilised in any form or by any electronic, mechanical, or other means, now known or hereafter invented, including photocopying and recording, or in any information storage or retrieval system, without permission in writing from the publishers.

Notice:
Product or corporate names may be trademarks or registered trademarks, and are used only for identification and explanation without intent to infringe.

Publisher's Note
The publisher has gone to great lengths to ensure the quality of this reprint but points out that some imperfections in the original copies may be apparent.

Disclaimer
The publisher has made every effort to trace copyright holders and welcomes correspondence from those they have been unable to contact.

ISBN 13: 978-0-367-00050-9 (hbk)
ISBN 13: 978-0-429-44479-1 (ebk)

INTERNATIONAL SOCIETY OF
STATISTICAL SCIENCE IN ECONOMICS

"Nec decipere, nec decipi."
(Neither to deceive, nor to be deceived.)

A professional society of members who are interested in the development of Statistical Science in Economics on the basis of epistemological foundations, the IS^3E was founded in 1982. Its objectives are:

To clarify statistical and mathematical applications and misapplications;

To effect a union of statisticians and economists;

To provide statistical training for business leaders and researchers in economics;

To conduct research programs on improvement of statistical methods; and

To organize seminars and conferences throughout the world.

Executive Committee

Vladislav V. Shvyrkov, Chairman

M. E. Charamko, Secretary

B. Kumar, Activities

R. C. Brown, Editor

T. H. Bonitsis, Associate Editor

REGIONAL COMMITTEES

Africa

H. David, Addis Ababa, Ethiopia
P. E. Ebelebe, Lagos, Nigeria
J. J. J. Roux, Pretoria, R.S.A.

Asia

A. Jafari-Samimi, Babolsar, Iran
M. B. Okamoto, Tokyo, Japan
A. K. Sinha, Patna, India
Y. Tingyi, Changchum, China
K. J. Yoon, Seoul, South Korea

Europe

K. Aleksandrov, Sofia, Bulgaria
A. Alonso, Madrid, Spain
O. D. Anderson, Nottingham, England
E. Gombos, Budapest, Hungary
Ch. Kamenidis, Thessaloniki, Greece
M. A. Korolev, Moscow, Russian Federation
E. Luparini, Pisa, Italy
P. S. Mortensen, Aarhus, Denmark
C. Otto, Berlin, Germany

Latin America

D. Braithwaite, Panama City, Panama
E. de Alba, Mexico City, Mexico
M. O. de Melo, Jr., Recife, Brazil
L. de Olarte, Bogota, Colombia

North America

S. Honig, New York, U.S.A.
J. C. R. Rowley, Montreal, Canada

Pacific

C. P. Fernandez, Manila, Philippines
W. D. Jones, Waverly, Australia
J. Marsh, Hilo, Hawaii

CONTENTS

CONTRIBUTORS

I. ABOUT THE EDITORS

Theologos Homer Bonitsis is an Associate Professor of Finance at the School of Management at New Jersey Institute of Technology as well as a member of The Graduate Faculty of Rutgers University. He holds a Ph.D. in Economics from The Graduate School of the City University of New York; a M.A. from Hunter College; and a B.A. degree, *magna cum laude*, from The Bernard M. Baruch College, where he received The President's Prize for Academic Excellence in Economics. He is a member of numerous professional organizations including the American Economic Association, Eastern Economic Association, Financial Management Association, and the International Trade and Finance Association. Dr. Bonitsis' main research interests center on the empirical testing of theoretical international financial and economic relationships with an emphasis on U.S. international competitiveness. Dr. Bonitsis' research findings have appeared in numerous publications, these include *The Journal of Applied Business Research, The Eastern Economic Journal, The International Journal of Finance,* and *The International Journal of Economic Studies.* He is a reviewer for several professional journals as well as a consultant in the areas of forensic economics and finance, having been qualified as an expert witness at securities arbitration and court cases. Dr. Bonitsis is listed in *Marquis Who's Who in Finance and Industry* and has been a Visiting Scholar at Columbia University in New York City.

Roy Chamberlain Brown is a member of the IS^3E Executive Committee and editor of the previous three volumes in this series. He has been a contributing editor to the Legal Briefs section of the *Journal of Marketing.* He holds an A.B. in English from Rutgers University, a M.B.A. in Marketing from Columbia University, and did doctoral level work in Communications at Temple University. Professor Brown is a member of the graduate and undergraduate marketing faculty at Allentown College, Center Valley, Pennsylvania; previously he has taught at Rutgers University, Trenton State College, Rider University, Fairleigh Dickinson University, Monmouth College, and Lehigh University. Professor Brown is Managing Principal of Chamberlain-Brown Associates, a marketing consultancy.

II. ABOUT THE CONTRIBUTORS

Petros Anastasopoulos is Associate Professor of Economics at Fairleigh Dickinson University, College of Business Administration, School of Hotel, Restaurant and Tourism Management, Teaneck-Rutherford, New Jersey. Dr. Anastasopoulos holds a Ph.D. in Economics from the New School for Social Research and teaches courses in economics, international business, and domestic and international tourism. He has published on topics such as tourism demand and tourism development in refereed journals and other publications. His research interests include tourism development in the Mediterranean and tourist demand modeling and forecasting.

Augustine Arize received his Ph.D. in Econometric Research and Management from North Texas State University and is currently a Professor of Statistics at the Department of General Business and Systems Management at Texas A&M University–Commerce. His research has appeared in numerous journals including *The International Review of Economics and Finance*, *Review of Quantitative Finance & Accounting*, *Journal of Post-Keynesian Economics*, and the *Southern Economic Journal*.

Kuang-Chian Chen is Associate Professor of Decision Sciences at Rider University in Lawrenceville, New Jersey. He has a Ph.D. in Water Resources and Operations Research from the University of Pittsburgh. Dr. Chen's articles have appeared in *Data Management*, *Journal of Small Business Management*, *Journal of Systems Management*, and *Managerial Planning*. His current research interests are in decision analysis and decision support systems.

Nikos I. Floros is a Lecturer at the Department of Economics at the University of Athens in Greece. He holds a Ph.D. degree in Economics from the London School of Economics. Dr. Floros' area is game theory and mathematical modelling in economics and finance. His research has appeared in several journals including the *Journal of Political Economy* and the *Journal of Applied Financial Economics*.

David T. Geithman is Professor of Economics at New Jersey Institute of Technology, where he served as Chair of the Department of Organizational and Social Sciences. Dr. Geithman, who received his Ph.D. in Economics from the University of Florida, has taught at several universities; they include the University of Florida, Tulane University, and Seton Hall University. He is the author, co-author, or editor of numerous books, monographs, and published professional articles. His latest book, *Economics, the Environment, and Environmentalism*, will be published by Kendall/Hunt in the Spring of 1997.

Renuka Jain completed her Ph.D. in economics at McGill University in Montreal, Canada. Dr. Jain joined the teaching faculty of Worcester State College in Massachusetts, where she is currently an Associate Professor of Business Administration and Economics. Her research interests include econometric methodology, quality improvement, information technology, and globalization.

Ioannis N. Kallianiotis is an Associate Professor of Finance at the School of Business at the University of Scranton, Scranton, Pennsylvania. Dr. Kallianiotis holds a Ph.D. in Economics from The Graduate School of the City University of New York. He specializes, and has several publications in professional journals in the area of international finance.

Krishna M. Kasibhatla, an Associate Professor and Chair of the Department of Business and Economics at Bennett College, Greensboro, North Carolina, received his Ph.D. in Economics from Rutgers University. Dr. Kasibhatla has numerous publications in professional journals in the area of international finance.

Joe H. Kim is an Associate Professor of Marketing, College of Business, Rider University. His primary teaching and research interests are in international marketing and health care marketing. His recent writings have appeared in the *Indian Journal of Economics* and *Health Services Management Research*. He received his Ph.D. from Saint Louis University.

Seth A. Kurland is a Fixed Income Analyst with Prudential Investments, a division of The Prudential. He has extensive experience in the financial services sector, having held positions at Mutual of New York, National Australia Bank, and First Fidelity Bank. Mr. Kurland has a M.B.A. from the Stern School of Business at New York University. He has also completed Level I of the Chartered Financial Analyst program.

John Malindretos has numerous publications in professional journals, books, and conference proceedings. Some of his research findings have appeared in *Advances in Quantitative Analysis of Finance and Accounting, Applied Economic Letters, Business Journal, International Journal of Finance*, and the *Journal of Business and Society.* He is currently an Associate Professor of Finance at St. John's University in New York. Dr. Malindretos has a Ph.D. in Economics from Rutgers University.

Gordian A. Ndubizu has a Ph.D. in Accounting from Temple University and is currently Professor of Accounting at Drexel University. Dr. Ndubizu has published extensively, his research has appeared in the *Journal of International Business Studies, Journal of Accounting, Auditing & Finance* and the *Review of Quantitative Finance & Accounting.* In addition, he has served on numerous editorial review boards of academic journals.

Nick L. Nicholas, Associate Professor of Marketing at St. Thomas University, Miami, Florida, has a Ph.D. in Marketing from the University of Florida. As a member of the editorial staff of *The Journal of Marketing* he has written case analyses describing the impact of legal decisions on marketing strategy. Dr. Nicholas has been a consultant and corporate trainer for a wide range of service organizations including AT&T, the International Marketing Institute, and state government agencies.

Maury R. Randall is Associate Professor of Finance at Rider University in Lawrenceville, New Jersey. He has a Ph.D. in Finance from the Graduate School of Business Administration at New York University. Dr. Randall has written articles which have appeared in a number of journals, including *Financial Management, Financial Review,* and *Financial Analysts Journal.* He is also the co-author of *Investment Analysis and Management,* published by Allyn and Bacon.

Farahmand Rezvani is Associate Professor of Economics at Montclair State University. Dr. Rezvani received his Ph.D. from The Graduate School of the City University of New York and has published in professional national and international journals such as the *Atlantic Economic Journal* and *The Journal of Mathematical Modeling* as well as a working paper by the National Bureau of Economic Research.

Luis Eduardo Rivera-Solis holds a Ph.D. in economics from the New School for Social Research and is currently an Assistant Professor of Finance at the School of Business at Dowling College, Oakdale, New York. His articles have appeared in *The Journal of Applied Business Research, International Journal of Finance,* and *The Journal of Business and Society.* Dr. Rivera has written extensively on the Spanish banking system.

J. C. Robin Rowley did his training at the London School of Economics where he received his Ph.D. in Economics. Dr. Rowley has taught at Canadian universities for more than two decades, served as a consultant to nine government agencies, and provided research findings for two major Commissions. Currently he is a Professor of Economics at McGill University in Montreal and is actively exploring econometric issues, monetary policy, and the history of economic thought.

Siamack Shojai is an Associate Professor of Economics and Finance and the former Chairperson of the Department of Economics and Finance at Manhattan College in New York. He has held teaching positions with Fordham University, where he received his Ph.D. in Economics, and Lafayette College. His articles have appeared in the *Journal of Energy and Development* and the *Journal of Economic Development.* Dr. Shojai's is the editor/co-editor of two books and is currently completing *Global Budget Deficits.*

Vladislav V. Shvyrkov was educated in the former U.S.S.R., where he obtained a M.S. in Economics from the State Financial Institute of National Economy and a D.Sc. in Statistics from Leningrad University. He is a former Chief Expert of the State Planning Committee (Gosplan) and Professor of Statistics at Moscow State University, where he developed models for forecasting consumer demand in the U.S.S.R. Dr. Shvyrkov has lectured at Humdoldt, Helsinki, Stockholm, Uppsala, Frankfurt, and Panama Universities. In the United States he has been a Research Scientist at New York University and has taught at Rider University, San Francisco State University, and the University of San Francisco. Dr. Shvyrkov has published extensively in the areas of demand analysis, applied probability, business forecasting, management science, time series analysis, and testing for data quality. He is a member of the American Statistical Association, the International Statistical Institute, Bernoulli Society, and Chairperson of the International Society of Statistical Science in Economics. Dr. Shvyrkov's biography appears in *Who's Who in the West* and *Who's Who in America*; he was nominated as International Man of the Year for 1992/93 by the International Biographic Center in Cambridge, England.

Richard Telofski, who holds a M.B.A., is currently President of The Becker Research Company, Inc., a business research firm specializing in competitor intelligence. Prior to founding this company, Mr. Telofski was a Senior Project Officer for the New Jersey Trade Adjustment Assistance Center, a unit of the U.S. Department of Commerce, which provided consulting services to American manufacturers negatively impacted by imports.

Demetri Tsanacas is Professor of Business and Chair of the Division of Business and Economics at Ferrum College, Ferrum, Virginia. Dr. Tsanacas, who holds a Ph.D. in economics from Rutgers University, has authored over a dozen published research papers, some appearing in the *Detroit Journal of Business*, *The Journal of Business Issues*, and the *Review of the Social Economy*. His areas of expertise are international trade and finance and money and banking. On two occasions Dr. Tsanacas was honored as the outstanding faculty member of the year and is the recipient of numerous grants from the Ford Foundation, the Mellon Foundation, and the Wal-Mart Foundation.

George P. Tsetsekos, Professor of Finance at Drexel University, holds a Ph.D. in Finance from the University of Tennessee. His research interests are in the areas of corporate restructuring, security offerings, and multinational financial strategy. Dr. Tsetsekos' numerous publications include articles appearing in *Financial Management, The Journal of Financial Economics,* and *The Journal of Financial Research.* He has also been involved in various specialized consulting assignments in the corporate finance area and has been retained as an advisor on matters involving corporate reorganizations and securitization.

Othmar W. Winkler is Professor Emeritus at Georgetown University's School of Business where he has been teaching for thirty-five years. His research deals with the theoretical foundation of statistics in economics and business, resulting in over forty published articles. He holds a doctorate from the Austrian School of Economics and has taught statistics since 1948. Fluent in three languages, he has taught in Venezuela, Chile and in the U.S. He is a member of ISI, the International Statistical Institute, ASA, IASS, IASI, SE-SSE, WSS, and is a regular participant in national and international statistical conferences.

INTRODUCTION

Given the frequent misapplication of statistical methodology, the International Society of Statistical Science in Economics (IS^3E) was founded by Dr. Vladislav V. Shvyrkov to "unite economists and statisticians to promote the development of statistical science in economics."

By 1984 and the First International Conference, in Princeton, New Jersey, the organization had broadened the scope of its mission, as well as its international audience, to include the proper use of statistical science in applied economics and in the other functional areas of business administration. It is this cross-disciplinary and qualitative-quantitative dimension that differentiates the International Society of Statistical Science in Economics.

The current national concern with quality control was anticipated in the title and content of the Society's research volume series, *Quantity and Quality in Economic Research*. Indeed, Volume IV continues in the tradition of the previous volumes, but reflects the growing emphasis on global issues. Hence, this volume is divided into three parts: international financial economics, statistical science and economics, and applied economics and finance. Below is a brief discussion of each paper as they appear in each section.

Part I of this volume consists of five chapters addressing timely international issues. Bonitsis and Kallianiotis address the thorny issue of the persistent U.S. trade deficit within the context of a two-country econometric model and find that a set of macroeconomic parameters have contributed to the external imbalance. This finding is in contrast to the one parameter culprit, e.g., an overvalued currency, offered by many. The paper by Kasibhatla shows that the loan pushing hypothesis does not explain international bank lending to Brazil, for he finds that syndicated Eurocurrency loans to Brazil are efficiently priced. Then the traditional theory of international finance is put under scrutiny by Malindretos and Tsanacas.

1

They comprehensively analyze the theory's shortcomings not to discredit it, but to strengthen its applicability by offering suggestions for the selection of the appropriate policies for external adjustment. The next paper by Rivera-Solis finds that multinational bank entrance decreased bank concentration in the long run in Spain. The final chapter of this section by Anastasopoulos examines alternative models of international trade within the context of international travel; this comparative study will be invaluable reading for serious researchers in tourism studies.

Three very thought provoking papers dealing with applications of statistical science are contained in Part II of this volume. First, Shvyrkov exposes the unwarranted assumption employed in the conventional statistical treatment of contingency tables; namely, that the influence of the unexplanatory factor is not significant on the relationship between two classification variables. He describes the new approach for the analysis of 2 x 2 tables derived from the New Quality Philosophy in statistics. Second, the paper by Winkler takes one on a comparative historical journey into the realm of statistics in the West and former East; one will be fascinated by how differently statistical science is treated in these two worlds. These two papers are well complemented by the third study by Jain and Rowley; their work adds to the growing body of literature that is exposing some of the haphazard axiomatic methodological basis of traditional econometrics. This paper, needless to say, is essential reading for anyone doing applied econometric work.

The third, and final, part of this volume consists of seven papers on various issues in applied economics and finance. Nicholas presents a method for comparing the effectiveness of different state lottery operations; Telofski and Kim, in contrast, construct an international service market opportunity index that can be used to rank individual countries in terms of their market potential. The following two studies deal with corporate restructuring issues: Floros and Tsetsekos find that differences across industries in abnormal returns at the announcement of stock splits are attributed to differences in cash flows and performance in each industry; Shojai and Kurland construct a logit model to predict the success of in-sample and out-of-sample takeover bids. Then a theoretical model is presented by Randall and Chen to calculate the net benefits attributed with the refinancing of a home mortgage loan. While Arize and Ndubizu conclude that the implementation of SFAS no. 52 decreased both the volatility of foreign currency translation gains/losses and analysts' forecast errors. This section closes with an examination of the economic determinants of juvenile crime in New York City by Rezvani, Bonitsis, and Geithman; this research is an application of the new economics of crime to a major U.S. metropolitan area.

It would be an act of remissness not to mention that the manuscript for this volume was prepared with the invaluable assistance of several graduate research students. They include Mr. Srinivas Munukutla and Mr. Vipul Patel as well as Mr. Mahendra Kumar Sagar and Mr. Manoj Amin–the last two individuals were indispensable in this volume's final preparation. IS^3E extends its gratitude to them. In addition, special thanks is extended to the reviewers and the members of the editorial board who so painstakingly reviewed, commented, and corrected the papers contained in this volume.

It is clear that this volume offers a cornucopia of research papers that will interest a wide and diverse audience; thus achieving IS^3E's goal of inspiring interdisciplinary research into the appropriate role statistical science has in economics and in the other functional areas of business administration.

Theologos Homer Bonitsis, Editor
School of Management
New Jersey Institute of Technology
and The Graduate Faculty of Rutgers University

Roy Chamberlain Brown, Co-editor
School of Business
Allentown College

June 1997

Part I

Issues in International Financial Economics

DECIPHERING THE U.S. TRADE DEFICIT: A TWO-COUNTRY MODEL APPROACH

Theologos Homer Bonitsis
New Jersey Institute of Technology
Ioannis N. Kallianiotis[1]
University of Scranton

I. INTRODUCTION

The U.S. merchandise trade balance has been in continuous deficit since the implementation of controlled floating exchange rates in the early 1970s. This suggests that the belief by some policymakers, Feldstein (1987), that market induced dollar exchange rate adjustments would be sufficient to achieve trade balance equilibrium were too optimistic. Recently, for example, the merchandise trade deficit widened to $166 billion in 1995 from $133 billion in 1993 and $96 billion in 1992.[2] As predicted by trade theory, imports were rising and exports were falling in the early 1980s while the dollar appreciated to reach its peak in February 1985. Subsequently, the U.S. dollar declined, stabilizing roughly for the period 1987–1993, and then depreciated with respect to major international currencies. However, throughout this period, paradoxically, the U.S. trade deficit persisted.

To explain these developments this research examines the persistence of the United States' merchandise trade deficit by empirically investigating a set of macroeconomic parameters which, as suggested by the literature, may contribute to a country's external trade imbalance. Specifically, by employing the two-country model suggested in this paper, parameter specific statistical inferences can be obtained

---

[1] The authors are grateful to Anton Boutchev and Karen Buholski for their research assistance and to Nancy Gownley for word processing assistance on previous drafts of this paper.

[2] *Federal Reserve Bulletin*, March 1996, Vol. 82, No. 3, p. A53.

to explain the trade balance between the United States and the rest of the world. The rest of the world is defined as the twelve largest trading partners of the U.S., footnote seven delineates the specifics on the construction of this composite parameter. The historical span covered in this study is for the period 1973.III–1992.II, where roman numerals refer to the particular quarter in the year. Empirical results are consistent with the thesis that the budget deficit, national debt, insufficient saving and investment levels, high monetary liquidity, high income elasticity, low unemployment, income growth, shifts in tastes towards foreign products, and a strong currency have all contributed to an increase in imports as well as to a dampening of exports. In short, a persistent trade deficit.

This paper now proceeds as follows: Section II gives a concise review of the literature. Section III presents the theoretical two-country augmented linear model employed to estimate the merchandise trade account as well as aggregate import and export functions. Next, section IV describes data sources and statistical methodology. Section V summarizes the empirical results of the model. Section VI discusses the economic implications of the empirical findings as well as presents some recommendations to remedy the persistent trade deficit. Finally, section VII presents some concluding remarks with regard to the paper's findings.

II. REVIEW OF THE LITERATURE

There is an extensive body of literature covering trade balance determination, it covers the venues of elasticity, commercial policies, and currency movements as well as forecasting. Bickerdike (1920) and Robinson (1947) initiated a theoretical approach now referred to as the elasticity approach; while Orcutt (1950) did a classic empirical research paper related to the price elasticity approach. In contrast, Johnson (1958) emphasized that the direction of the trade balance depends on the income elasticity of demand for imports. A study by Houthakker and Magee (1969) estimated elasticities under a fixed exchange rate regime; Warner and Kreinin (1983) produced elasticities estimates under floating exchange rates.

An alternative analysis by Gregory (1971) and Artus (1973) examined the link from income to trade by employing delivery lags and inventory ratios. A study by Magee (1975) argued that trade flows respond differently to secular and business cycle income changes. Khan and Ross (1975) and Dunlevy (1980) decomposed income into trend, deviation-from-trend, and changes in deviation-from-trend. Miles (1979), taking a multivariate approach, related changes in the trade balance to changes in the exchange rate, income, and the money supply.

Haynes and Stone (1983) estimated two standard demand and supply equations for trade by decomposing income into trend and deviation-from-trend, they concluded that the information of the responses is ambiguous. Marquez and McNeilly (1988) estimated income and price elasticities of non-oil exports of developing countries. Kallianiotis and Patel (1990) provided price and income elasticities between the U.S and twelve European Community (EC) countries and tested the Marshall-Lerner conditions for each EC country with respect to the United States.

Recently, Hooper (1991) ventured an explanation for the persistence of the U.S. trade deficit in the late 1980s; he attributed the deficit to a decline in the U.S. capital stock. Orr (1991), in contrast, estimates that the surge in foreign direct investment, e.g., the establishment of Japanese automobile subsidiaries, into the U.S. in the second half of the 1980s may have increased U.S. imports by about $5 billion in recent years in the form of capital equipment and components.[3] Hickok and Hung (1991–92) concluded that the factor responsible for the weak U.S. trade balance in the late 1980s is a structural change in world trade and capital stock developments. While Kallianiotis (1993) suggested a more favorable commercial policy by the U.S. towards its citizens is needed to ameliorate the trade imbalance. Others, e.g., D'Andrea Tyson (1992) and Thurow (1992) view the trade deficit has a reflection of a decline in U.S. competitiveness; Krugman (1996), however, disputes such arguments.

There are several other studies of interest. Mahdavi and Sohrabian (1993), for example, performed tests of Granger causality between the nominal and real exchange rates and the U.S. trade balance and its price and quantity components. Clarida (1994) used a two-good rational-expectations permanent-income model to estimate the parameters of the demand for imported nondurable consumer goods.

---

[3] This small increase in U.S. imports suggests, of course, that foreign direct investment did not make a substantial contribution to the net deterioration in the trade balance.

Backus, Kehoe, and Kydland (1994) documented some of the properties of short-term fluctuations in the trade balance and the terms of trade and concluded that the trade balance is uniformly countercyclical and negatively correlated with current and future movements in the terms of trade, but positively correlated with past movements.

The research presented in this study differs from other work by formulating aggregate import demand and export supply models as well as a trade balance relationship. As presented in the following section, imports, exports, and the trade balance are modelled as functions of a comprehensive set of macroeconomic variables; variables that reflect an economy's external competitive position.

III. A THEORETICAL TWO-COUNTRY MODEL

This section presents a theoretical aggregate trade demand and supply model so as to explain the recent historical stylized deficit of the U.S. trade balance. Like all theoretical paradigms, this model has several assumptions that require delineation. First, there are two countries, a home or focus country and a composite country, referred to in the literature as "the rest of the world." Second, it assumes the existence of three markets; the goods, money, and foreign exchange markets. Third, demand and supply schedules are considered relatively stable; fourth, importable and exportable are perfect substitutes for domestic and foreign commodities. Fifth, exchange rates and prices are assumed flexible, they are market determined. Sixth, expectations of the future price level play a dominant role in the determination of real income, terms of trade, volume of trade, interest rates, and policy effectiveness.

In this model, it follows that the quantity of imports demanded by the home country is equivalent to the quantity of exports supplied by the rest of the world to the home country. Hence, the function that represents the home country's demand for foreign currency is equivalent to the home country's own-currency supply to the rest of the world. A linear representation of this conceptional framework is given by equations (1)–(3), which are the aggregate import, export, and trade balance functions, respectively:

$$m_t{}^d \equiv x_t^{*s} = \alpha_0 + \alpha_1 y_t + \alpha_2 q_t + \alpha_3 p_t + \alpha_4 bd_t + \alpha_5 nd_t + \alpha_6 ta_t$$

$$+\alpha_7 m2_t + \alpha_8 s_t + \alpha_9 i_t + \alpha_{10} u_t + \sum_{i=0}^{n} \lambda_i e_{t-1} + \varepsilon_{1t}. \tag{1}$$

$$x_t{}^s \equiv m_t^{*d} = \beta_0 + \beta_1 y_t^* + \beta_2 q_t + \beta_3 p_t^* + \beta_4 bd_t + \beta_5 nd_t + \beta_6 ta_t$$

$$+\beta_7 m2_t + \beta_8 s_t + \beta_9 i_t + \beta_{10} u_t + \sum_{i=0}^{n} \mu_i e_{t-1} + \varepsilon_{2t}. \tag{2}$$

$$ta_t \equiv -ka_t = \gamma_0 + \gamma_1 y_t + \gamma_2 y_t^* + \gamma_3 q_t + \gamma_4 p_t + \gamma_5 p_t^*$$

$$+\gamma_6 bd_t + \gamma_7 nd_t + \gamma_8 ta_{t-1} + \gamma_9 m2_t + \gamma_{10} s_t$$

$$+\gamma_{11} i_t + \gamma_{12} u_t + \sum_{i=o}^{n} \zeta_i e_{t-i} + \varepsilon_{3t}. \tag{3}$$

Where m_t is the quantity of real imports, x_t represents the volume of real exports, ta_t is the real trade balance–exports less imports, ka_t is the capital account balance, y_t is real income, q_t is the terms of trade,[4] p_t is the domestic price level, bd_t is the budget deficit, nd_t represents national debt, $m2_t$ the money supply (M2), s_t is saving, i_t is investment, u_t is the unemployment rate, and e_t is the effective exchange rate in the form of direct quotes, e.g., \$/FC. The lagged values of the exchange rate in the above equations are given by the term $\sum_{i=0}^{n} z_i e_{t-i}$ for $z = \lambda$, μ, and ζ. This term is used for testing the J-curve effect on the home country's imports and exports, i.e., the intertemporal effect of a devaluation on the trade balance.[5] Employing the notation used in the literature, parameters with an asterisk denote the composite, rest of the world, foreign country; superscripts d and s denote demand and supply, respectively; subscripts t-1, t, and $t+1$ indicate the prior, current, and following time period, respectively.

---

[4] The terms of trade (q_t) are defined as follows: $q_t \equiv p_m - p_x = e_t + p_t^* - p_t$. Where p_m and p_x are the price of imports and exports, respectively.

[5] For a devaluation to have a positive effect on the trade balance, the Marshall-Lerner condition must hold: $|\varepsilon_p^*| + |\varepsilon_p| > 1$. In short, the direct effect of a currency devaluation on the trade balance will be positive only when the absolute sum of the price elasticities of domestic exports and imports exceed unity.

The *a prior* signs of the coefficients for the aggregate import function are: $\alpha_1 > 0$, $\alpha_2 < 0$, $\alpha_3 > 0$, $\alpha_4 > 0$, $\alpha_5 > 0$, $\alpha_6 > 0$, $\alpha_7 > 0$, $\alpha_8 < 0$, $\alpha_9 < 0$, $\alpha_{10} < 0$, and $\lambda_i < 0$. Similarly, the *ex ante* signs of the aggregate export equation's parameters are: $\beta_1 > 0$, $\beta_2 > 0$, $\beta_3 > 0$, $\beta_4 < 0$, $\beta_5 < 0$, $\beta_6 < 0$, $\beta_7 < 0$, $\beta_8 > 0$, $\beta_9 > 0$, $\beta_{10} < 0$, $\mu_i > 0$. Finally, the *a prior* signs of the trade balance function's parameters are as follows: $\gamma_1 < 0$, $\gamma_2 > 0$, $\gamma_3 > 0$, $\gamma_4 < 0$, $\gamma_5 > 0$, $\gamma_6 < 0$, $\gamma_7 < 0$, $\gamma_8 > 0$, $\gamma_9 < 0$, $\gamma_{10} > 0$, $\gamma_{11} > 0$, $\gamma_{12} > 0$, $\zeta_i > 0$. It is essential to emphasize that the traditional and monetary approaches to the balance of trade do not necessarily agreed on the affect of each parameter on the trade balance. An empirical country case study by Bonitsis, Kasibhatla, and Malindretos (1995) extensively discusses this point.

IV. DATA AND METHODOLOGY

The data for this study come from three major sources: (1) *Survey of Current Business*, U.S. Department of Commerce, (2) *Main Economic Indicators*, Organization for Economic Cooperation and Development (OECD), and (3) *International Financial Statistics*, International Monetary Fund (IMF). All of the data are reported on a quarterly basis covering the historical period 1973.III to 1992.II. The home country in this study is the United States. The composite country, referred to as the rest of the world, consists of a trade weighted average of the twelve major trading partners of the United States. In essence, those countries for which the U.S. has the highest volume of trade; where total trade volume is defined to be the sum of exports and imports, $(T = X + M)$.[6] The trade data for the construction of the weights are from various volumes of the IMF's *Direction of Trade Statistics Yearbook* for the period 1981–1987.[7]

The empirical methodology of this research is to obtain econometric estimations for the model presented in section III, this will determine which *ex ante* parameters explain the persistence of the U.S. trade deficit. These parameters are, of course, all the independent

---

[6] These countries and their weights are: Canada ($W_C = .329$), Japan ($W_J = .268$), Germany ($W_G = .09$), United Kingdom ($W_{UK} = .084$), France ($W_F = .048$), Italy ($W_I = .041$), the Netherlands ($W_N = .037$), Belgium-Luxembourg ($W_{B+L} = .026$), Australia ($W_A = .025$), Switzerland ($W_{SW} = .02$), Spain ($W_S = .017$), and Sweden ($W_{SD} = .016$).

[7] The weight of country j and the composite world variable are as follows: $W_j = T_j / \sum_{j=1}^{12} T_j$ and $\sum_{j=1}^{12} W_j = 1$; i.e., $Y^* = \sum_{j=1}^{12} W_j Y_j$.

variables in equations (1)–(3). The empirical equations are specified in double natural log form, this implies that all regression coefficients are elasticities, and are estimated using ordinary least squares (OLS) with the Time Series Processor (TSP) software package. The estimated equations appear in Tables 1, 2, and 3 of the following section. To complement these empirical findings, Granger (1969) causality tests are conducted among several of the trade account parameters to determined the direction of their causal relationship. These results are reported in Appendix A.

For further clarification, it is noteworthy to mention how two specific parameters are empirically defined and constructed. First, changes in tastes and preferences are embodied in the model by including a time trend variable. Second, the effective exchange rate for this study is calculated as an index that includes only the currencies of the major industrial countries as reported in *International Financial Statistics*.

V. EMPIRICAL RESULTS

This section presents the econometric estimations for equations (1)–(3) by employing a quarterly data base for the period 1973.III–1992.II. The results for the U.S. demand for imports, equation (1), are given in Table 1. Similarly, estimations for the U.S. supply of exports function, equation (2), are presented in Table 2. Finally, Table 3 relates the regression findings for the U.S. trade balance model, i.e., equation (3). All reported results are for alternative specifications of each model. In general, econometric results are consistent with the *a prior* sign and statistical significance of the various parameters on their respective endogenous parameters, i.e., either real imports, exports, and/or the trade balance, with R^2s, in general, in excess of ninety-five percent.

With regard to the import function, Table 1 relates that real domestic income, the domestic price level, the national debt and deficit, the trade account balance, the money supply, investment, and unemployment all are statistically significant in explaining real imports for the historical period under review. There is also, but not reported, statistical significance between real imports and tastes, represented by a time trend variable, as well as the effective exchange rate; with the signs of the current and several lagged effective exchange rates

13

Table 1
Aggregate Import Function

$$m_t^d = \alpha_0 + \alpha_1 y_t + \alpha_2 q_t + \alpha_3 p_t + \alpha_4 bd_t + \alpha_5 nd_t + \alpha_6 ta_t$$

$$+\alpha_7 m2_t + \alpha_8 s_t + \alpha_9 i_t + \alpha_{10} u_t + \sum_{i=0}^{n} \lambda_i e_{t-i} + \rho_1 \varepsilon_{t-1} + \rho_3 \varepsilon_{t-3} + \eta_{1t}.$$

α_0	–	8.578* (.387)	–	3.709* (1.453)	−2.546* (1.238)	3.376* (1.448)
α_1	1.264* (.037)	–	1.007* (.107)	.423* (.233)	1.278* (.180)	.469* (.232)
α_2	–	–	−.111 (.144)	–	–	–
α_3	–	1.077* (.296)	–	–	–	–
α_4	.021 (.015)	.027* (.013)	−.004 (.017)	–	–	–
α_5	–	–	.201* (.075)	–	–	–
α_6	−.398* (0.78)	−.370* (.065)	–	–	–	–
α_7	–	−.434* (.203)	–	–	–	–
α_8	.008 (.024)	–	–	$-.032^N$ (.024)	$-.027^R$ (.026)	–
α_9	–	–	–	$.482^{*N}$ (.078)	$.393^{*R}$ (.112)	.451* (.076)
α_{10}	−.031* (.014)	−.075* (.010)	–	–	–	–
λ_0	–	–	–	–	–	–
ρ_1	.845* (.052)	.760* (.064)	.989* (0.19)	.869* (.086)	.879* (0.94)	.873* (.085)
ρ_2	–	–	–	–	–	–
ρ_3	–	–	−.199* (.080)	−.199* (.077)	−.139* (.073)	−.199* (0.77)
R^2	.982	.987	.966	.980	.973	.979
$S.E.$	.037	.031	.047	.039	.042	.039
$D-W$	1.731	2.242	1.926	2.176	2.095	2.168
$L(.)$	143.522	153.850	104.446	138.658	127.634	137.643
$F_{K-1,N-K}$	529.164	865.452	323.000	667.594	460.130	823.378

*Statistically significant up to the 10% level, standard errors are in parentheses, N and R are nominal and real variables, respectively. The empirical results are for alternative specifications of the model. See text for definitions of variables.

Table 2
Aggregate Export Function

$$x_t^s = \beta_o + \beta_1 y_t^* + \beta_2 q_t + \beta_3 p_t^* + \beta_4 bd_t + \beta_5 nd_t + \beta_6 ta_t + \beta_7 m2_t + \beta_8 s_t$$

$$+ \beta_9 i_t + \beta_{10} u_t + \beta_{15} trend + \sum_{i=0}^{n} \mu_i e_{t-1} + \rho_1 \varepsilon_{t-1} + \rho_2 \varepsilon_{t-2} + \rho_3 \varepsilon_{t-3} + \eta_{2t}.$$

β_0	–	6.535* (1.148)	4.401* (1.785)	5.321* (2.347)	8.517* (1.580)	6.336* (.950)
β_1	1.154* (.351)	.722* (.333)	1.480* (.489)	1.128* (.440)	.129 (.322)	.780* (.317)
β_2	−.933* (.469)	–	–	–	–	–
β_3	2.661* (.569)	1.203* (.364)	–	–	–	1.585* (.325)
β_4	.031* (.015)	.031* (.013)	.004 (.017)	−.007 (.014)	–	.028* (.013)
β_5	.764* (.339)	–	−.229* (.124)	−.201 (.335)	–	–
β_6	.720* (.077)	.653* (.063)	–	.474* (.090)	–	.628* (.060)
β_7	−1.144* (.551)	−.813* (.237)	–	–	–	−.938* (.247)
β_8	.005 (.022)	–	–	–	−.004 (.018)	–
β_9	–	.195* (.104)	–	–	.136* (.080)	–
β_{10}	−.077* (.014)	−.048* (.014)	–	–	–	−.066* (.011)
β_{15}	−.036* (.008)	–	–	.007 (.011)	–	–
μ_0	1.056* (.485)	.103 (.089)	–	–	–	–
ρ_1	.597* (.138)	.620* (.126)	.871* (.061)	.832* (.071)	1.172* (.063)	.590* (.126)
ρ_2	.327* (.157)	.307* (.139)	–	–	–	.306* (.137)
ρ_3	−.402* (.142)	−.331* (.120)	–	–	−.185* (.060)	−.255* (.121)
R^2	.954	.975	.882	.923	.964	.973
S.E.	.033	.030	.048	.039	.033	.030
$D-W$	2.088	2.137	1.806	1.698	2.050	2.073
$L(.)$	131.833	158.815	102.758	116.116	145.318	156.813
$F_{K-1,N-K}$	69.558	215.184	106.901	110.745	347.084	256.751

*Statistically significant up to the 10% level, standard errors are in parentheses. See text for definitions of variables.

being positive, this is suggestive of a J-curve effect. In contrast, the export function results reported in Table 2 indicate that real foreign income, the terms of trade, the foreign price level, the national debt and deficit, the trade balance, unemployment rate, tastes, and the exchange rate are statistically significant in explaining real imports.

Finally, the trade balance results in Table 3 suggest that foreign real income, the terms of trade, domestic and foreign price levels, the national debt and deficit, the immediate past trade balance, the money supply, saving, investment, unemployment, and tastes all have statistically significant explanatory power. In addition, although not reported here, the effective exchange rate has a significant effect on the trade account, the coefficient of the current effective exchange rate was negative. This suggests a possible weak J-curve effect.

VI. ECONOMIC IMPLICATIONS

This paper finds that the factors primarily responsible for the persistent U.S. trade deficit are the budget deficit, national debt, low saving and hence low capital investment, monetary liquidity, dependence on foreign investment, relative high substitutability between domestic and foreign goods, high income elasticity for imports, low unemployment, relative high real income growth, a shift of tastes towards foreign products, a strong dollar, inadequate "rest of the world" real income growth, and a decline in the proclivity of foreigners for U.S. products.

The income elasticity for U.S. imports is between 1.120 and 1.626, but the same elasticity for the "rest of the world" is between .722 and 1.480. This is an indication that Americans prefer foreign over domestic products. The price elasticities are for the U.S. between -.042 and -.191[8] and for the "rest of the world" between -.642 and -.933; this indicates that there is no price effect for U.S. imports, but there is foreign price sensitivity for imports. The sum of the two elasticities is between -.684 and -1.124; hence, the Marshall-Lerner condition is, allowing for measurement errors, roughly satisfied. A devaluation of the dollar may marginally improve the trade account.[9]

---

[8] These two elasticities are, however, statistically insignificant.

[9] Further, Granger causality tests, reported in Appendix A of this paper, indicate that the effective exchange rate causes the trade account, i.e., dollar depreciation improves the trade balance.

Table 3

Trade Balance Function:
Empirical Results for Alternative Specifications

$$ta_t = \gamma_0 + \gamma_1 y_t + \gamma_2 y_t^* + \gamma_3 q_t + \gamma_4 p_t + \gamma_5 p_t^* + \gamma_6 bd_t + \gamma_7 nd_t + \gamma_8 ta_{t-1}$$

$$+\gamma_9 m2_t + \gamma_{10} s_t + \gamma_{11} i_t + \gamma_{12} u_t + \gamma_{15} trend + \sum_{i=o}^{n} \zeta_i e_{t-i} + \epsilon_{3t}.$$

γ_0	17.688*	4.512	10.135*	10.313*
	(6.753)	(4.807)	(5.794)	(3.785)
γ_1	.771	−.535	.406	−.319
	(.990)	(.811)	(.661)	(.758)
γ_2	.071	1.418*	–	–
	(.898)	(.710)		
γ_3	−.013	.327*	–	.362*
	(.132)	(.113)		(.110)
γ_4	2.970*	–	.794	–
	(1.556)		(.726)	
γ_5	−6.438*	–	–	–
	(2.097)			
γ_6	−.029	−.040*	−.056*	−.026
	(.034)	(.020)	(.018)	(.016)
γ_7	−2.094*	−.736	−.497	−1.040*
	(.752)	(.479)	(.371)	(.468)
γ_8	–	–	.336*	–
			(.102)	
γ_9	−1.010	–	−2.311*	–
	(1.007)		(.547)	
γ_{10}	.013	.150*	.096*	.166*
	(.053)	(.047)	(.036)	(.047)
γ_{11}	.241	−.529*	−.350*	−.549*
	(.265)	(.152)	(.149)	(.153)
γ_{12}	.108*	.025	.022	–
	(.036)	(.018)	(.022)	
γ_{15}	.122*	.020	.059*	.035*
	(.024)	(.014)	(.016)	(.012)
R^2	.961	.926	.962	.919
S.E.	.044	.061	.046	.062
$D - W$	2.047	1.126	2.134	1.074
$L(.)$	96.113	91.179	111.521	88.593
$F_{K-1,N-K}$	50.242	72.137	92.279	87.990

*Statistically significant up to the 10% level, standard errors are in parentheses. See text for definitions of variables.

These findings suggest that the United States appears to have experienced a decline in competitiveness due to a low saving rate (and consequently low capital investments), low foreign income effect and changes in foreign tastes away from American products. On the U.S. export side, increased foreign competition in high technology applications and goods may have reduced the foreign demand for U.S. manufactured (capital) goods exports.[10]

To summarize, several important implications may be drawn from the findings of this research, these are:

(1) The trade balance will improve with declines in the budget deficit and reductions in the national debt.

(2) The trade account deficit implies that spending exceeds income (production) in the U.S. economy. This suggests that external imbalances have a macroeconomic aspect and their solution must encompass policies that restore the balance between income and spending.

(3) The saving rate and investment from domestically produced capital goods must increase so as to augment production, relative competitive position, and consequently exports.

(4) The trade balance will improve with further depreciation of the dollar.

(5) The trade balance will significantly improve when relative composite foreign growth exceeds domestic growth.

(6) Continued domestic consumption proclivity for foreign products will impede improvements in the trade account.

(7) With the growing global integration of national economies, U.S. products are likely to face greater competition at any given exchange rate, price level, and income growth rate.

It is important to emphasize that saving in the U.S. has undergone a dramatic downturn since the mid-1980s. The net national saving rate, which measures the fraction of the net national product that is not consumed and that can be devoted to the formation of new capital, averaged 9.0 percent in the 1960s, fell to 8.5 percent in the 1970s, and declined to 5.8 percent in the first half of the 1980s. The average for 1985–89 was a paltry 3.6 percent.[11] This development

---

[10] Related to this point is a study by Bonitsis (1995) that suggests that there is no long-term equilibrium, cointegration, relationship between defense and non-defense R&D expenditures and U.S. export performance.

[11] See *Economic Trends*, Federal Reserve Bank of Cleveland, August 1993, p. 13.

is disturbing because a current low saving rate implies a smaller future capital stock, lower productivity and external competitiveness as well as persistent, and perhaps higher, trade deficits. As a result future capital per worker and hence productivity and real wages will be lower than they otherwise would be, this has obvious adverse implications for the future standard of living. However, since countries can borrow from abroad, a low domestic saving rate may not constrain domestic investment in the short run, but capital inflows improve the capital account only to deteriorate the current account. Indeed, the results of this research indicate a positive effect between investment and imports, but a negative relationship between investment and the trade balance. This may reflect that a sizable amount of U.S. investment comes from direct foreign investment activity, but is recorded as imports of manufacturing goods.

Dependence on foreign investment for sustaining high domestic capital formation has its risks; for international capital flows respond fairly rapidly to new opportunities and to changes in relative rates of return. Foreign capital inflows did augment net domestic investment in the 1980s, but cannot do so indefinitely. Indeed, net foreign investment rates in the U.S. plummeted during the late 1980s and into the early 1990s. In short, a low net national saving rate may constrain domestic investment and thus adversely affect social welfare.

VII. CONCLUDING REMARKS

In this study an augmented demand for imports, supply of exports, and trade account models have been presented as a tool to investigate the persistence of the U.S. trade deficit for the historical period 1973.III to 1992.II. The sharp deterioration in the U.S. trade balance during this period is attributable, among other factors, to budgetary deficits[12] and national debt, low saving and investment levels, a favorably change in tastes by domestic consumers for foreign products, a greater U.S. income elasticity of demand for imports relative to the foreign income elasticity of demand for U.S. exports, and to a strong U.S. currency. These results suggest that there have been structural

---

[12] This is the dual deficit hypothesis: large budgetary deficits crowd out domestic saving which increases domestic interest rates, this increases the foreign portfolio demand for U.S. dollars ensuring a capital inflow and capital account improvement which results in a current account deterioration.

changes in the U.S. that have adversely affected the U.S. trade balance for the period under review. Indeed, over all, the model fits the trade data very well with robust R^2s and statistically significant regression coefficients that are consistent, in general, with the theory presented in this paper. Hence, the model in this study can be employed to obtain out-of-sample predictions with regard to the future path of the U.S. trade account conditional on the expected magnitudes of the independent parameters.

Many economists support the conclusion that structural shifts in U.S. trade relations in the 1980s have led to a deterioration in the U.S. trade position, but few suggest drastic corrective measures. Trade issues are politically controversial and hence are frequently avoided by well-intended individuals. Who will be affected by an ostrich-like policy stance? One can argue the entire country through a potential deterioration in the standard of living.

REFERENCES

Artus, J. R., "The Short-Run Effects of Domestic Demand Pressure on Export Delivery Delays for Machinery," *Journal of International Economics* (February 1973), Vol. 3, No. 1, pp. 21–36.

Backhus, D. K., Kehoe, P. J., and Kydland, F. E., "Dynamics of the Trade Balance and the Terms of Trade: The J-curve?," *American Economic Review* (1994), Vol. 84, No. 1, pp. 84–103.

Bickerdike, C. F., "The Instability of Foreign Exchange," *Economic Journal* (1920), Vol. 30, No. 117, pp. 118–22.

Bonitsis, Theologos Homer, "Research and Development Expenditures, Export Performance, and United States' International Competitiveness," Chapter 8 in *International Finance in the New World Order*, H. Peter Gray and Sandra C. Richard, editors, (Oxford, U.K.: Pergamon Press, Elsevier Science Ltd., 1995), pp. 103–117.

Bonitsis, Theologos Homer, Kasibhatla, Krishna M., and Malindretos, John, "A Comparison of the Monetary and Traditional Approaches to International Competitive Adjustment: The Case of South Korea," *Journal of International Economic Studies* (March 1995), No. 9, pp. 123–138.

Clarida, Richard H., "Cointegration, Aggregate Consumption, and the Demand for Imports: A Structural Economic Investigation," *American Economic Review* (1994), Vol. 84, No. 1, pp. 298–308.

D'Andrea Tyson, Laura, *Who's Bashing Whom: Trade Conflict in High-Technology Industries* (Washington, D.C.: Institute for International Economics, 1992), pp. xviii + 324.

Dunlevy, J. A., "A Test of the Capacity Pressure Hypothesis within a Simultaneous Equation Model of Export Performance," *Review of Economics and Statistics* (1980), Vol. 62, No. 1, pp. 131–135.

Feldstein, Martin, "Correcting the Trade Deficit," *Foreign Affairs* (Spring 1987), Vol. 65, No. 4, pp. 795–806.

Granger, C. W., "Investigating Casual Relations by Econometric Cross-Spectral Methods," *Econometrica* (1969), Vol. 37, No. 3, pp. 424–438.

Gregory, R. G., "United States Imports and Internal Pressure of Demand: 1948-1968," *American Economic Review* (1971), Vol. 61, No.1, pp. 28–47.

Haynes, S. and Stone, J., "Secular and Cyclical Responses of U.S. Trade to Income: An Evaluation of Traditional Models," *Review of Economics and Statistics* (1983), Vol. 65, No. 1, pp. 87–95.

Hickok, Susan and Hung, Juann, "Explaining the Persistence of the U.S. Trade Deficit in the Late 1980s," *Quarterly Review* (Winter 1991–92), Federal Reserve Bank of New York, Vol. 16, No. 4, pp. 29–46.

Hooper, Peter, "Comment," *International Adjustment and Financing: The Lessons of 1985-91*, C. Fred Bergsten, editor (Washington, D.C.: Institute for International Economics, 1991), pp. 103–112.

Houthakker, H. S. and Magee, S. P., "Income and Price Elasticities in World Trade," *Review of Economics and Statistics* (1969), Vol. 51, No. 2, pp. 111–125.

Johnson, H. G., *International Trade and Economic Growth* (Cambridge, Massachusetts: Harvard University Press, 1958).

Kallianiotis, I. N., "Trade Deficit Persistence, Currency Devaluation, and Welfare Policy: An Empirical Approach and a Provlepsis," University of Scranton, School of Management, *Research Report Series No. 9303* (December 1993), pp. 1–39.

Kallianiotis, I. N., and Patel, Ashish, "Income and Price Elasticities: U.S. Imports from and Exports to E.C. Countries," *Northeast Decision Sciences Institute 1990 Proceedings* (April 1990), Paul Mangiameli, editor, pp. 115–117.

Khan, M. S. and Ross, K. Z., "Cyclical and Secular Income Elasticities of the Demand for Imports," *Review of Economics and Statistics* (1975), Vol. 57, No. 3, pp. 357–361.

Krugman, Paul, *Pop Internationalism*, (Cambridge, Massachusetts: The MIT Press, 1996), pp. xiv + 221.

Magee, S. P., "Prices, Incomes, and Foreign Trade," in *International Trade and Finance: Frontiers for Research*, Peter Kenen, editor, (Cambridge, England: Cambridge University Press, 1975), pp. 175–252.

Mahdavi, Saeid and Sohrabian, Ahmad, "The Exchange Value of the Dollar and the U.S. Trade Balance: An Empirical Investigation Based on Cointegration and Granger Causality Tests," *Quarterly Review of Economics and Finance* (1993), Vol. 33, No. 4, pp. 343–358.

Marquez, J. and McNeilly, C., "Income and Price Elasticities for Exports of Developing Countries," *Review of Economics and Statistics* (May 1988), Vol. 70, No. 2, pp. 306–314.

Miles, M. A., "The Effects of Devaluation on the Trade Balance and the Balance of Payments: Some New Results," *Journal of Political Economy* (1979), Vol. 87, No. 3, pp. 600–620.

Orcutt, Guy H., "Measurement of Price Elasticities in International Trade," *Review of Economics and Statistics* (1950), Vol. 32, No. 2, pp. 117–121.

Orr, James, "The Trade Balance Effects of Foreign Direct Investment in U.S. Manufacturing," *Quarterly Review* (1991), Federal Reserve Bank of New York, Vol. 16, No. 3, Summer, pp. 63–76.

Robinson, Joan, "The Foreign Exchanges," (1947) reprinted in *Collected Economic Papers, Joan Robinson, Volume Four* (Cambridge, Massachusetts: The MIT Press, 1980), pp. 212–228.

Thurow, Lester C., *Head to Head: The Coming Economic Battle Among Japan, Europe, and America* (New York, New York: Morrow Press, 1992), pp. 336.

Warner, D. and Kreinin M. E., "Determinants of International Trade Flows," *Review of Economics and Statistics* (1983), Vol. 65, No. 1, pp. 96–104.

APPENDIX A

GRANGER ECONOMETRIC TESTS OF CAUSALITY

To complement the theoretical model and empirical findings of this research bidirectional Granger causality tests are conducted among the various parameters discussed in this research. Succinctly stated, by way of an example, Granger causality may be tested with equation system (A1)–(A2):

$$ta_t = \alpha + A(L)ta_t + B(L)bd_t + \varepsilon_{1t}. \qquad (A1)$$

$$bd_t = \beta + \Gamma(L)ta_t + \Delta(L)bd_t + \varepsilon_{2t}. \qquad (A2)$$

Where A(L), B(L), Γ(L) and Δ(L) are the polynomials in the lag operator. Parameter bd causes ta if $B(L) \neq 0$, while ta causes bd if $(L) \neq 0$. If both conditions hold, then bidirectional causality between the parameters exists; if one condition holds then there is only unidirectional causation. Empirically, a Wald test is performed to test the null hypothesis of no causation between hypothesized causal and caused parameters. Given the limitations of space, test results for all parameters are not reported here, but are available from the authors as well as in Kallianiotis (1993). The reported Wald test findings are for bidirectional causality between the trade balance and the following parameters: national budget deficit and debt, nominal (ns) and real saving (rs), nominal (ni) and real investment (ri), and the effective exchange rate.

Turning to the empirical findings, Table A1 reports Granger causality tests between the various variables under study. These results indicate that the budget deficit, the national debt, and the effective exchange rate Granger-cause the trade account deficit. Interestingly, however, there is no Granger-causality between saving and the trade account; real investment, in contrast, causes the trade account. Specifically, an increase in U.S. investment deteriorates the trade account, this may be indicative of the fact that some U.S. investment goods are imported, e.g., direct foreign investments. These findings, in general, are consistent with the empirical results discussed in the body of the paper; namely, the model's explanatory parameters affect the trade account balance.

Table A1

Granger Econometric Causality Tests for the Trade Account: Bidirectional Results with Alternative Lag Specifications

Lag lengths	$bd \to ta$ / $ta \to bd$	$nd \to ta$ / $ta \to nd$	$ns \to ta$ / $ta \to ns$	$rs \to ta$ / $ta \to rs$	$ni \to ta$ / $ta \to ni$	$ri \to ta$ / $ta \to ri$	$e \to ta$ / $ta \to e$
1	3.807*	2.007	.026	1.723	.090	.416	15.828*
	1.195	4.093*	.515	.857	3.084*	.210	7.261*
2	1.807	1.358	1.164	1.113	1.756	2.609*	8.915*
	.933	2.517*	.273	.524	1.482	.262	2.135
3	2.736*	3.078*	1.261	.934	1.398	2.481*	6.541*
	.933	1.813	.177	.300	1.505	.535	2.220*
4	1.963	2.711*	.962	.705	1.083	1.904	4.541*
	.825	1.375	.478	.462	1.087	.500	1.056
5	4.394*	4.479*	.935	.598	1.064	1.467	3.421*
	.716	1.267	.378	.396	.882	.596	.777
6	4.121*	4.380*	.787	.462	1.137	1.101	2.730*
	.674	1.021	.638	.978	.705	.489	.845
7	3.662*	6.624*	.934	.521	.940	.872	2.178*
	.514	.766	.392	.532	.742	.456	.586
8	4.363*	5.952*	.868	.522	.921	2.036*	1.775*
	.689	.558	.495	.561	.649	.444	.369
9	4.156*	5.064*	.764	.446	.842	1.891*	1.789*
	.714	.359	.441	.494	.566	.391	.344
10	3.760*	4.321*	.745	.391	.688	1.466	1.592
	.691	.304	.414	.529	.567	.471	.330
11	3.478*	5.530*	.911	.438	.673	1.170	1.481
	.670	.350	.375	.417	.597	.399	.289
12	3.099*	4.881*	.800	.410	1.000	1.097	1.437
	.804	.324	.380	.447	.533	.340	.311
13	3.073*	4.924*					
	.788	.354					
14	3.203*	4.406*					
	.692	.588					
15	3.615*	4.292*					
	.523	.639					

*Statistically significant up to the 10% level; $\to$ implies Granger-causes. See text for definitions of variables.

2

PRICING OF SYNDICATED EUROCURRENCY LOANS TO BRAZIL

Krishna M. Kasibhatla
Bennett College

I. INTRODUCTION

Various hypotheses have emerged in the wake of the international debt crisis. The most popular among them was the "loan pushing" hypothesis. Pushing loans implies a drastic softening of terms relative to the expectations of the potential borrowers. According to this view, spreads charged on bank loans to LDCs bear no correspondence to the risks associated with such lending. Proponents of this "doctrine," e.g., Darity (1986), suggest that banks have engaged in self-victimization by advancing credit to foreign borrowers who have less than a prayer of making repayment.

One way to examine the validity of the "loan pushing" hypothesis is to first conduct an empirical investigation with reference to a major LDC borrower and see if spreads charged on the loans to that country bear any relationship to the risks associated with those loans; secondly, examine whether or not the spreads charged reflect efficient pricing of lending risks. These two aspects are examined in this paper. The country selected for this investigation is Brazil, and the market is the syndicated eurocurrency market.

Section II deals with an empirical model to investigate whether spreads charged on syndicated eurocurrency loans to Brazil bear any correspondence to the risks associated with such lending during the period 1966–1985. In Section III the analysis is extended to examine whether or not the actual spreads charged reflect efficient pricing of country lending risks. This analysis is important because the "loan pushing" hypothesis also seems to imply that the syndicated eurocurrency market is consistently inefficient. Section IV offers a summary and the conclusions of this research paper.

II . RELATIONSHIP BETWEEN SPREADS AND RISKS

(A) Lenders' Perception of Risks

Since a good deal has already been written on this aspect, I will confine only to the popular response of the multinational banks to the question: On what basis lenders formulate their perceptions of lending risks? On several occasions banks have stated that they take into account various factors relating to the country concerned before they make the decision to lend to that country. A majority of these factors deal with quantifiable variables dealing with the overall economic performance of the country in general, and its external debt situation, in particular. Further, banks have argued that spreads charged on loans to different groups of country-borrowers reflect the differences in the perceived risks. Multinational banks deny the allegation that they have "pushed" poor quality loans.

(B) The Empirical Model

There are two popular conceptual approaches to measuring risks associated with lending to LDCs, namely, the debt service approach, and the monetary approach. The major focus of the first approach is the debt service charge relative to a country's export earnings and the fluctuations in these earnings. The monetary approach looks at the borrowing country's domestic monetary and credit policies, rather than the structural variables.

In examining the lending risks it is important to take into account both the structural and monetary indicators of risk. The risk indicators selected for this study include the rate of inflation in Brazil, its debt service ratio (ratio of interest and amortization payments on outstanding debt to export earnings), and the ratio of current account balance to gross domestic product (GDP). The selection of these indicators is not entirely subjective but based on ample empirical evidence contained in some of the recent studies on this subject, Sergen (1976) and Frank and Cline (1971).

It is postulated that the return (spread) on eurocurrency loans depends on the cost of funds to the lender and on the degree of risk associated with the loans. The general expression for the regression model is:

$$SPRD = f(LIBOR, IR, DSR, CAB). \tag{1}$$

Where $SPRD$ is the premium over the London interbank offer rate

($LIBOR$) , IR is the inflation rate in Brazil, DSR is the debt service ratio, and CAB is the ratio of current account balance to GDP.

It is hypothesized that the spread, the dependent variable, is a linear function of the cost of funds, and the three country risk indicators. The equation estimated has the following form:

$$Y = \alpha + \beta_1 X1 + \beta_2 X2 + \beta_3 X3 + \beta_4 X4 + \epsilon. \tag{2}$$

Where Y is spread, and $X1$ through $X4$ are $LIBOR$, IR, DSR and CAB, respectively, and ϵ is the error term.

In estimating the equation (2) the three country risk variables, IR, DSR, and CAB are lagged one time period, i.e., one year, because this is the information lending institutions will have when formulating their lending decisions in the current period, see for example Haegele (1980). The regression coefficients are estimated using the OLS method for the data on all the variables for the time period 1966–1985.

It is anticipated that the relationship between LIBOR and the spread is negative. Goodman (1980) argues that participating banks in the syndicated eurocurrency market can lower spreads when the LIBOR rises and still maintain their target return on equity. When nominal interest rates go up, the opportunity cost of holding required reserves for banks operating in regulated markets in the industrialized countries will go up. Banks in the euromarket are not required by law to keep reserves against their deposits. As the gap between the opportunity cost in the eurocurrency market and the regulated market widens, domestic banks will shift funds into the euromarket, and with unchanged demand for funds in the euromarket and with these additional funds, the spreads will have to decline. So higher nominal rates ($LIBOR$) imply lower spreads.

The relationship between the three country risk indicators and the $SPRD$ is expected to be positive. Other things being equal, higher rates of inflation are a reflection of expansionary monetary policy and is associated with balance of payments difficulties, and lenders will require a larger risk premium, Haegele (1980). Likewise, as the debt service ratio rises, either due to a rapid increase in debt service payments or due to a decline in export earnings or both, there is a high likelihood that the country will experience liquidity problems. Lenders seek higher margins on loans to such countries. Finally,

27

larger current account deficits mean higher borrowing needs and the subsequent increase in debt outstanding. An increase in the ratio of current account balance to GDP is an early warning of a trend toward deterioration in the ability of a country to meet its debt service obligations. Further, if the current account deficits grow it indicates the need for structural adjustment policies. Lenders in such circumstances require higher premiums on loans.

The sources for the data on the six-month LIBOR are: *Eurocredit Summary* of the World Bank, *Federal Reserve Bulletin* and *International Financial Statistics*. The spreads used are the weighted averages, the weights being the size of the loans. Various sources were used for the information on spreads to Brazilian loans including *Borrowing in the International Capital Markets* (World Bank), *International Financial Market Trends* (OECD), *Euromoney*, and *Conjuntura Economica* (F.G.V., Brazil). For the data on inflation, debt service, exports, current account balances, and GDP, the main source was *Boletim*, published by the Central Bank of Brazil.

(C) Empirical Results

The estimated results are presented below with the t-values in parenthesis.

$$\widehat{Y}_t = 0.0076 - 0.1272 LIBOR_t + 0.0047 IR_{t-1} + 0.0232 DSR_{t-1}$$
$$(-4.7) \qquad\qquad (2.9) \qquad\qquad (2.6)$$

$$\tag{3}$$

$$+0.1521 CAB_{t-1}.$$
$$(4.5)$$

$$\bar{R}^2 = 0.75, \; DW = 2.79, \; SER = 0.0028.$$

All the estimated coefficients have the expected signs, and all are significant at the one percent level. Together the independent variables explained seventy-five percent of the total variation in the spread charged on syndicated eurocurrency loans to Brazil.

As the Durbin–Watson statistic is above 2.0 indicating negative first order serial correlation, the regression estimates are corrected for serial correlation using the Cochrane–Orcutt method. The results obtained after this correction are presented below with t-values in parenthesis.

$$\widehat{Y_t} = 0.00683 - 0.14914 LIBOR_t + 0.004381 IR_{t_1} + 0.02853 DSR_{t-1}$$
$$\quad\quad (-8.4) \quad\quad\quad\quad (3.9) \quad\quad\quad (4.9)$$

$$(4)$$

$$+0.1567 CAB_{t-1}.$$
$$(7.2)$$

$$\bar{R}^2 = 0.82, \, DW = 2.1, \, SER = 0.0024.$$

There is a significant improvement in the overall explanatory power of the model as the adjusted R^2 rose from seventy-five to eighty-two percent and the t-values show a marked increase. The Durbin–Watson statistic has declined from 2.7 to 2.1. The t-values indicate that all the estimated coefficients are statistically significant at the 0.5% level.

The elasticity of spread with respect to each explanatory variable is computed at the point of the mean of each of these variables. A one percent increase in DSR will result in a 1.01% increase in the spread, while a one percent increase in $LIBOR$ will lead to a 0.89% decrease in spread. Spread is found to be less sensitive with respect to variations in CAB (0.28) and IR (0.16), significantly less than one in absolute terms. The order of importance in terms of elasticity is: DSR, $LIBOR$, CAB, and IR.

The above results clearly indicate that in the case of Brazil the spreads charged by banks on syndicated eurocurrency credits during the period 1966–1985 bore a close association with the cost of funds to the banks and the three risk indicators. The "loan pushing" hypothesis, that loan spreads bore no correspondence to the risks is not valid in the case of Brazil. In other words, multinational banks did take into account the risks in their lending decisions to Brazil.

Although nothing can be said as to whether the banks were adequately or reasonably compensated for the risks based on the above results, it may be inferred that even if the pricing of risks may not be efficient in the earlier years of lending, the spreads charged in the subsequent years may be considered efficient, or reasonable. The efficiency aspect of pricing the lending risks is examined in the next section.

29

III. DO SPREADS REFLECT EFFICIENT PRICING OF RISKS?

After establishing a close empirical relationship between the risk indicators and the spreads, the next step is to examine whether the actual spreads charged in the syndicated loan market are efficient or inefficient. Even if it is assumed that the eurocurrency market was inefficient in pricing lending risks in the earlier years of lending, it can be determined as to how long it would take the market to learn the mistake and correct the error. This, in effect, involves finding the time taken for the convergence of the actual spread with the "desired" or " efficient" spread.

The model employed to find this convergence is the "partial adjustment" model by Nerlove (1958). Let us say that the efficient spread, $SPRD^*$, is a linear function of $LIBOR$, IR, DSR, and CAB as follows:

$$SPRD_t^* = \alpha + \beta_1 LIBOR_t + \beta_2 IR_{t-1} + \beta_3 DSR_{t-1} + \beta_4 CAB_{t-1} + \epsilon_t. \quad (5)$$

Since the coefficient or desired spread, $SPRD^*$, is not directly observable, let us postulate the following partial adjustment process:

$$SPRD_t - SPRD_{t-1} = \lambda(SPRD_t^* - SPRD_{t-1}). \quad (6)$$

λ is the coefficient of adjustment $(0 \leq \lambda \leq 1)$, and $(SPRD_t - SPRD_{t-1})$ is the actual change, and $(SPRD_t^* - SPRD_{t-1})$ is the desired change.

The adjustment process states that the actual change in the spread in any given time period t is a fraction of λ of the desired change in spread for that period. If $\lambda = 1$, it means that the actual spread is equal to the efficient spread instantaneously in the same time period. If $\lambda = 0$, it implies that convergence does not occur. Typically, it is expected to lie between these two extremes since adjustment toward the efficient market will take time.

The adjustment mechanism described above can also be written as:

$$SPRD_t = \lambda SPRD_t^* + (1 - \lambda)SPRD_{t-1}. \quad (7)$$

Which states that the observed spread on loans at time t is a weighted average of the efficient spread at that time and the observed spread in the previous time period. The weights are λ and $(1 - \lambda)$, respectively.

Substitution of equation (7) into equation (5) gives:

$$SPRD_t = \lambda(\alpha + \beta_1 LIBOR_t + \beta_2 IR_{t-1} + \beta_3 DSR_{t-1} + \beta_4 CAB_{t-1} + \epsilon_t)$$
$$+ (1 - \lambda)SPRD_{t-1},$$

or

$$SPRD_t = \lambda\alpha + \lambda\beta_1 LIBOR_t + \lambda\beta_2 IR_{t-1} + \lambda\beta_3 DSR_{t-1}$$
$$+ \lambda\beta_4 CAB_{t-1} + \lambda\epsilon_t + (1-\lambda)SPRD_{t-1}. \tag{8}$$

Equation (8), the partial adjustment model, is estimated using the OLS method. The estimated results, with t-values in parenthesis, are presented below:

$$\widehat{SPRD}_t = 0.0057 - 0.1326 LIBOR_t + 0.00343 IR_{t-1} + 0.0245 DSR_{t-1}$$
$$\qquad\qquad (-7.1) \qquad\qquad (3.0) \qquad\qquad (4.3)$$

$$\tag{9}$$

$$+0.1466 CAB_{t-1} + 0.1796 SPRD_{t-1}.$$
$$\quad (7.3) \qquad\qquad (1.8)$$

$\bar{R}^2 = 0.85$, $D.W. = 2.3$, $1-\lambda = 0.1796$, $\lambda = 0.8204$, $SER = 0.0022$.

The estimated coefficients including the lagged spread have the expected signs. The t-values indicate that $LIBOR$, IR, DSR, and CAB are significant at the 0.5% level, while the lagged spread is significant at the five percent level. The model explained eighty-five percent of the variation in the spread.

The Durbin–Watson statistic cannot be used to detect the first order serial correlation as the dependent variable appears on the right-hand side of the equation (9), lagged one period. Durbin's h-statistic is used to test for first order serial correlation.[1]

The computed h-value is 0.73. At the five percent level of significance the critical value from the normal distribution table is 1.645. Since the computed h-value is less than the critical h-value, we may accept the hypothesis that there is no first order serial correlation. However, as the h-statistic is for large samples, its application to small samples of size 20 is not strictly justified. As such, the evidence of no serial correlation in this case is not conclusive.

The coefficient of adjustment (λ) is 0.82, which implies that eighty-two percent of the discrepancy between the efficient and actual spread is eliminated in a year. Since the time taken for convergence is relatively small, we can say that the eurocurrency market was not inefficient in pricing lending risks on syndicated loans to Brazil.

---

[1] $h = (1 - \frac{1}{2}d)\sqrt{\frac{N}{1 - N(var.\hat{\alpha})}}$, where d is the Durbin–Watson statistic, N is the number of observations, and $(var.\hat{\alpha})$ is the variance of the estimated coefficient of the $SPRD_{t-1}$.

The above results provide ample evidence to reject the contention that banks pushed loans by lowering spreads, especially in the case of Brazil. Further, there is proof to believe that the market was efficient to a high degree as indicated by the short adjustment lag. Hence, the return for banks on their loans to Brazil can be considered reasonable, or appropriate.

IV. SUMMARY AND CONCLUSIONS

The empirical model employed in finding the determinants of spreads charged on syndicated eurocurrency loans to Brazil during 1966–1985 has shown that lenders' cost of funds, inflation rates in Brazil, debt service ratio, and the ratio of current account balance to GDP to be major factors. The model has explained eighty-two percent of the variation in spreads. The statistically strong evidence of the relationship between the spread and the three risk indicators, apart from the cost of funds to lenders, permits us to reject the contention of the "loan pushing" hypothesis that "spreads charged on syndicated eurocurrency loans bore no correspondence to the risks involved in lending to LDCs." This is found not to be true in the case of Brazil. The empirical findings show that the spread is relatively very sensitive to the changes in the country's debt service ratio relative to the other explanatory variables. It is interesting to note that in spite of several sophisticated methods of evaluating country risk, the most important indicator that lenders take into account in the final analysis appear to be very few. At least this is true in the case of Brazil.

The "partial adjustment" model used to examine whether or not there is any convergence toward efficient pricing of risks, has yielded very good results to the effect that the market, as far as pricing of lending risks to Brazil, is relatively efficient, for the adjustment lag is short.

The empirical results allow us to invalidate the contention that the market consistently underpriced the risks as far as Brazil is concerned.

It can be concluded that the syndicated loan market priced lending risks to Brazil appropriately. However, although the hypothesis is not valid in the case of Brazil, we cannot say that it is invalid in the case of other borrowers unless empirical evidence on lending decisions and spreads charged to those countries is collected and analyzed.

REFERENCES

Central Bank of Brazil, *Boletim*, various issues, 1965–1986.

Darity Jr., William, "Did the Commercial Banks Push Loans on the LDCs?" in *World Debt Crisis*, Michael P. Claudon, editor (Cambridge, Massachusetts: Ballinger, 1986), pp. 200–201.

Euromoney, various issues.

F. G. V., *Brazil, Conjuntura Economica*, various issues, 1971–1986.

Federal Reserve Board, *Federal Reserve Bulletin*, various issues, 1971–1987.

Frank Jr., Charles R. and Cline, William R., "Measurement of Debt Servicing Capacity: An Application of Discriminant Analysis," *Journal of International Economics* (August 1971), Vol. 1, No. 3, pp. 327–344.

Goodman, Laurie S., "Pricing of Syndicated Eurocurrency Credits," *Quarterly Review* (Summer 1980), Federal Reserve Bank of New York, pp. 39–48.

Haegele, Monroe J., "The Market Still Knows Best," *Euromoney* (May 1980), pp. 121–128.

International Monetary Fund, *International Financial Statistics* (Washington, D.C.), various issues, 1966–1987.

Nerlove, Mark, *Distributed Lags and Demand Analysis for Agricultural and Other Commodities* (June 1956), monograph, U.S. Department of Agriculture.

OECD, *International Financial Market Trends*, various issues, 1973–1984.

Sargen, Nicholas, "Commercial Bank Lending to Developing Countries," *Economic Review* (Spring 1976), Federal Reserve Bank of San Francisco, pp. 20–31.

World Bank, *Borrowing in the International Capital Markets*, various issues, 1967–1980.

World Bank, *Eurocredit Summary*, various issues, 1972–1980.

A POLICY ORIENTATION OF THE CRITICISMS OF THE TRADITIONAL THEORY OF INTERNATIONAL FINANCE IN THE CONTEXT OF FIXED EXCHANGE RATES

John Malindretos
St. John's University
Demetri Tsanacas
Ferrum College

I. INTRODUCTION

The traditional theory of international finance and trade flows is a good and respected theory of international disequilibrium and adjustment. However, the Keynesian theory is incomplete on a number of points and as such its policy applications become problematic. In this study we hope to analyze the flaws of the traditional theory systematically and comprehensively. Part II of the study deals with the validity of the assumptions. Part III explores the importance of the other accounts besides the current account. Part IV examines the nature of the real and monetary disturbances and the policies and costs of dealing with those disturbances. Part V comments on the validity of a general equilibrium framework and Part VI summarizes the paper's general conclusions.

II. ASSUMPTIONS

The Keynesian international payments theory is based on a number of unrealistic assumptions.

The perfectly competitive markets assumption of the Keynesian international theory results in perfectly substitutable inputs and in homogeneous products, thus, making an expenditure switching policy successful. Gray (1976) has pointed out that the imperfections that exist in the product and the inputs markets would render expenditure switching policies ineffective because of the lack of flexibility.

The exclusion of the nation's size from the adjustment process has been criticized by Miles (1978a) and Laffer (1972). The assumption of equal size implies an equivalent impact on the balance of payments on monetary and fiscal policy and on exchange rate policy in the course of adjustment. Such an assumption is not true in real life.

All nations are not of equal importance. The reserve country status was introduced by Kemp (1975) and was expanded by Swoboda (1978). Swoboda was the first to point out that nations whose currencies serve in an international currency status capacity may not experience decreases in money supply as non-reserve nations under a fixed exchange rate regime. The pursuit of monetary policy by a non-reserve country as opposed to a reserve country would lead to a differential impact on the money supply in both nations. Further, the willingness to hold on to currency as an international reserve would result in different implications for the money supply.

That all nations hold only their own currency and have monetary independence under a flexible exchange rate system as suggested by Friedman (1953), was challenged by Miles (1978b) citing evidence from Canada and the United States. Currency substitution existence, although debatable (Husted, 1981), indicates monetary interdependence among countries under a flexible exchange rate system. Recent modelling by MacDonald and Taylor (1993) to capture the distinction between long run equilibrium and short term dynamics does, however, offer strong support to monetary models.

III. OVEREMPHASIS AND OMISSION OF ACCOUNTS

The balance of payments consists of a number of accounts. The Keynesian theory emphasizes the trade balance and adjustments through relative prices and income; it excludes the transfer account (Keynes, 1929) as well as interest and dividend flows associated with the services account (Cooper, 1966). The disregard of these flows can be detrimental especially if the transfers–aid to LDCs, war reparations, and the interest and dividend flows resulting from past foreign investment–are indeed substantial. Such disequilibrium in the balance of payments can not be handled by the traditional approach.

The non-embodiment of the capital account (KA) into the core theory is a major omission considering the size of the capital account which has resulted from the globalization and integration of world financial markets (Roosa, 1970). The capital account consist of two sections: short-term liquid and long-term illiquid assets. The long run capital account is further divided into foreign portfolio investment (FPI), representing investments in financial assets with maturities of over a year, i.e., bonds and stocks (with less than 10% ownership) and foreign direct investment. The former flows are influenced by the relative interest rate, wealth and the marginal propensity to acquire foreign securities. It is clear that the Keynesian theory to be a complete theory needs to explicitly introduce portfolio investment into its discussion.

The foreign direct investment (FDI) account represents the acquisition of real assets and of common stock above the ten percent limit. The motives for foreign direct investment are classified as: strategic, behavioral and economic. Many researchers have made contributions in this area. An excellent summary of their contributions appears in Eiteman, Stonehill and Moffett (1995). The traditional theory is in desperate need of a framework to analyze the reasons for pursuing FDI.

To the Keynesian theory the official reserve transactions balance (ORTB) or money account is accommodating in its nature and as such has not been properly emphasized. The monetary approach to the balance of payments (MA) advanced by Johnson (1977) has given preeminence to the money account. According to the monetary approach to the balance of payments an excessive money supply or an insufficient demand for money, would cause a deterioration of the balance of payments under a fixed exchange rate regime. In fact, any disturbance in the international accounts must go through the money market. Even though the monetary approach is extreme in its argumentation it, nevertheless, complements the traditional approach which is essentially a theory of the trade balance.

The traditional approach discards the notion that the balance of payments is a monetary phenomenon even though money is essentially introduced in each of the accounts. Further, money, as the vehicle used in the disposal either of tariff revenue, or of export tax proceeds, could neutralize the policy by increasing the consumption of foreign goods following the reduction in income taxes. The financing of an export subsidy, necessary to improve the competitiveness of exports, through the imposition of an income tax could lead to a decrease in the demand for imports, as after tax income falls, thus improving the trade balance. The trade balance will improve if the price elasticity of demand for exports is higher than one minus the marginal propensity to import of the focus nation.

IV. DISTURBANCES, ADJUSTMENTS, COSTS

A major weakness of the traditional approach in its explanation of disequilibrium is that it only dwells on the intermediate determining variables such as: relative prices, incomes and interest rates and not on the forces affecting these variables. The appropriate policy necessitates knowledge of the root cause of the disturbance, not simply knowledge of the vehicle of transmission of the disturbance.

James E. Meade (1970) has elaborated on price and income adjustments, and even though his work is brilliant, it remains incomplete. Modern theorists such as Machlup (1956), Roosa (1970), and Gray (1974) have attempted to incorporate the nature of the root cause of the disturbance into the traditional approach, though they do not delve deeply enough.

(A) Types of Disturbances
The categorization and grouping of the root disturbances is absolutely essential for any meaningful explanation. Following Lary (1957), Gray (1974) and Kindleberger (1969a) one can define the following seven kinds of disturbances:
1. Random and seasonal
2. Structural
3. Cyclical
4. Over absorption
5. Uncompetitiveness
6. Capital accounts or securities account
7. Official reserves transactions balance or money account

The differences among the disturbances are associated with the root cause of the disturbance and the types of accounts which they affect. Similarities among the disturbances exist, either in the intermediate cause of the disturbance, even though they may differ in the root cause, or in the root cause. In the second case identical causes could lead to different responses. For example, assume a loss of a substantial technological lead; depending on the reaction of the indigenous entrepreneurs, the outcome could be a structural over-absorption or a competitiveness disequilibrium.

In theory, we often distinguish *ad nauseum*. The real world is indeed more integrated than our analysis would indicate. There are repercussions and feedback among the disturbances. A successful analysis of international flows must integrate the kinds of disturbances.

This study will proceed to examine the cause of the disturbances and the selection and costs of the appropriate adjustment policies.

1. *Random and Seasonal Types of Disturbances*: Random and seasonal disturbances affect mainly the current account, since they impact the international flow of good and services. Random disturbances could also affect foreign direct investment if they relate to a discovery/exhaustion of a natural resource or a breakthrough in technology.

2. *Structural Disequilibrium*: International trade and financial flows are influenced by changes in the distribution of income in the export/import markets (MacDougall, 1957), alteration of tastes, and changes in the availability of products offered by foreign suppliers (for exports) and domestic suppliers (for imports) (Lary, 1967). In view of these structural changes it is expected that an efficient market economy will alter its production and tailor it to the new realities. Artus and Young (1979) indicated that this may not happen, citing as reasons for the non-occurrence the possibility of insufficient and/or inappropriate relative price and resource adjustments. If this occurs, the nation develops a balance of payments deficit or surplus and adjustment is needed.

3. *Cyclical Disequilibrium*: Cyclical over-absorption occurs when demand exceeds production during the expansion phase of the business cycle (Robinson, 1947, ch. 1). The expansion is usually due to expansionary demand management policies: monetary policy, fiscal policy, and industrial policy (Meade, 1970).

The above policies will have a different yet negative affect on the trade balance. The reason is that, absorption rises faster than production in the case where demand management policies are undertaken (Alexander, 1952).

4. *Over-absorption Disturbances*: At times, a nation does not produce enough or it absorbs too much. Thus, relative to production

there is an excessive demand or relative to demand there is an insufficiency of production (Johnson, 1961).

The reason for the noncyclical (secular) over-absorption are, insufficient production and excessive absorption. Insufficient production is caused by insufficient capacity (Machlup, 1956), lack of technical know-how (Marsden, 1970) and lack of sufficiently skilled laborers (Barbison, 1962).

Excessive absorption could be caused by cultural reasons affecting thriftiness (Nurkse, 1953), insufficient savings because of poverty (Lewis, 1954), excessive spending out of current income associate with increased wealth, high terms of trade affecting the income level (Alexander, 1952), and inflationary expectations by consumers and producers (Houthakker and Taylor, 1970).

5. *Uncompetitiveness Disequilibrium*: The impact of uncompetitiveness on disequilibrium was introduced by Swan (1963). The ratio of competitiveness of a nation is defined as follows:

$$C = (\frac{P_f}{P_d})ER, \tag{1}$$

where P_f is the foreign price level, P_d is the domestic price level, and ER is the exchange rate (units of domestic currency given per unit of foreign currency).

An increase in the ratio indicates increased international competitiveness while a decrease indicates that the nation's ability to compete has fallen. The competitiveness ratio depends on relative prices and the exchange rate. There are five factors which could affect competitiveness and would have an impact on the balance of payments.

The five determinants of competitiveness (Gray, 1974, chapters 3–5) are associated with the inability (ability) of a nation to compete internationally because of: one, higher prices due to inflationary pressure resulting from monetary expansion or excessive wage and profit increases (Keynes, 1936); two, higher prices due to higher cost resulting from either the depletion of natural resources and/or the loss of a lead in technology (Hoffmeyer, 1958); and three, factors affecting and keeping the value of the domestic currency high for political reasons, central bank intervention, expectations and an influx of funds under the capital account (Keynes, 1929).

6. *Capital or Financial Account Disequilibrium*: The capital account represents of the flow of securities internationally. It has been decomposed into three sub-accounts:

 a. The short-term capital account

 b. The illiquid portfolio investment

 c. The illiquid direct investment account (Kindleberger, 1969b)
Disturbances in any of the sub-accounts will lead to external disequilibrium.

7. *Official Reserves Transactions Balance (ORTB) or Money Disequilibrium*: The Keynesian theory of international disequilibrium and adjustment followed the path of the domestic Keynesian theory in that it de-emphasized the money sector. This is unfortunate because Keynes believed that money matters. It is probable that international Keynesianism, as domestic Keynesianism, went astray because of the success on the employment front which was achieved in the forties, fifties and sixties (Davidson, 1978). Also, as Gray indicates, Keynes never fully developed a comprehensive theory of international disequilibrium and adjustment which essentially included money (Gray, 1974, chapter 3). Robert Mundell (1968), Harry Johnson (1961) and Jacob Frankel (1976) developed a monetary theory of the international financial accounts. Under the monetary approach to the balance of payments (MABOP) the official reserves transactions balance (ORTB) and money demand and supply are the key variables of international disequilibrium and adjustment. An excess supply (demand) of money in the focus nation will worsen (improve) its official reserves transactions balance. An increase in money supply, interest rates, and the value of the currency as well as a drop in income and prices would worsen this account, because they would engender an excessive money supply. Any movement in the opposite direction for the above variables would improve the account. The monetary approach to the balance of payments, however, cannot explain the adjustments occurring in the other international accounts. Its main emphasis is the money account.

(B) Appropriate Policies for Adjustments to Disturbances
  and Their Respective Costs
There are numerous ways to address the different types of disturbances. This survey will examine only the optimal policies of attacking the root cause of disequilibrium.

1. *Appropriate Policies and Costs to deal with Random and Seasonal Disturbances*: Both seasonal and random forces of balance of payments disequilibrium are reversible, thus necessitating the use of an optimal policy tool. Financing is such a policy (Machlup, 1964). The pursuit of financing is a passive response to the disequilibrium. *Ceteris paribus*, the classical mechanism would be allowed to work through the twofold prongs of the reduction in prices and demand; hence, the focus economy will move towards external equilibrium.

The costs of pursuing the policy of financing to remedy random and seasonal disturbances are:

a. Loss of wealth (Barro, 1974),

b. Negative influence on income (Gervaise, 1956); and,

c. Crisis due to insufficiency of reserves (Gray, 1976).

The costs are less burdensome if the disequilibrium is reversible (Gray, 1974), and if money is not considered net wealth (Miles 1978a, ch. 11). Further, a reserve currency country could defer the cost to a later date and presumably could pay with a devalued and/or an inflated currency thus drastically reducing its cost (Laffer and Miles, 1982).

2. *Appropriate Policies and Their Cost to Deal with Structural Disturbances*: Policy making in view of structural disturbances is aimed at:

a. Alteration of relative product prices in the right direction, rapidly, and sufficiently.

b. The price alteration must result in a resource movement in the right direction rapidly and sufficiently.

c. The demand alteration desired by the government must take place quickly, by the correct amounts and for the targeted products (Artus and Young, 1979). A number of policies have been proposed. Their costs are determined mainly by the relative price and resource adjustments in the affected sectors.

Proposal 1: The enhancement of free trade domestically and the allowance of competition (Guitian, 1982; Schydlowsky, 1982). Free trade and a reduction in monopoly power would lead to price adjustments and to a more efficient utilization of resources. The costs of the transition between structures is small.

Proposal 2: The pursuit of flexible and dynamic resource markets (Serpick, 1987). Flexibility in the factor market would lead to the expansion of the "right" industries. To achieve that the economic authorities should undertake policies of: a) job training; b) subsidization of workers attempting to change vocations; and c) disallowance of monopsonization of factor markets. The costs of training the population would be paid through taxes with repayment at a later date. A reduction of monopsony power would benefit both resource users and consumers through lower product costs. Any losses in wages by the workers employed in the monopsonistic market would be offset by employment longevity in those markets.

Proposal 3: Industrial policy (Corden, 1955 and Samuelson, 1980). Industrial policy is an attempt by government to increase the level of investment through the use of accelerated depreciation allowances, investment and R&D tax credits. The benefits are: an increase in the level of income, a product mix more in line with worldwide consumption patterns and an improvement in the balance of payments. The cost are income redistribution to business, and shifts in consumption from the present to the future. Both of these are offset if production and consumption increase enough intertemporally.

Proposal 4: Commercial policy (Metzler, 1949). Commercial policy, whether of the tariff or non-tariff barrier type, has a price and an income effect. The price effect is a change of relative prices leading to an improvement in the terms of trade and a resource reallocation towards tradables. The income effect is a decline in income and purchasing power which should improve the trade balance due to the decrease of imports (Johnson, 1961).

The costs of commercial policy are a reflection of the two effects relative price changes lead to, i.e., changes in consumer tastes and in income distribution, which in turn cause a reallocation of resources (Corden, 1955). The policy of commerce chosen by the government leads to protectionism costs in consumption and in production. The costs of production can be heavy. Excluding all other arguments for protectionism except the infant industry, the senile industry or the diversification argument, the protection should eventually be removed and the protected industry should be allowed to compete with foreign industries. There is always the threat of indefinite protection owing to the firms political lobbying power.

The costs of a tariff identified by Fleming (1951) are: the misallocation of production, the misallocation of consumption and retaliation by foreigner countries. The size of the costs depend on the rate of protection extended to the firm. The benefits of a tariff are: improvements in the allocation of resources (Haberler, 1950), the terms of trade (Metzler, 1949), and in the trade balance and employment (Myint, 1958).

3. *Cyclical Over-absorption Policies and Costs*: Monetary and fiscal policy are the two policies used to deal with cyclical over-absorption. A reduction in spending and/or an increase in taxes will have a positive influence on the gap between production and spending. Two variables are necessary to determine the efficacy of fiscal policy on the trade balance and the balance of payments: capital mobility and the extent of exchange rate variability (Mundell, 1968).

The pursuit of a tight monetary policy, unlike a tight fiscal policy, would raise interest rates. Further, the efficacy of monetary policy depends on the mobility of capital and exchange rate flexibility.

The pursuit of a tight monetary policy will result in:

    a. Reduction of nominal and real income

    b. Decrease in the price level

    c. Rise in interest rates

    d. Revaluation of the currency

    e. Reallocation of resources

A tight monetary policy will reduce income, decrease the price level of the nation which is the *raison d'etre* of the policy, and induce the focus currency to revalue which will offset the fall of domestic prices. If the foreign exchange authority intervenes, however, it can disallow the revaluation to wholly offset the drop of internal prices.

This disinflationary policy is appropriate because it deals with the root problem of the deficit which is the higher inflation of the focus country due to excessive money increase in the past.

The cost of a tight fiscal policy is a loss of income. On the benefits side, interest rates will fall and the level of investment will rise. Tight monetary policy will not lead to a fall in interest rates and it might not produce the anticipated results.

4. *Policies and Costs of Adjusting to Noncyclical Overabsorption*: There are two sets of policies to deal with noncyclical overabsorption: demand management policies and trade controls/commercial policy.

The demand management policies are of the fiscal and/or the commercial policy type. The intent is to reduce demand and enhance savings (Kimzey, 1983) through a variety of tax measures. The major cost is the possibility of a recession, *ceteris paribus*. Supplementing the policy with one which stimulates employment, i.e., an investment policy, would be beneficial. If the investment takes the form of foreign direct investment, both the wealth and the balance of payments of the focus nation will be positively affected over time. The pursuit of commercial policy and trade controls seeks to diminish absorption and to enhance production. The costs of controls are many and depend on the type of control. The misallocation of consumption and production could have serious repercussions on the economy. The possibility of increasing comparative advantage through the use of industrial policy would obviously offset the costs.

5. *Policies and Costs to Cure Uncompetitiveness*: The policy needed to cure uncompetitiveness is dictated by the cause of the uncompetitiveness disequilibrium (Machlup, 1964):

a. Inflation

If the cause is inflation two policies are recommended: tight monetary policy and devaluation. A tight monetary policy over a period of years would extinguish inflation at the possible cost of unemployment and resource misallocation (Casell, 1928). A reduction in the value of the currency would restore competitiveness to the level that existed prior to the rise of the domestic price level. The cost of devaluation would be a greater feeding of inflation. The benefits of devaluation, in contrast to a tight monetary policy, is that there is no loss of jobs (Robinson, 1947, chapter 1). In addition, it reduces the real wage by raising prices instead of nominal wages, which is more appealing from a political point of view, and it is less likely to cause a financial crisis (Gray, 1974).

b. Excess wage rates and monopoly power profits

Keynes refers to inflation caused by excessive wages and monopoly power as an incomes type of inflation. The policy which address the root reason for price increases is wage and price controls, provided that enough flexibility is allowed to enable the system to continue its allocative efficiency (Keynes, 1936).

Encouraging R&D through tax incentives will eliminate the need for raising prices and will improve labor productivity (Magaziner and Reich, 1982).

Devaluation will enhance competitiveness if it has fallen due to inflation. However, a devaluation will mean a lower standard of living for workers, profit recipients, and renters, because it does not enhance the nation's productivity. Furthermore, it could lead to increase borrowing abroad to sustain real consumption (Mendoza, 1992, table 1).

c. Exhaustion of natural resources

Pursuing R&D through tax credits to boost the output of natural resources and their embodiment into the production process will mean less revenues during the period of support, but higher revenue once the resource industries recover (Lawrence, 1980).

d. High currency values

An overvalued currency has an impact on competitiveness. A devaluation although it worsens the terms of trade, it improves competitiveness and it increases the level of income offsetting the impact of the terms of trade.

e. Technology losses

Magaziner and Reich (1982) recommend generous tax credits and allowances in cases where a nation is losing its technological lead or technological parity. Accelerated depreciation, investment tax credits, and R&D tax credits will enable firms to invest and to adapt new technologies which will improve competitiveness by either cutting down costs and/or increasing productivity.

6. *Policies to Use to Improve the Long Term and the Short Term Capital Account and their Costs.*:

a. Long term capital account

Deficits in the long-term portfolio account are caused by either lower interest rates at home or greater wealth and a high propensity to buy foreign securities. Capital controls and/or higher interest rates on intermediate and long run financial instruments will address the problem (Branson, 1985). Capital controls will affect future money flows and they could result in capital flight while higher interest rates affect investment and employment. In case of a financial crisis, its cost warrants the imposition of controls on capital.

Deficits in the foreign direct investment account originate in sources identified in the previous section of this paper. Policies of forced repatriation of profits and/or disallowances of investing abroad have been proposed. Their costs exceed the cost of other capital account restrictions (Larry, 1967).

b. Short term capital account

Short run international financial flows depend on interest rate differentials, on wealth and on the propensity to acquire short run assets (Branson and Hill, 1971). Three policies are available for improving the short run capital account:

    i. Capital outflows disallowance
    ii. Repatriation
    iii. Raising of interest rates

The major cost of these policies are the inefficiencies of the suboptimal allocation of resources.

7. *Policies and costs to cure money account disequilibrium*: A declining value of the currency created by an excessive money supply and/or an insufficient money demand could be cured by a combination of tight monetary policy and an increase in the demand for money (Mundell, 1961). The major cost of a tight monetary policy is recessionary pressure on the economy, while the cost in the second case is inflation and "crowding out," due to an expansionary fiscal policy to raise GNP.

V. GENERAL EQUILIBRIUM

The traditional theory assumes a world of general equilibrium. Davidson (1978) has indicated that the world of international finance is characterized by uncertainty, the passage of irreversible time, and money, which point to a continuous disequilibrium in the international financial system. In addition, the existence of exogenous disturbances and the frequency of their occurrence contribute to continuously changing expectations (Gray, 1974). This continual alteration of expectations creates an environment where general equilibrium is not ubiquitously present, if partially present. A real world analysis must embody into the core theory the elements mentioned above.

The few types of disturbances accounted for in the traditional theory are corrected once the adjustment process is allowed to take place. This is clearly unrealistic since the disequilibrium causes are numerous and continuous. The adjustment process could only be completed in a static, not a dynamic environment. Natural events, political factors and economics variables are the causes of a state of continuous disequilibrium. Hallwood and MacDonald (1994) advance the institutional aspects of change and disequilibrium and the resulting instability in the world economy.

Natural events occur randomly and frequently enough to disturb the international financial accounts especially of developing nations.

Political factors are essential to a discussion of international financial flows and to adjustments in these flows since they affect their size, direction, and speed of adjustment. The following political factors will have a profound impact:

a. The nullification of self-correction by the national authorities especially if the course of adjustment brings a temporary recession which is politically unacceptable.

b. Commercial policy measures to protect domestic producers from increased foreign competition.

c. An artificially high value of the focus currency for prestige reasons and/or fear of inflation.

d. The formation of trade groups leads to trade creation/trade diversion effects and in changes the size and direction of financial flows (Tsanacas, 1989).

e. The formation of financial systems and currency blocks is a political creation which has economic implication for the balance of payments and the exchange rate. The cooperation and the coordination of the economies of the block nations in trade and financial matters reduces the deterioration of the balance of payments of individual countries.

Changes in the values of certain economic variables could lead to a disequilibrium in the international financial accounts. According to Malindretos (1984) these are:

a. The rate of saving
b. The rate of international investment and its return
c. The rate of productivity change
d. The rate of advancement in transportation
e. Alterations of tastes.

These variables affect consumption, production and investment patterns. Changes in financial flows which parallel these patterns could very well lead to financial adjustments. A world of general equilibrium becomes irrelevant in such a dynamic framework.

VI. CONCLUSION

The traditional approach of international finance is a commendable and useful theory. It is a core theory in that it explains an important part of disturbances and policies of adjustment. It is not, however, a comprehensive theory of international finance for several reasons: first, it is based on restrictive assumptions; second, it does not distinguish between different root causes of a disturbance; third, the theory over emphasizes the trade balance at the expense of other accounts; fourth, it does not separate real and monetary variables; and fifth, the theory assumes a general equilibrium framework in a world where disturbances are frequent and severe. Therefore, any theoretical and/or empirical contributions that supplement and qualify the traditional approach to the balance of payments will increase its acceptability as well as its policy application.

REFERENCES

Alexander, Sidney, "Effects of a Devaluation on a Trade Balance," *Staff Papers* (April 1952), International Monetary Fund, Vol. 2, pp. 263–278.

Artus, Jacques R. and Young, John H,. "Fixed and Flexible Exchange Rates: A Renewal of the Debate," *Staff Papers* (December 1979), International Monetary Fund, Vol. 26, No. 4, pp. 659–667.

Barbison, Frederick H., "Human Resources Development, Planning, Modernizing Economies," *International Labour Review* (May 1962), Vol. 85, No. 5, pp. 1–23.

Barro, Robert J., "Are Government Bonds Net Wealth," *Journal of Political Economy* (November 1974), Vol. 82, pp. 343–348.

Branson, William H., "Causes of Appreciation and Volatility of the Dollar," in *The U.S. Dollar: Recent Developments, Outlook and Policy Options* (1985), Federal Reserve Bank of Kansas City, pp. 33–53.

Branson, William H. and Hill, Jr., Raymond D., *Capital Movements in the OECD Area: An Econometric Analysis*, OECD Economic Outlook Occasional Studies (Paris, France: Organization for Economic Cooperation and Development, 1971).

Cassel, Gustav, *Post War Monetary Stabilization* (New York, New York: Columbia University Press, 1928).

Cooper, Richard N., "The Balance of Payments in Review," *Journal of Political Economy* (August 1966), Vol. 74, No. 4, pp. 379–395.

Corden W.M., "The Economic Limits to Population Increases," *Economic Record* (November 1955), Vol. XXXI, pp. 242–260.

Davidson, Paul, *Money and the Real World*, second edition (London, England: The Macmillan Press Limited, 1978).

Eiteman, Stonehill and Moffett, *Multinational Business Finance* (New York, New York: Addison-Wesley, 1995).

Fleming, John M., "On Making the Best of Balance of Payments Restriction on Imports," *Economic Journal* (March 1951), Vol. LVI, pp. 48–71.

Frenkel Jacob, "A Monetary Approach to Exchange Rates: Doctrinal Aspects and Empirical Evidence," *Scandinavian Journal of Economics* (1976), pp. 200–224.

Friedman, Milton, "The Case for Flexible Exchange Rates," *Essays in Positive Economics* (Chicago, Illinois: University of Chicago Press, 1953), pp. 157–203.

Gervaise, Isaac, "The System or Theory of the Trade of the World," (1720) reprinted in *Economic Tracts* (Baltimore, Maryland: Johns Hopkins University Press, 1956).

Gray, Peter H., *An Aggregate Theory of International Payments Adjustment* (London, England: The Macmillan Press Limited, 1974).

Gray, Peter H., *The Monetary Approach to International Payments Theory: A Critique* (March 1976), Mimeo, Rutgers University.

Guitian, Manuel, "Economic Management and International Monetary Fund Conditionality," in *Adjustment Financing in the Developing World: The Role of the International Monetary Fund*, Tony Killick, editor (Washington, D.C.: International Monetary Fund, 1982).

Haberler, Gottfried, "Some Problems in the Pure Theory of International Trade," *Economic Journal* (June 1950), Vol. 60, pp. 223–240.

Hallwood, Paul and MacDonald, Ronald, *International Money and Finance* (London, England: Blackwell, 1994).

Hoffmeyer, Erik, *Dollar Shortage and the Structure of U.S. Foreign Trade* (Copenhagen, Denmark: E. Munksgaard, 1958).

Houthakker, Hendrik S. and Taylor, Lester D., *Consumer Demand in the U.S.: Analyses and Projections* (Cambridge, Massachusetts: Harvard University Press, 1970).

Husted, Stephen, *A Transactions Model of Currency Substitution* (October 1981), Mimeo, Department of Economics, University of Pittsburgh.

Johnson, Harry G., "Towards a General Theory of the Balance of Payments," in *International Trade and Economics Growth: Studies in Pure Theory*, Harry G. Johnson, editor (Cambridge, Massachusetts: Harvard University Press, 1961), pp. 153–168.

Johnson, Harry G., "The Monetary Approach to the Balance of Payments: A Nontechnical Guide," *Journal of International Economics* (August 1977), Vol. 7, No. 3, pp. 251–268.

Kemp, Donald S., "A Monetary View of the Balance of Payments," *Review* (April 1975), Federal Reserve Bank of St. Louis, pp. 14–22.

Keynes, John M., "The German Transfer Problem," *Economic Journal* (March 1929), Vol. 39, pp. 1–7.

Keynes, John M., *A Treatise on Money* (London, England: Macmillan, 1930).

Keynes, John M., *The General Theory of Employment, Interest, and Money* (New York, New York: Harcourt Brace, Inc., 1936).

Kimzey, Bruce W., *Reaganomics* (St. Paul, Minnesota: West Publishing Company, 1983).

Kindleberger, Charles P., "Measuring Equilibrium in the Balance of Payment," *Journal of Political Economy* (November/December 1969a), Vol. 77, No. 6, pp. 873–91.

Kindleberger, Charles P., *American Business Abroad: Six Lectures on Direct Investment* (New Haven, Connecticut: Yale University Press, 1969b).

Laffer, Arthur B., "Monetary Policy and the Balance of Payments," *Journal of Money, Credit and Banking* (February 1972), Vol. 4, pp. 13–22.

Laffer, Arthur B. and Miles, Marc A., *International Economics in an Integrated World* (Glenview, Illinois: Scott, Foresman and Company, 1982).

Lary, Hal B., *Problems of the United States as World Trader and Banker*, Studies in International Economic Relations, No. 1, National Bureau of Economic Research (New York, New York: Columbia University Press, 1957).

Lawrence, Franco, *European Industrial Policy Past, Present, and Future* (February 1980), The Conference Board in Europe.

Lewis, Arthur W., "Economic Development with Unlimited Supplies of Labour," *The Manchester School of Economics and Social Studies* (May 1954), Vol. 22, pp. 139–191.

51

MacDonald, R. and Taylor, M. P, "The Monetary Approach to the Exchange Rate Rational Expectations, Long-Rum Equilibrium and Forecasting," *Staff Papers* (1993), International Monetary Fund, Vol. 40, pp, 89–107.

MacDougall, Donald, *The World Dollar Problem A Study in International Economics* (New York, New York: St. Martin's Press, 1957).

Machlup, Fritz, "The Terms of Trade Effects of Devaluation Upon Real Income and the Balance of Trade," *Kyklos Fasc.* (1956), Vol. 4.

Machlup, Fritz, "Adjustment, Compensatory Correction, and Financing of Imbalances in International Payments," in *Trade, Growth, and the Balance of Payments Essays in Honor of Gottfried Haberler*, Richard E. Caves, Harry G. Johnson and Peter B. Kenen, editors (Chicago, Illinois: Rand McNally and Company, 1964).

Magaziner, Ira C. and Reich, Robert B., *Minding America's Business: The Decline and Rise of the American Economy* (New York, New York: Vintage Books, 1982).

Malindretos, John, "The Traditional and Monetary Approaches to the Balance of Payments: A Theoretical Comparison," *American Business Review* (June 1984), Vol. 2, No. 1, pp. 31–42.

Marsden, Keith, "Progressive Technologies for Developing Countries," *International Labour Review* (May 1970), pp. 475–502.

Meade, James Edward, *The Theory of International Economic Policy The Balance of Payments, Volume 1* (London, England: Oxford University Press, 1970).

Mendoza, E. G., "The Effect of Macroeconomic Shocks in a Basic Equilibrium Framework," *Staff Papers* (December 1992), International Monetary Fund, Vol. 39, No. 4, pp. 885–889.

Metzler, Lloyd A., "Tariffs, The Terms of Trade, and The Distribution of National Incomes," *Journal of Political Economy* (February 1949), Vol. LVII, No. 1, pp. 1–29.

Miles, Marc A., *Devaluation, The Trade Balance and The Balance of Payments* (New York, New York: Marcel Dekker Inc., 1978a).

Miles, Marc A., "Currency Substitution, Flexible Exchange Rates, and Monetary Independence," *American Economic Review* (June 1978b), Vol. 68, No. 3, pp. 428–436.

Mundell, Robert, "A Theory of Optimum Currency Areas," *American Economic Review* (November 1961), Vol. 51, pp. 509–517.

Mundell, Robert A., "Barter Theory and The Monetary Mechanism of Adjustment," in *International Economics*, Robert A. Mundell, editor (New York, New York: Macmillan Publishing, Co., Inc., 1968).

Myint, Hla, "The Classical Theory of International Trade and the Underdeveloped Countries," *Economic Journal* (June 1958), Vol. LXVIII, No. 270, pp. 317–337.

Nurkse, Ragnar, *Problems of Capital Formation in Underdeveloped Countries* (New York, New York: Oxford University Press, 1952).

Robinson, Joan, "The Foreign Exchanges," in her *Essays in The Theory of Employment*, second edition (Oxford, England: Basil Blackwell, 1947).

Roosa, Robert V., "Capital Movements and Balance of Payments Adjustment," in *Men, Money and Policy: Essays in Honor of Karl R. Bopp*, David. P. Eastburn, editor (Federal Reserve Bank of Philadelphia, 1970), pp. 171–194.

Samuelson, Paul, "On Mobility," *National Journal* (August 16, 1980).

Schydlowsky, Daniel M., "Alternative Approaches to Short Term Economic Management in Developing Countries," in *Adjustment and Financing in The Developing World*, Tony Killick, editor (Washington, D.C.: International Monetary Fund, 1982), pp. 105–134.

Serpick, Joanne, "Job Training's Iffy Track Record," *The Washington Times* (March 9, 1987), pp. 20–21.

Swan T. W., "Longer-Run Problems in the Balance of Payments," in *The Australian Economy: A Volume of Readings*, H. W. Arndt and M. W. Corden, editors (Melbourne, Australia: Chesire Press, 1963).

Swoboda, Alexander K., "Gold Dollars, Euro Dollars, and The World Money Stock Under Fixed Exchange Rates," *American Economic Review* (September 1978), Vol. 68, No. 4, pp. 625–642.

Tsanacas, Demetri P., "Market Share Effects of the Lome Convention and GSP," in *The Modern International Environment*, H. Peter Gray, editor (Greenwich, Connecticut: JAI Press, 1989), pp. 129–208.

4

THE INFLUENCE OF MULTINATIONAL BANK ENTRY ON HOST COUNTRY MARKET STRUCTURE: A CASE STUDY OF SPAIN

Luis Eduardo Rivera-Solis
Dowling College

I. INTRODUCTION

(A) The Problem

In recent years, industrial market structure and its relationship to foreign investment has been extensively researched. The primary focus of the research has been on the kinds of market structures that favor the growth of multinational firms (MFs) mostly in the context of advanced economies. The effect of MF entry on host market structure has received little attention. The theoretical literature has dealt with this on few occasions (Caves, 1974; Dunning, 1974); with a few empirical studies in developed countries (Bonitsis and Rivera-Solis, 1993; Clark and Speaker, 1992; Smirlock and Brown, 1986; Steuer, 1973; Dunning, 1973; Rosenbluth, 1970) and in developing countries (Lall, 1979; Newfarmer, 1978; Connor and Mueller, 1977; Newfarmer and Mueller, 1975).

In most cases, no attempt was made to determine how the entry of MFs influenced on market concentration within a comprehensive model of the determinants of industrial structure. Lall's (1979) case study on Malaysia attempted to do this using cross-section analysis. According to Lall, without such a model it is difficult to determine whether the presence of MFs influences market structure independently of those industrial variables that are commonly believed to influence it, whether it is "merely associated with structural characteristics that are inherent in different industries, or whether it speeds up the process of structural change which may occur even in its absence" (Lall, 1979, p. 326). In a recent study, Cho (1990) examined whether and how foreign banking presence influenced market concentration in Indonesia. Cho's study showed that foreign banking presence contributed to increased banking competition.

One of Lall's main findings was that "higher foreign presence in an industry is associated with higher levels of concentration" (1979, p. 344). However, Lall used cross-section analysis of industrial structure at a given point in time, and he asserted that this may not be the best way of evaluating an MF's repercussion on host country market structure. A more appropriate method would be a before and after analysis "using time series data for particular industries and making specific international comparisons" (Lall, 1979, p. 345). Caves indicated that it is unlikely that the long-run effect of the multinational corporation on market structure and performance can be uncovered "except through the patient assembly of information on individual industries over time" (Caves, 1974, pp. 142–143). Both Caves and Lall raise an important issue that needs to be considered: What is the long-run repercussion of multinational firm entry on host country market structure? It is this issue that was examined in this study.

The purpose of this study was to test the hypothesis that the entry of multinational banks (MBs) has made Spanish banking structure, as measured by concentration, less competitive and evaluate this in connection with conventional economic theory. The alternate hypothesis was whether Spanish banking structure has been made more competitive by the presence of multinational banks. In this connection, it was necessary to examine the influence of multinational banks on net interest margins. As to the effect that can be expected upon the banking structure, there are three possibilities. First, in the short run, concentration may be reduced as the number of competing banks increases. Second, in the long run, concentration may be increased by raising barriers to entry, as a result of the MBs' access to foreign financial markets. Third, the process of concentration may actually be accelerated.

(B) The Data

Spain provides a good case study for our purpose. This is due to that country's restrictive policy towards multinational bank presence for one period (1960–1978). Since then Spain has adopted a fairly liberal policy. There was sufficient information on Spanish banking to make this study feasible. In both periods there has been a consistent growth of foreign bank activities.

The *Anuario Estadistico de la Banca Privada: 1981* provided ample data on domestic and foreign banks such as total assets, foreign and local currency deposits, and net worth. Similar data were available in the *Balances y Estadisticas de la Banca Privada*, a monthly publication. Both of these are published by the Consejo Superior Bancario (Higher Banking Board), a consultative body with representatives from the private banking sector.

Data on lending and borrowing rates for Spain were obtained from the *Financial Statistics Monthly (OECD)*. Because banks have different lending and borrowing rates depending on the tenor of the loan or deposit a weighted average was taken of each and subtracted from each other to obtain the industry net interest margin. In view of the volatility of interest rates and their influence on net interest margins, the data were compiled on a semi-annual basis during the period of January 1974 to December 1983.

II. THE INFLUENCE OF MULTINATIONAL BANK ENTRY ON CONCENTRATION IN SPANISH BANKING

(A) Introduction

As indicated above, the influence of multinational firm entry on host country market structure has received little attention. This section examines the response of concentration levels in Spanish banking to changes in the level of multinational bank presence. The level of concentration is useful in determining the degree of competition in an industry; that is whether it is an oligopoly, pure competition, or some variant thereof.

(B) Purpose of the Study

First of all, a model explaining the determination of the levels of banking concentration was constructed, taking into account multi-national bank presence. Second, the hypothesis was tested that the entry of multinational banks (*MBs*) has made Spanish banking structure, as measured by concentration, less competitive, and third, the results were evaluated in connection with conventional economic theory.

(C) The Variables

It was important to answer the following questions: "How well do changes in foreign bank presence explain the variations in concentration, as measured by total assets or loans?" and "Are these changes in foreign bank presence statistically significant?" To answer these questions, it was necessary to specify a model, or models, that incorporate most of the determinants of industrial structure as well as foreign bank presence. The statistical tool employed is ordinary least squares regression.

The multivariate model is specified below:

$$C_5 = \beta_0 + \beta_1 MG + \beta_2 MEBS + \beta_3 MB + \beta_4 MSS. \tag{1}$$

According to Lall (1979) the variables specified in the above model "incorporate practically all the determinants of structure which have been tried for the developed countries" (p. 333). The following variables were used for that reason.

The dependent variable, C_5, is the concentration ratio in Spanish banking as measured by the proportion of total bank assets accounted for by the five largest Spanish banks. Concentration ratios were computed for the five largest banks rather than the standard four firm concentration ratio since this has been the usual practice in Spain. In addition, some of the available statistics are computed in this manner. During the time period 1960–1983, the concentration ratio for the five largest banks in Spain decreased from 55.6% in 1960 to 36.8% at the end of 1983.

The independent variables are: MB, multinational bank presence, as measured by the foreign bank share of total bank assets in Spain; MG, market growth, as measured by the percentage growth in total bank loans; MSZ, market size, as measured by the total bank loans outstanding; $MEBS$, minimum efficient bank size, as measured by the average capital asset ratio for the industry. This ratio provides a concrete measure of minimum acceptable capitalization. This measure assumes that a minimum degree of capitalization is required to achieve efficiency. Since the legal capital asset ratios vary by class of bank, the average capital asset ratio was used.

The above variables incorporated the major determinants of industrial structure.

(D) Empirical Analysis

This section presents the results for the Spanish banking industry. None of the variables were transformed, except market growth (MG).

MG was expressed in natural logarithms. The time period used was 1960–1983.

A regression analysis was performed to test the hypothesis that banking concentration in Spain for the five largest banks (C_5, the dependent variable) is a function of market growth (MG), minimum efficient bank size ($MEBS$), multinational bank presence (MB), and market size (MSZ).

The computer run using all four independent variables yielded the following results:

$$C_5 = 107.11 - 9.3MG + 4.38MEBS - 1.25MB + 0.003MSZ.$$
$$(36.09) \quad (14.04) \quad (2.25) \qquad (5.9) \qquad (4.11)$$

$$\tag{2}$$

$$R^2 = .985, SER = 0.80, D - W = 2.01, F - ratio = 356.8, d.f. = 19.$$

It appears that the signs of the coefficients are correct, since an increase in market growth and multinational could be expected to affect banking concentration. We note a high R^2 of 98.5%, meaning that 98.5% of the variation in concentration is explained by the variation of the independent variables. The critical F-value from the statistical tables is 2.90 at a significance level of five percent and nineteen degrees of freedom. Since the computed F-value is 356.8, we conclude that the regression is statistically significant at both levels. From the statistical tables we find that the critical t-value (which are in parenthesis under equation (2)) for $\alpha = 0.01$ under a probability of $\frac{\alpha}{2} = .005$, with nineteen degrees of freedom, the critical value is 2.861. Since the t-test ratios for MB, MG, and MSZ are greater, we can conclude that the variables are statistically significant at the one percent level of significance. However, $MEBS$ does not appear to be significant at the one percent level. At the five percent level of significance the critical t-value is 2.093, and at that level all of the variables are statistically significant. It is evident that first order autocorrelation is not present since the Durbin–Watson statistic is 2.01.

In general, the findings suggest that multinational bank presence serves to decrease concentration, although market growth appears to have a more significant influence upon concentration. Despite the fact that concentration in Spanish banking has decreased and it appears that multinational bank presence has had some influence, it does not necessarily mean that banking has become more competitive. We need to explore the impact on net interest margins, which is evaluated in the section below.

III. MULTINATIONAL BANK INFLUENCE ON NET INTEREST MARGINS

(A) Introduction

In view of the relationship between multinational bank presence and concentration in Spanish banking, it was necessary to examine the effect of multinational bank presence on net interest margins. Caves (1974) indicated that the "presence of subsidiaries disposes the industry toward venting its competitive animal spirits through non-price rather than price competition" (p. 124). In other words, the effect of multinational bank presence would be to shift competitive conduct toward product and away from pricing strategies.

Examined in this section is the response of net interest margins to changes in the level of multinational bank presence. The net interest margin is determined by comparing the loan-deposit spreads. The difference between interest rates earned on its assets and interest rates paid on its liabilities covers the banks' costs and provides them with the necessary profits to finance expansion.

(B) Purpose of the Study

This section has a twofold purpose. The first is to construct a model which explains the determination of net interest margins, taking into account multinational bank presence. Second, the model is used to test the hypothesis that multinational bank presence in Spain has had a significant influence on the net interest margin. If this is the case, then the conclusion to be drawn is that competitive conduct has not shifted away from pricing strategies as Caves would suggest. The alternate hypothesis is that multinational bank presence has not had a significant repercussion on net interest margins. In this case, the conclusion to be drawn is that competitive conduct is toward product and away from pricing strategies.

(C) The Model

Fluctuations in the net interest margin are influenced by both endogenous and exogenous factors. The former include the degree of managerial risk aversion, reflected by the asset-liability composition of the banks; the maturity and quality of loans; and the maturity and cost of attracted funds while the latter include general economic conditions and the level of interest rates (Graddy and Karna, 1984; Hempel et al., 1983; and Ho and Saunders, 1981).

To test the hypothesis that multinational bank presence has had a significant effect on the net interest margin in Spain, it was necessary to construct a multivariate model incorporating these exogenous and endogenous factors. The statistical tool employed was ordinary least squares. The multivariate model is specified below:

$$NIM = \beta_0 + \beta_1 MB + \beta_2 IB + \beta_3 GRH + \beta_4 SR + \beta_5 GVT. \qquad (3)$$

The dependent variable, NIM, is net interest margin, the weighted average of the lending rate minus the weighted average of the deposit rate. During the period 1974 to 1983 net interest margins increased from 4.58% to 6.08%.

The independent variables are: MB, multinational bank presence, as measured by the percentage of total loans accounted for by foreign banks; IB, weighted average of the lending rate; GRH, growth rate of loan assets, as measured by the percentage growth of total bank loans; SR, sensitivity ratio, rate sensitive loans divided by total loans, or alternately, rate sensitive liabilities to total loans; GVT, dummy variable, from 1974 to 1980 equal to zero, and from 1981 to 1983 equal to one.

According to Graddy and Karna (1984), resource growth is both a result of bank managers' discretionary actions as well as external changes in the money market. In both cases revenues and costs are influenced by marginal changes in the balance sheet. Although not every change in the balance sheet can be considered discretionary "asset liability managers probably have better control over this determinant of the risk-return position than the other two (asset-liability composition and interest rate movements" (p. 285).

In this model, there are two kinds of assets and liabilities: rate sensitive and fixed rate. Rate sensitive assets and liabilities are influenced by the volatility of interest rates. In other words, a loan or deposit is sensitive if cash flows from the loan or deposit "change in the same direction and general magnitude as the change in short term rates" (Hempel et al., 1983, p. 491). There are various measures that can be used to measure sensitivity. One such measure, the sensitivity ratio or the ratio of sensitive assets divided by sensitive liabilities. Another measure is rate sensitive assets to assets. According to Hempel, with rising short-term rates, if sensitive assets exceed sensitive liabilities, net interest margins will decrease. The implications of this are that a bank's asset-liability mix is influenced by interest rate movements, and that there is a desired sensitivity position. It is assumed that exogenous to the model are the level and fluctuations of interest rates which are determined in the loanable funds market.

In view of the above, the effect of the sensitivity ratio on net interest margins cannot be predicted on *a priori* grounds. Its effect on the sign of the coefficient has to be determined empirically.

The government variable (GVT) was introduced into the equation because in January 1981 the Spanish government liberalized interest rates (Government Decree 1224, January 17, 1981) on both loans and deposits. It was expected that the sign of the coefficient for this variable to be positive, since liberalization of interest rates should increase net interest margins.

The growth rate of loan assets (GRH) coefficient was expected to be negative, since market growth may lead to more competition and hence, lower net interest margins. The lending rate (IB) coefficient was expected to be positive, as an increase in lending rates may lead to increased net interest margins.

Finally, the multinational bank (MB) presence coefficient should be negative, since an increase in multinational bank presence was expected to decline interest margins.

(D) Regression Results

The computer run using all five independent variables yielded the following regression equation results:

$$NIM = 20.2 - 0.82MB + 1.17IB - 3.0GRH - 3.1SR + 3.15GVT. \tag{4}$$
$$(2.55)(2.0)\quad (4.4)\quad (3.25)\quad (2.18)\quad (1.97)$$

$R^2 = .75, SER = 0.82, D-W = 1.94, F-ratio = 8.4, d.f. = 14.$

It appears that the signs of the coefficients were correct. The R^2 was .75, meaning that seventy-five per cent of the variation in the net explained by the variation in the independent variables.

To compare the overall significance, the F-value calculated by the computer run was compared with the corresponding upper tail critical value of the F-distribution. The critical F-value from the statistical tables was 2.96, at a significance level of five percent and fourteen degrees of freedom. Since the computed F-value is 8.43 it was concluded that the regression was statistically significant at both levels.

It is also important to test for the reliability and significance of each independent variable with all other variables are held constant. For these tests the standard error of the regression coefficient and the t-test ratios, reported in parenthesis under equation (4), given above were used. From the statistical tables the critical t-values for $\alpha = 0.05$ and fourteen degrees of freedom is 2.145. Since the t-test ratios for IB, GRH, and SR were greater, It was concluded that the variables were statistically significant at the five percent level of significance. However, multinational bank presence (MB) and (GVT) did not appear to be statistically significant at the five percent level. However, since the t-value for MB was 2.0 compared to the critical value of 2.145, it was concluded that it was significant at the .06 level. In addition, at the ten percent level of significance, the critical t-value is 1.761 and all of the variables were statistically significant. Since the Durbin–Watson statistic is 1.95, no autocorrelation is present.

In general, the findings suggest that net interest margins are influenced by market rates, market growth, and the banks' asset-liability mix, supporting the findings of Graddy and Karna (1984) and Ho and Saunders (1981). In addition, multinational bank presence was found to be statistically significant, lending support to the hypothesis that multinational bank presence had a significant influence on net interest margins. The conclusion can be drawn that competitive conduct has not shifted away from pricing strategies as Caves would suggest.

IV. CONCLUSION

Based on the above findings, it appears that the presence of multinational banks in Spain have had some effect on the levels of concentration and net interest margins. However, it is not clear whether or not Spanish banking has become more or less competitive as a result. It is hoped that the results that have been obtained, which seem plausible and interesting, will provide incentive for further work in the area, since the question is still an open one.

REFERENCES

Bonitsis, Theologos Homer and Rivera-Solis, Luis E., "External Liberalization and Industrial Concentration: The Evidence from Spain," *Journal of Applied Business Research* (Summer 1995), Vol. 11, No. 3, pp. 7–15.

Caves, R. E., "Industrial Organization," in *Economic Analysis and the Multinational Enterprise*, John H. Dunning, editor (New York, New York: Praeger Publishers, 1974), pp. 115–146.

Cho, Kang Rae, "Foreign Banking Presence and Banking Market Concentration," *The Journal of Development Studies* (October 1990), No. 1, pp. 98–112.

Clark, Jeffrey and Speaker, Paul, "The Impact of Entry Conditions on the Concentration–Profitability Relationships in Banking," *Quarterly Review of Economics and Finance* (Winter 1992), Vol. 32, No. 4, pp. 44–66.

Connor, John M., and Muller, William F., *Market Power and Profitability of Multinational Corporations in Brazil and Mexico*, Report to the Subcommittee on Foreign Economic Policy, U.S. Senate, 95th Congress First Session (1977), Washington, D.C.

Consejo Superior Bancario, *Anuario Estadistico de la Banca Privada: 1981* (1982), Madrid, Spain.

Consejo Superior Bancario, *Balances y Estadisticas de la Banca Privada* (December 1975–December 1983), Madrid, Spain.

Dunning, J. H., "The Determinants of International Production," *Oxford Economic Papers* (November 1973), pp. 289–336.

Dunning, J. H., "Multinational Enterprises, Market Structure, Economic Power and Industrial Policy," *Journal of World Trade Law* (1974), Vol. 8, pp. 575–613.

Graddy, Duane B. and Adi S. Karna, "Net Interest Margin Sensitivity Among Banks of Different Sizes," *Journal of Bank Research* (Winter 1984), pp. 283–290.

Hempel, George, et al., *Bank Management Text and Cases*, second edition (New York, New York: John Wiley & Sons, 1983).

Ho, S. Y. and Saunders, Anthony, "The Determinants of Bank Interest Margins: Theory and Empirical Evidence," *Journal of Finance and Quantitative Analysis* (November 1981), Vol. XVI, No. 4, pp. 581–600.

Lall, Sanjaya, "Multinationals and Market Structure in an Open Developing Economy: The Case of Malaysia," *Weltwirt-Schaftliches Arc* (1979), 115, pp. 325–348.

Ministry of Economy and Commerce, "The Liberalization of Interest Rates and Bank Dividends," *Ministerial Order 1224* (January 19, 1981).

Newfarmer, Richard S. and Mueller, William F., *Multinational Corporations in Brazil and Mexico: Structural Sources of Economic and Noneconomic Power*, Report to the Subcommittee on Multinational Corporations of the Committee on Foreign Relations, U.S. Senate, 94th Congress, First Session (1975), Washington, D.C.

Newfarmer, Richard S., "TNC Takeovers in Brazil: The Uneven Distribution of Benefits in the Market for Firms," *Working Paper*, University of Notre Dame, Indiana (1978).

OECD, *Financial Statistics Monthly* (December 1983).

Rivera-Solis, Luis Eduardo, "Multidimensional Banks and Market Structure: The Case of Spain," *The International Journal of Finance* (Autumn 1993), Vol. 6, No. 1, pp. 709–715.

Rosenbluth, G., "The Relation Between Foreign Control and Concentration in Canadian Industry," *The Canadian Journal of Economics* (1970), Vol. 1, pp. 14–38.

Smirlock, Michael and Brown, David, "Collusion, Efficiency and Pricing: Behavior Evidence from the Banking Industry," *Economic Inquiry* (January 1986), pp. 85–96.

Steuer, Max D., *The Impact of Foreign Direct Investment on the United Kingdom* (London, England: HMSO, 1973).

5

MODELS OF INTERNATIONAL TRADE AND OF INTERNATIONAL TRAVEL: A COMPARATIVE REVIEW

Petros Anastasopoulos
Fairleigh Dickenson University

I. ECONOMETRIC MODELS OF INTERNATIONAL TRADE

(A) Justifying the Qualification of International Relationships

The various econometric models developed in studies of international trade over the past fifty years have served a variety of theoretical and practical purposes. While the theoretical merits of these models, which have been among the most numerous to appear in the relevant literature, have not been overlooked, their great popularity and growth is primarily due the their broad applicability.[1] Moreover, the fact that statistical data in this particular branch of economics have been kept in great detail undoubtedly facilitated and encouraged econometric investigation. According to S. J. Prais, researchers have had accessibility to statistical information with regard to international trade for several countries. This availability of information has existed over a long period of time and in some cases over centuries (Prais, 1962).

International trade studies have traditionally focused on the estimation of price elasticities of demand with regard to a country's imports and exports. Also, income elasticities have gained theoretical and practical importance, particularly for expanding economies (Houthakker and Magee, 1969; Kreinin, 1967). For example, an income elasticity of demand for a country's imports measures the extent to which changes in its national or disposable income affects the volume of its imports.

---

[1] Particularly with regard to policies concerning the balance of payments, tariffs, exchange rates, etc.

With respect to the development of world trade models, a general justification that has often been advanced is the need to remedy the over-simplified Keynesian model (Taplin, 1967). For example, the Keynesian model while it was extended to capture domestic economic interdependencies, it did not include variables reflecting international interdependencies of trade flows and capital movements among nations.

Finally, one important concern in international trade studies has been specifically expressed in connection with a country's balance of payments. In a world of increasing international interdependencies domestic and international developments may adversely affect the future direction of a country's balance of payments. As a consequence, this may impose important constraints on national economic policies which are aimed at promoting economic growth.

The connection between the direction of the balance of payments and the magnitude of price and income elasticities has been stressed in several studies. One such argument advanced by Harry G. Johnson seems especially important (Johnson, 1958). Johnson argued that imbalances in the balance of payments may occur in countries with balanced trade, constant prices and constant rates of growth, if the elasticities of demand for their imports and exports differ. For example, let us assume that in country A the income elasticity of demand for its imports is greater than that of its exports. Then, under the assumptions of balanced trade, constant prices and constant growth, we will expect country A's imports to exceed its exports over time. Consequently, country A will develop a trade deficit as its imports will be growing faster than its exports. Furthermore, in cases where this discrepancy in income elasticities is large enough, even a relatively slow growth in A's economy will not be sufficient to reverse this unfavorable trend.

(B) Econometric Research in International Trade:
   The Debate Over the Validity of the OLS Method

Among the first to estimate price elasticities in connection with international trade studies was the pioneer in the field of econometrics, Jan Tinbergen (Cheng, 1959). His extensive writings on this particular topic include a 1937 publication in which he presented a 22 equation model attempting to describe the function of the Netherlands economy (Tinbergen, 1937).

In the subsequent two decades, with the exception of the World War II period, a large number of similar studies were published. The majority of these studies, which appeared in the early 1950's, primarily confirmed the strong relationship existing between a country's national income and its imports (Cheng, 1959). However, with regard to the role of the relative prices of imported and exported goods, this research did not produce any significant results. In a number of cases, the estimates of the relative price coefficients did not pass the significance test, and in several others, even the signs were opposite from the ones being anticipated.

What became of primary importance during that period was Orcutt's article which cast doubt on the validity of time series analysis in international trade (Orcutt, 1950). This article triggered a discussion which later became part of what is known today in econometric theory as the identification problem. Orcutt had cited five sources of possible bias which tend to lower the estimates of price elasticities derived by the customary methods (Prais, 1962).

This article and the discussion which ensued had quite an inhibiting effect on later work. For example, Hans Neisser who in 1953 had just completed an extensive study on international trade using time series analysis, was compelled to state that "... the traditional multiple regression analysis of time series ... is dead" (Neisser, 1958; Neisser and Modigliani, 1953). Nevertheless, the subsequent suggestions and procedures which attempted to ameliorate these problems became a constructive tool for further research. The new approaches which were later proposed and the research generated brought a greater awareness of the conditions under which the classical method could still be meaningfully applied. For example, Orcutt, by his own criticism, elucidated a number of conditions under which the least squares estimates would be unbiased. For instance, he argued that the estimates of the demand elasticities will be closer to their true values if the variance of the residual factors affecting demand could be substantially reduced. This, of course, could be achieved with the inclusion of more relevant variables. Also, he argued that the demand estimates would be more accurate in the case where the supply schedules shift widely, while that of demand shift moderately. As a consequence, in the special case where the supply schedule becomes infinitely elastic, while the shifts in the demand schedule are independent of the shifts in supply, the bias will disappear completely. Finally, the use of statistical tests for the purpose of assessing the validity of econometric results became an integral part of econometric analysis.[2]

Klein, the economics Nobel Laureate who has written extensively on simultaneous equations systems and their applications, seems to agree with the appropriateness of the OLS single equation method in international trade under certain conditions. In international trade relationships, Klein argued, a country's supply and demand functions can be properly estimated by the OLS as long as the country's participation in the world market remains relatively small. Under such circumstances, Klein explicated that a country's internal economic conditions will be expected to have only a minimal effect upon the world market. Consequently, the world prices will be considered by that country as given and the volume of its trade will adjust to these externally determined prices, rendering the OLS an appropriate estimating tool (Klein, 1960).

In conclusion, and in light of the recent vast econometric research in the fields of international trade and tourism, it has become apparent that this early criticism on time series analysis had a constructive and stimulative effect. The variety of methods introduced led to the refinement of the estimating procedures. Moreover, it was the development and the customary use of statistical tests on the significance of the estimated parameters which increased the method's practical importance.

(C) World Trade Models

The world trade models present an ambitious effort to interrelate the flow of goods, services and capital on a global scale. Attempts have been made by several authors to link these flows to a number of economic variables such as incomes, relative prices, the volume of investments, etc., and to non-economic ones, e.g., population, distance, trade agreements, etc.

World trade models resemble the inter-industry analysis of the Leontief type where the investigation focuses on the relative shares of imports and exports among the various trading countries and regions (Beckerman, 1956; Fleming and Tsiang, 1956; League of Nations,

---

[2] No tests of significance were performed on the estimated coefficients in the early econometric studies of international trade.

70

1942). Furthermore, a strong Keynesian influence becomes apparent in several world trade models, where through a system of simultaneous equations the domestic and foreign sectors of interrelated economies are linked through a mechanism of successive transmissions (Rhomberg and Boissonneault, 1964; Polak, 1954; Neisser and Modigliani, 1953; Metzler, 1950).

Finally, world trade models have been presented in the Walrasian scheme of a general equilibrium model. However, while in Walras' original model the trading volumes of goods and services take place in a domestic market, in a Walrasian type world trade model a set of relative prices are linked to the exports and imports of trading countries.

II. ECONOMETRIC MODELS OF INTERNATIONAL TOURISM

(A) Forecasting Methods in Tourism Studies

Three basic methods have been employed in tourism studies in connection with forecasting. These methods are:

  a. the Delphi method;
  b. the gravity and trip-generation models; and
  c. the multi-variable model.

First, the Delphi method is not a strictly scientific technique, but a process whereby ideas and opinions regarding the forecasting of an event are exchanged among specialists in the field. This process of disseminating and exchanging views ceases when a relatively satisfactory consensus of opinions is reached among the participants (Archer, 1976; Linstone and Turoff, 1975).

Originally developed by the Rand Corporation in the early 1960's, the Delphi method was first utilized to forecast technological events. It is relatively recently that its use in forecasting has been extended to the tourist industry.

Secondly, the gravity and trip-generation models are based on the assumption that several natural constraints such as population size and the distance among regions, primarily determine the amount of travel. For example, a typical gravity model will assume the number of trips undertaken between regions to be directly related to the size of the populations of these regions and inversely to their distance. Therefore, a gravity model will be formulated as follows:

$$T_{ij} = \alpha \frac{P_i P_j}{D_{ij}^b}. \tag{1}$$

Where T_{ij} is the number of trips between regions i and j, P_i and P_j are the populations of the two regions and D_{ij} is their distance; a and b are the parameters to be estimated which reflect the unique and qualitative characteristics of the study.

When considering the formula which depicts the Newtonian law governing the motion of bodies in physics, its resemblance with the gravity model formula becomes apparent. For example, Newton's law states that the intensity (F) with which two bodies are attracted or repelled is directly related to their masses (m_1) and (m_2) and inversely related to their distance (r) in the following form:

$$F = K \frac{m_1 m_2}{r^2}. \tag{2}$$

Where K is a constant. The gravity models in practice, of course, are not being used in the simplified form as presented above. Very often, a number of relevant variables will be added, as for example, incomes, traveling costs, the degree of car ownership, etc., together with a set of parameters reflecting the unique features of a destination. A typical gravity model, as the one described above, can be alternatively expressed in a logarithmic form as follows:

$$log T_{ij} = log a + log P_i + log P_j - log D_{ij}. \tag{3}$$

Therefore, a gravity model can easily be transformed into a cross-sectional, multiple regression analysis.

Ultimately, the gravity models, the trip-generation models and the multi-variable regression models are all similar in form. Nevertheless, the differences lie in the hypothesis upon which each model is formulated. For example, gravity models are rigid in form by placing particular emphasis on the constraints which are imposed by distance and population size. On the other hand, the multi-variable regression models which are not as rigid, base their specification primarily on the principles of economic theory.

The trip-generation models represent a combination of the gravity and the multi-variable regression models, i.e., they are either derived from gravity models or they are a refined form of consumer demand equations. Regarding the statistical estimating technique, the OLS method has been almost exclusively applied in all these three types of models.

In the present comparative review only the multi-variable regression models of tourism will be presented. The intention is to demonstrate that these tourism demand models represent simple extensions and/or specific applications of the general international trade models which were developed earlier.

(B) Multiple Regression Models in International Travel and Tourism

One of the first quantitative estimations of the demand for tourism was made by Gunter Menges in 1957. Therefore, this study preceded the majority of similar travel studies by at least a decade (Menges, 1957).

Menges, writing during an era in which Keynesian economics had reached its pinnacle, examined the tourism sector of Switzerland by heavily relying on the Keynesian consumption function model. Through a sequence of disaggregations of this latter model, he formulated his final macroeconomic tourist equation as follows:

$$Y = (C_n + C_t + C_g) + (I_n + I_t) + [(EX_n + EX_t) - (IM_n + IM_t)] - A.$$

(4)

Where Y, C, I, EX, and IM stand for the traditional macroeconomic variables of national income, consumption, investment, exports, and imports, respectively. The subscripts t, n and g represent the tourism, the non-tourism and the government sectors respectively, while A denotes the government's activity in terms of the amount of direct taxes minus that of total subsidies. Further, Menges continued his analysis by constructing econometric equations to estimate the tourist consumption (C_t) and tourist investment (I_t) variables, among other estimations relating to the tourist investment multiplier and acceleration functions. This early study by Menges, despite its serious limitations with reference to the rather small number of observations and lack of statistical tests was, nevertheless, significant for its attempt to examine the tourist sector of Switzerland in connection with the other sectors of its economy. In contrast, the majority of econometric studies on tourism which appeared much later focused exclusively on a county's tourism demand. These models were much more detailed and exhibited a higher level of refinement than Menges' work. However, the latter studies were undertaken in isolation from the rest of the economy. These econometric models, which in their great majority were formulated as single equation demand models, were primarily designed to fulfill specific practical objectives.

In the remaining section of this review, Peter Gray's study on the demand for international travel by the United States and Canada will be reviewed in detail since it is among the earliest and most representative econometric studies on international tourism. Further, other studies from the early development of econometric travel models will be presented with a brief description of their purpose and findings. These studies are listed in chronological order according to publication date since no other organizational order was meaningful.

III. REVIEW OF SALIENT LITERATURE

Peter Gray (1966), a pioneer author in the field of tourism, published his article on the demand for international travel by U.S. and Canadian residents, showing a full awareness of the industry's dynamic potential and its increasing importance with regard to the balance of payment accounts.

Gray's primary aim was to estimate the income and exchange rate elasticities of demand for international travel by American and Canadian tourists bilaterally as well as in relation to the rest of the world.

He stressed the importance of the magnitude of these elasticities due to the valuable information they provide in explicating the relationship which exists between a country's rate of economic growth and the import leakage expected from foreign travel. Aware of the difficulties associated with the estimation process of the demand equation as highlighted in Orcutt's article, Gray made the appropriate assumptions necessary for the proper identification of the demand schedule. For example, he assumed that the supply equation for travel exports are perfectly elastic for any short period of time. Therefore, it becomes possible for the demand equation to be identified. With respect to the price variable, Gray selected the exchange rate which he asserted to be reflective of the responses of the demand for travel. This, he argued, is true because the prices of services and commodities used by foreign visitors are ordinarily determined in advance and in some cases subject to government regulations. Further, he assumed tastes to be reasonably constant and negated the significance of a separate analysis for business travel since this comprises a small percentage (approximately ten per cent) of the total travel account.

The basic equations of Gray's study are as follows:

$$MCU = \alpha_1 Y_c^{b_1} R^{c_1} e^u, \tag{5}$$

$$MCO = \alpha_2 Y_c^{b_2} R^{c_2} T^{d_2} e^u, \tag{6}$$

$$MUC = \alpha_3 Y_u^{b_3} \left(\frac{1}{R}\right)^{c_3} e^u, \tag{7}$$

$$MUC = \alpha_4 Y_u^{b_4} T_u^{d_4} e^u, \tag{8}$$

$$MUC = \alpha_5 Y_u^{b_5} T_u^{d_5} e^u. \tag{9}$$

Where MCU and MCO, are the actual imports on the Canada travel account by Canadian travelers in the United States and the rest of the world, respectively; MUC and MUO are the actual imports on the U.S. travel account by the American travelers in Canada and the rest of the world, respectively; Y_c and Y_u are the disposable per capita income of Canada and the U.S., respectively, measured in constant dollars; R is the rate of exchange; and T_c and T_u represent the cheapest round-trip air fare from Montreal to London and New York to Paris, respectively.

The data employed were annual for the years 1951 to 1963 (i.e., thirteen observations), and the basic results were as follows:

Income elasticities: $b_1 = 1.94$, $b_2 = 6.60$, $b_3 = 2.28$, $b_4 = 5.64$.

Price elasticities: $c_1 = -2.14$, $c_2 = -2.40$, $c_3 = -1.22$.

The high income elasticities of overseas travel (b_2, b_4) were attributed to the large influx of immigrants to Canada and the U.S. from Europe since World War II; while the difference in the price elasticities for the Canadian travelers to the U.S. and the American travelers to Canada (c_1, c_3), was attributed to the success of the depreciation of the Canadian dollar. The transportation cost variable was found not to be significant due to the negative correlations existing between the transport cost and the income variable. Finally, the omission of the transportation cost variable was found to cause an upwards bias.

In conclusion, Gray suggested that the travel account is likely to assume increasing importance, particularly in the event that domestic economic growth policies become restrained by balance of payment considerations.

Blackwell (1970) stated the aims of his study to be : (1) the projection of tourist arrivals to Ireland for the period 1969 to 1978; (2) the study of the determinants of tourist demand in general; (3) the projection of accommodation requirements; and (4) the estimation of the sensitivity of accommodation projections to the length of stay of visitors.

His projections were based on multi-variable regression equations as well as on simple linear extrapolations of past trends. The regression equations presented in Blackwell's study solely refer to the British visitors to Ireland and the American visitors to Europe. He therefore attempted by the use of this latter regression to indirectly estimate American arrivals to Ireland.

Blackwell attempted a variety of specifications which ultimately produced unsatisfactory results. Despite the fact that the obtained R^2s exhibited relatively high values, the only variable with significant coefficients at the 95% level was disposable personal income. In his concluding remarks concerning the projections of future tourists to Ireland and future accommodation needs, Blackwell points to the tentative nature of his findings due to the lack of an adequate data base and the exclusion of other non-quantifiable important variables such as special policy factors, etc.

Jacques R. Artus (1970) attempted to estimate the determinants of expenditures of German travelers abroad, as well as the determinants of German receipts from foreign visitors to Germany. Specifically, he placed emphasis on the October 1969 revaluation of the Deutsche mark and its impact on the foreign travel component of Germany's balance of payments.

He also expressed interest in the price elasticities of foreign travel which he found to be high. For example, the price elasticity coefficients of the German foreign travel receipts and expenditures equations were found to be 3.40 and 2.20, respectively. Further, the income elasticity of German expenditures on foreign travel was also high (1.74). Nevertheless, this elasticity was not as high as the equivalent income elasticities of U.S. and Canadian travelers abroad estimated in Gray's study to be between 1.94–6.60.

Artus interpreted his findings to indicate the deterioration of the German foreign travel account in the near future due to the revaluation of the Deutsche mark.

Hossein Askari's (1971) study focused exclusively on the demand for package tours by American travelers. He pursued a cross-section regression analysis which confirmed that incomes, price per day, and number of attractions per day for a particular tour were among the most important determinants of the demand for package tours. The values of the income elasticity coefficient were very high in comparison to the general income coefficients for travel. Askari attributed this discrepancy to the fact that people with increasing incomes have a tendency to first take a number of tours before they will embark on an independent trip. Also, the coefficients of the price per tour variable were very high.

Kevin Barry and J. O'Hagan (1972) in their study attempted to investigate the factors influencing the demand for tourism and recreation in Ireland. The primary intent of the authors was to derive estimates of the determinants of British tourist expenditures to Ireland, which approximately account for fifty per cent of Ireland's total tourist receipts. However, the study was based on expenditures by tourists of all nationalities who travel to Ireland via Britain, due to the difficulty the authors encountered in collecting exclusive British data.

The time period this study covered was from 1956 to 1969 and the most serious problem encountered was that of multicollinearity. Due to multicollinearity, no more than three variables were regressed at a time. Among the various equations tested, the most reliable involved the income and price variables which yielded income and price elasticities of 1.66 and 1.12, respectively. However, the authors suggest that they may have overestimated the true parameters, due to the omission of theoretically important variables such as marketing expenditures and credit restrictions. Finally, the equations which employed data on tourist arrivals rather than tourist expenditures in the dependent variable, yielded superior results.

S. Y. Kwack's (1972) study has as its focal point of an investigation the U.S. travel account which had incurred a deficit of one billion dollars between 1960–1967. Specifically, Kwack expressed an interest in the role which the determinants of travel to and from the U.S. had upon the balance of payments.

For the purpose of his analysis and in order to bring out, as he claims, "far more clearly the variations and patterns of travel spending abroad," Kwack employed quarterly data instead of the customarily used annual data in the econometric studies of travel.

As in most relevant studies both the income and price variables were found to be significant explanatory variables in determining travel expenditure with prices playing a lesser role. Income alone was found to satisfactorily explain real travel expenditure abroad. However, the inclusion of the relative prices reduced the residual variance.

The findings of this investigation suggested that a given rate of increase in U.S. income and prices will raise the deficits with prices exerting a greater impact. Further, in his final recommendations regarding a U.S. policy which would reduce the foreign travel deficit Kwack is not optimistic. From the two relevant variables, namely incomes and prices, which are connected with the deficit of the U.S. travel account only the latter can be incorporated to a U.S. policy. For example, it was estimated that a 1% decrease of the relative price levels in the U.S. will cause a 3.2% decrease in the deficit. However, due to the marginal role attributed to prices in explaining U.S. travel spending, the above assertion may be considered an overstatement.

J. S. Artus (1972), in a second study on tourism, attempts to examine international travel movements in the context and structure of the world trade models previously examined. The econometric model consists of a set of bilateral and multilateral relationships which attempt to explain the short-run determinants of international travel flows. The bilateral relationships refer to travel flows between the United States and Canada, as well as between the latter two countries and Western Europe. The multilateral relationships primarily refer to travel flows among developed countries, and it is precisely among these countries that the great bulk of international travel takes place. Two types of equations, travel expenditures and travel receipts, were employed to assess the determinants of foreign travel. The travel expenditures (travel imports) equations were expressed in a country's national currency and reflected expenditures by its nationals for traveling abroad. The travel receipts equations (travel exports) reflected a country's receipts from its foreign visitors. In his conclusion, Artus pointed out the clear indications of his study's findings with regard to the role of the relative prices in international travel. Between the two types of relative prices considered, i.e., the relative prices of foreign travel, as expressed by the appropriate CPIs, and those of relative exchange rates, the latter was found to reflect more accurately changes of travel flows.

The income elasticities were also high and significant for most international travel flows. For example, for the Western European countries the average income elasticity was estimated to range between 1.16–2.30. In contrast, the travel flows from North America to Western Europe were not found to be particularly influenced by incomes. The latter observation was attributed to the use of national aggregate rather than threshold income data of those income groups who actually travel.

B. V. Bechdolt, Jr. (1973) in his research derives cross-sectional estimates of the demand functions for travel to Hawaii by U.S. visitors. The period under consideration was from 1961 to 1970. During this period, more than ninety per cent of the visitors arrived via air, while ninety-five per cent of the nearly one million surveyed stated the purpose of their trip to be pleasure and/or other non-business activities. Consequently, the study is primarily focusing on the demand for air travel to Hawaii by U.S. tourists.

The results of the study consistently indicated that incomes, expressed either in aggregate or in per capita form, and airline fares were the most significant determinant of the demand for travel to Hawaii.

The aggregate income elasticity was approximately equal to 1, while the per capita income elasticity was approximately equal to 3. The air fare price elasticity was estimated to be approximately -3. This high price elasticity indicated that a reduction in the air fares to Hawaii not only would potentially increase the number of visitors there, but also airlines revenues.

Finally, an examination of the per capita demand for travel to Hawaii revealed a negative time trend in the per capita income elasticity. The above indicated that travel to Hawaii was becoming less attractive and less responsive to per capita income increases among the various states in the U.S. over time. Further, a positive time trend in the price elasticity indicated that per capita demand was becoming less responsive to changes in airline fares over time.

Donald G. Jud and Hyman Joseph (1974) in their research were concerned with the development of tourism in Latin America and its economic potential. By means of an econometric analysis, estimates of the income, price, and travel cost elasticities of the demand for travel to Latin America by foreigners were derived for seventeen selected Latin American countries. The ultimate aim of the study was to provide information regarding the potential contribution of tourism to a strategy of economic development.

The demand of tourism by foreigners in Latin America was assessed in two sets of equations. In the first set, travelers of all nationalities were considered. The second set, included only U.S. travelers who in 1967 accounted for seventy-two percent of all visitors to Latin America. The travel cost elasticities were estimated by pooling time series and cross-sectional data due to the high degree of multicollinearity between the air fare and income variables. The time period under examination was from 1958 to 1968. With respect to the empirical results, the income and price elasticities were very high and they were interpreted to indicate a favorable long-run growth potential as well as a high degree of competitiveness of tourism in Latin America. Also the high values of the travel cost elasticity coefficient suggested the potential benefits from a reduction in air fare costs to both airlines and the tourist industries in Latin America.

This brief presentation of econometric travel models represents the early efforts of tourism researches to understand and quantify the rapid expansion of international travel in the 1960s. Over the last twenty years, the econometric research on international travel has continued to grow. This research is extensive in terms of the large variety of tourist destinations it examines; nevertheless, it is similar in scope and methodology to this study.

IV. CONCLUSIONS

As a result of this comparative review the following conclusions can be drawn: (1) The econometric models of international travel represent specific applications and extensions of the econometric models of international trade which had been developed much earlier. (2) Orcutt's criticism on the time series multiple regression analysis in 1950 had a temporary dampening effect on econometric research on international trade. However, this criticism resulted in the refinement of the estimating procedures and ultimately contributed in enhancing research in the field. (3) Econometric models in international tourism were shown to have a broad applicability, despite their relatively small number. (4) The major determinants of demand for international tourism as well as trade were shown to be disposable incomes and, to a lesser degree relative prices. (5) The income elasticities of the demand for international tourism were found to be high, indicating tourism to be in the category of luxury services. (6) The price elasticities of tourism studies were also high, particularly with respect to the rate of exchange, indicating the competitiveness of the industry, and the potential effects which changes in the rate of exchange may have upon the balance of payments. (7) Inadequate and unreliable statistical data on international travel have had an inhibiting effect on research, and in many instances led researchers into doubting the reliability of their findings.

REFERENCES

Archer, Brian H., *Demand Forecasting in Tourism* (North Wales, United Kingdom: University of Wales Press, 1976).

Artus, J. R., "The Effect of Revaluation on the Foreign Travel Balance of Germany," *IMF Staff Papers* (1970), International Monetary Fund, Vol. 17, pp. 602–617.

Artus, J. R., "An Econometric Analysis of International Travel," *IMF Staff Papers* (1972), International Monetary Fund, Vol. 19, pp. 579–614.

Askari, Hossein, "Demand for Package Tours," *Journal of Transport Economics and Policy* (January 1971), Vol. 5, No. 1, pp. 40–51.

Barry, Kevin and O'Hagan, John, "An Econometric Study of British Tourist Expenditure in Ireland," *Economic and Social Review* (January 1972), Vol. 2–3, pp. 143–161.

Bechdolt, V. Burley, Jr., "Cross-Sectional Travel Demand Functions: U.S. Visitors to Hawaii, 1961–1970," *Quarterly Review of Economics and Business* (Winter 1973), Vol. 13, Part 4, pp. 37–47.

Blackwell, John, "Tourist Traffic and the Demand for Accommodation: Some Projections," *Economic and Social Review* (April 1970), Vol. 1, No. 3, pp. 322–343.

Calatone, J. R., di Benedetto, C. A. and Bojanic, D., "A Comprehensive Review of the Tourism Forecasting Literature," *Journal of Travel Research* (1987), Vol. XXVI, No. 2.

Cheng, Hang S., "Statistical Estimates of Elasticities and Propensities in International Trade: A Survey of Published Studies," *IMF Staff Papers* (1959), International Monetary Fund, Vol. 7, pp. 107–158.

Fleming, J. M. and Tsiang, S. C., "Changes in Competitive Strength and Export Shares of Major Industrial Countries," *IMF Staff Papers* (1956), International Monetary Fund, Vol. V, pp. 218–248.

Golzales, P., and Moral, P., "Analysis of Tourism Trends in Spain," *Annals of Tourism Research* (1996), Vol. 23, No. 4.

Gray, Peter H. "The Demand for International Travel by the United States and Canada," *International Economic Review* (January 1966), Vol. 7, No. 1, pp. 83–92.

Houthakker, S. H. and Magee, Stephen P., "Income and Price Elasticities in World Trade," *The Review of Economics and Statistics* (May 1969), Vol. LI, No. 2, pp. 111–125.

Johnson, H. G., International Trade and Economic Growth (Cambridge, Massachusetts: Harvard University Press, 1958).

Jud, Donald G. and Hyman, Joseph, "International Demand for Latin American Tourism," *Growth and Change* (January 1974), pp. 25–31.

Klein, R. L., "Single Equation vs. Equation System Methods of Estimation in Econometrics," *Econometrica* (October 1960), Vol. 28, No. 4, pp. 866–871.

Kreinin, Mordechai E., "Price Elasticities in International Trade," *The Review of Economics and Statistics* (1967), Vol. 49, pp. 510–516.

Kwack, Y. Sung, "Effects of Income and Prices on Travel Spending Abroad: 1960 III–1967 IV," *International Economic Review* (June 1972), Vol. 13, No. 2, pp. 245–256.

League of Nations, *The Network of World Trade* (Princeton, New Jersey: League of Nations, 1942).

Linstone, H. A. and Turoff, M., editors, *The Delphi-Method: Techniques and Applications* (Boston, Massachusetts: Addison-Wesley, 1975).

Little, J. S., "International Travel in the U.S. Balance of Payments," *New England Economic Review* (May/June 1980), pp. 42–55.

Menges, Gunter, "Macro-Economic Approaches to the Problem of Investment in the Tourist Industry," *The Tourist Review* (1957), No. 4, pp. 153–159.

Metzler, L. A., "A Multiple-Region Theory of Income and Trade," *Econometrica* (1950), Vol. 18, pp. 329–354.

Neisser, Hans, "Comment," *Review of Economics and Statistics* (supp.) (May 1958), 40, 129, quoted in S. J. Prais, (1962), op. cit.

Neisser, Hans and Modigliani, F., *National Income and International Trade: A Quantitative Analysis* (Urbana, Illinois: University of Illinois Press, 1953).

Orcutt, H. G., "Measurement of Price Elasticities in International Trade," *Review of Economics and Statistics* (1950), Vol. 32, 2, pp. 117–132.

Polak, J. J., *An International Economic System* (Chicago, Illinois: Chicago University Press, 1953).

Prais, S. J., "Econometric Research in International Trade: A Review," *Kyklos* (1962), Vol. XV, pp. 560–579.

Rhomberg, Rudolf, and Boissonneault, Lorette, "Effects of Income and Price Changes on the U.S. Balance of Payments," *IMF Staff Papers* (March 1964), International Monetary Fund, Vol. XI, pp. 59–124.

Smeral, E. and Witt, S. F., "Econometric Forecasting of Tourism Demand," *Annals of Tourism Research* (1996), Vol. 23, No. 4.

Taplin, B. Grant, "Models of World Trade," *IMF Staff Papers* (1967), International Monetary Fund, Vol. XIV, pp. 433–453.

Tinbergen, J., *An Econometric Approach to Business Cycle Problems* (1937), S. J. Paris, in H. S. Cheng, op. cit.

Part II

Issues in Statistical Science and Economics

6

THE ANALYSIS OF 2 X 2 TABLES

Vladislav V. Shvyrkov
Sonoma State University

I. INTRODUCTION

The object of this paper is a contingency table with two classification variables and four cross-classifications, i.e., a 2 x 2 table. Conventional statistics teaches that the contingency table can be used when a researcher is interested in whether there is a relationship between two classification variables. The first step to the solution of this problem, according to conventional statistics, is the formulation of the null hypothesis of independence: the two classification variables are independent, i.e., there is no relationship between them.

To test 2 x 2 tables for independence, different methods are used: the Pearson χ^2 test, Fisher's exact test, McNemar's test, Cochran's method, Mantel-Haenszel test, the Lancaster-Irwin method, the likelihood ratio statistic, the Freeman-Tukey χ^2 method (Everitt, 1977), and the Akaike information criterion (Sakamoto et al., 1986).

All these methods are built upon one or more of the following three logical pitfalls of conventional statistics (Shvyrkov, 1997):

1. The prior knowledge of the model of cause is rejected. The prior cause is replaced by an unknown population, which is estimated by employing the sampling distribution method. This method is not reliable since it is based on heterogeneous samples with respect to their distributions (Shvyrkov and Persidsky, 1988).

2. The logical problem of cause-effect is replaced by the statistical formal problem of testing the null hypothesis.

3. The analysis of representativeness of a sample with respect to the population is replaced by testing agreement between the observed cell frequencies and the expected cell frequencies. This test is not reliable since: (a) The expected frequencies represent a fictitious population; and (b) Differences between observed frequencies and expected frequencies do not answer the question: Is the sample

representative of the population? Moreover, the concept of representativeness is not defined. These pitfalls of conventional statistics can be discerned by the following words of Prof. R. Little (1989): we need "to think carefully about the foundations of our methods."

II. THE PRIOR HOMOGENEOUS INVISIBLE POPULATION

From a practical point of view, the main purpose of contingency tables is the analysis of the influence of the explanatory variable. Therefore, we suggest to replace the name of "contingency tables" by the name of "explanatory tables." The analysis of explanatory tables has to be founded on the basis of the prior knowledge regarding the population. This knowledge must be consistent with our understanding of the universe. We agree with Dr. Busu (1988, p. 23) that our contingent and cognitive universe is finite. Therefore, the population of finite realities has to be a causal discrete distribution. According to the principle of minimum, this distribution must be represented by the Bernoulli probability distribution. This Bernoulli probability distribution represents the homogeneous invisible population (HIP). The HIP is a set of homogeneous invisible causes. This set of causes is homogeneous if causes have equal chances to occur. The HIP consists of successful causes (S) and unsuccessful causes (U). Each type of causes has its own constant influence on the effect. Let us assume that the influence of homogeneous successful causes on the effect is greater than the average, and the influence of homogeneous unsuccessful causes on the effect is equal to or less than the average.

In conclusion, it is important to underline that the HIP can be an one-dimensional distribution or a n-dimensional distribution. The one-dimensional HIP consists of one variable which is a cause. The two-dimensional HIP consists of two variables: a cause and an effect.

III. INVISIBLE SAMPLES

To represent a one-dimensional HIP, the sample size must be equal to two, and the number of possible invisible samples (IS) must be equal to four in the following combinations: U∩U, S∩S, S∩U, U∩S. These combinations or the IS are generated under the influence of the random factor. The first two of the IS are not representative of the HIP. Therefore, they are designated by 0 which is the value of representativeness. The next two of the IS are representative of the HIP. Therefore, they are designated by the value of representativeness which is equal to 1. As a result of these designations, the set of the IS in terms of the theoretical values of representativeness can be written as follows: 0, 0, 1, and 1. According to the principle of representativeness, this set is a representative set of invisible samples (RSIS) with respect to the HIP since it contains fifty percent of representative invisible samples.

The IS, drawn from a two-dimensional HIP, make up the same set of the theoretical values of representativeness (TVR). These TVR are to be transformed into the theoretical relative frequencies (TRF) in order to create a pattern for comparison with empirical relative frequencies, Table 1.

Table 1
The Two-Dimensional Homogeneous Invisible Population

Panel A: Theoretical Values of Representativeness

y

x	U	S	Total
U	$U \cap U = 0$	$U \cap S = 1$	1
S	$S \cap U = 1$	$S \cap S = 0$	1
Total	1	1	2

Panel B: Theoretical Relative Frequencies

y

x	U	S	Total
U	0.0	0.5	0.5
S	0.5	0.0	0.5
Total	0.5	0.5	1.0

Note: x is cause and y is effect.

The relation between cause and effect of a two-dimensional HIP is functional. Therefore, the marginal relative frequencies are the same and joint relative frequencies, generated under the influence of the disturbance factor, are equal to zero.

IV. PROBABILISTIC NATURE OF A STATISTICAL DATUM

To construct a bridge between the HIP and a statistical sample, a statistical datum has to be considered as a product of the influence of two types of homogeneous causes: successful (S) and unsuccessful (U). In this case a statistical datum consists of two events, and therefore it is considered as a sample. This sample is indivisible. The indivisible sample, drawn from the HIP, can be presented by one of four possible combinations between U and S.

Taking into account the probabilistic nature of a statistical datum, we can consider an empirical two-dimensional distribution, i.e., a 2 x 2 table, as an approximation to the theoretical two-dimensional distribution. To estimate this approximation, empirical joint relative frequencies must be comparable with the theoretical joint relative frequencies. This comparison is possible if causal marginal distributions of both data sets are the same. To meet this condition, empirical joint relative frequencies must be recomputed according to the following formula:

$$g(\bar{A} \cap \bar{B}) = \frac{f(\bar{A} \cap \bar{B})Q}{f(\bar{A})}, \tag{1}$$

where $Q = 0.5$. The compared new relative frequencies are called the comparable empirical relative frequencies (CERF).

V. TEST FOR HOMOGENEOUS REPRESENTATIVENESS

We are given a 2 x 2 explanatory table, Table 2. This table is built upon the postulate: the education (x) is an explanatory factor, the job position (y) is a response variable. According to this postulate the hypothesis is formulated as follows: the education (x) exerts significant influence on the job position (y), and the influence of the disturbing factor is not significant.

Table 2
Distribution of Employees

| Education, x | Job position, y | | |
	Nonsupervisory position ($\bar{B}$)	Supervisory position (B)	Total
Without college degree ($\bar{A}$)	0.46	0.09	0.55
With college degree (A)	0.07	0.38	0.45
Total	0.53	0.47	1.00

To test this hypothesis, we need to operate with two comparable two-dimensional distributions. Two-dimensional distributions are comparable if their causal marginal distributions are the same. This means that the causal marginal distributions of both data sets are to be uniformly distributed. To meet this condition, comparable empirical relative frequencies (CERF) are computed, see Table 3, according to the formula given by equation (1).

Now we can compare the CERF with the TRF. This comparison is carried out through two stages. At the first stage, we analyze the tendency of the CERF distributed according to the increasing order of TVR, see Table 4. The situation is considered to be normal if the tendency of the CERF is characterized by a continuous increase.

Table 3
Comparable Empirical Relative Frequencies

| Education, x | Job position, y | | |
	$\bar{B}$	B	Total
$\bar{A}$	0.418	0.082	0.50
A	0.078	0.422	0.50
Total	0.496	0.504	1.00

Note:

$$g(\bar{A} \cap \bar{B}) = \frac{f(\bar{A} \cap \bar{B}).Q}{f(\bar{A})} = \frac{(0.46)(0.5)}{0.55} = 0.418.$$

At the second stage, we deal with the analysis of the shape of the two distributions: the TRF and the CERF. These distributions are symmetrical. The TRF distribution is perfectly uniform. The CERF distribution is not perfectly uniform. But the difference between these two distributions is not significant since the CERF distribution resembles the TRF distribution by more than fifty percent. The resemblance between these two distributions is measured by the kurtosis coefficient. The kurtosis coefficient of the TRF distribution is equal to one:

$$Kr = \frac{\sum(g - \bar{g})^4}{ns^4} = 1 \qquad (2)$$

The kurtosis coefficient of the CERF distribution is equal to 1.01. This means that the representativeness coefficient is equal to 99%: $Rc = (2 - Kr) = 2 - 1.01 = 0.99$.

In conclusion, the empirical two-dimensional distribution is representative of the HIP and the cause-effect coefficient is equal to 98%:

$$Cec = \frac{g(\bar{B})}{g(B)} = \frac{0.496}{0.504} = 0.98 \qquad (3)$$

This coefficient indicates that the influence of the education on the job position is very strong. The influence of the disturbance factor on the job position constitutes only two percent.

Table 4
Distribution of the TRF and the CERF
According to the TVR

TVR	TRF	CERF
0	0.0	0.078
0	0.0	0.082
1	0.5	0.418
1	0.5	0.422

VI. DISCUSSION

The explanatory table analyzes the cause-effect relationship between two variables. With the help of this table statisticians can test the hypothesis of significant dependence of the response variable on the explanatory variable. The reliability of this test depends upon the data set quality. The quality of the data set is characterized by its representativeness with respect to the HIP. The cause-effect coefficient can be computed and the influence of the explanatory factor can be measured only on the basis of such a data set. Inferences regarding the cause-effect relationship are always specific with respect to the sample. To illustrate the effectiveness of this test, we have computed the Kr, the Rc, and the Cec for different examples published in the scientific literature, Table 5.

The first example, Table 6, was employed by R. Little (1989). In this example the relationship between two variables is functional. Therefore, the Rc and the Cec are equal to one, Table 6.

The second example, Table 7, was employed by R. A. Fisher (1954, p. 95). There are two inferences that can be made regarding this example. First, the data set is representative of the HIP. Second, the influence of the cause (x) on the effect (y) is significant since the $Rc > 0.5$.

The third example, Table 8, was analyzed by Y. Sakamoto and others (1986, p. 121). Employing our test for homogeneous representativeness, we came to the conclusion that the data are not representative of the HIP since the $Rc < 0.5$. Therefore this data set cannot be used for the analysis of the relationship between sex and response.

The fourth example, Table 9, was analyzed by M. Dykes and P. Meier (1975). This analysis was based on a study carried out in Toronto by T. W. Anderson in 1971–1972. The study analyzed the influence of ascorbic acid on the common cold. On the basis of this study and others, Dykes and Meier came to the conclusion that "no clear, reproducible pattern of efficacy has emerged from the review of all the evidence." This conclusion is wrong and misleading since it is based on data which are not representative of the HIP. The reason that these data do not meet the conditions of the homogeneous representativeness is: the optimum amount of ascorbic acid, according to Dr. L. Pauling (1986, pp. 2–8), is different for each individual;

93

since volunteers in the above test took the same amount of ascorbic acid, the dependent variable was, at least, under the influence of two factors. This caused the two-dimensional distribution to be not representative of the HIP.

Our fifth example, Table 10, was analyzed by R. A. Fisher (1954, p. 85). Having computed the χ^2 test statistic ($= 56.234$), Fisher makes the conclusion that y depends significantly on x. This conclusion is not valid since the data are not representative of the HIP.

Table 5

Test of 2 x 2 Tables for Homogeneous Representativeness

Contents	Kurtosis coefficient	Resemblance coefficient	Cause-effect coefficient	Homo-geneous represent-ativeness
1. Explanat-ory Table (Little)	1.0	1.0	1.0	yes
2. Monozygo-te and conviction (Fisher)	1.13	0.87	0.79	yes
3. Sex and responses (Sakamoto and others)	1.78	0.22	not valid	no
4. Ascorbic Acid and Common Cold (Dykes and Meier)	1.92	0.08	not valid	no
5. Inoculation and Attack (Fisher)	1.92	0.08	not valid	no

Table 6

Panel A: Explanatory Table

x	$\bar{B}$	B	p(x)
		y	
$\bar{A}$	0.5	0.0	0.5
A	0.0	0.5	0.5
p (y)	0.5	0.5	1.0

Panel B: Distribution of the TRF and CERF According to the TVR

TVR	TRF	CERF
0	0.0	0.0
0	0.0	0.0
1	0.5	0.5
1	0.5	0.5

Note to Panel A: This example was analyzed by Little (1989).

Note to Panel B: (1) $Kr(g) = 1.0$; (2) $Rc = 1.0$; (3) $Cec = 1.0$.

Table 7

Panel A: Monozygote and Conviction

x	Convicted $\bar{B}$	Not convicted B	Total
Monozygotic $\bar{A}$	0.33	0.01	0.34
Dizygotic (A)	0.06	0.50	0.56
Total	0.39	0.51	1.00

(column header) y

Panel B: Comparable Empirical Relative Frequencies

x	$\bar{B}$	B	Total
$\bar{A}$	0.39	0.12	0.5
A	0.05	0.44	0.5
Total	0.44	0.56	1.0

(column header) y

Panel C: Distribution of the TRF and the CERF According to the TVR

TVR	TRF	CERF
0	0.0	0.05
0	0.0	0.12
1	0.5	0.39
1	0.5	0.44

Note to Panel A: This example was analyzed by R.A. Fisher (1954, p. 95) by χ^2 test statistic.

Note to Panel C: (1) $Kr(g) = 1.13$; (2) $Rc = 0.87$; (3) $Cec = 0.79$.

Table 8

Panel A: Sex and Response

(If you could be born again, would you rather be a man or a woman?)

Sex x	**Response** y **Male** $\bar{B}$	**Female (B)**	**Total**
Male $\bar{A}$	0.39	0.04	0.43
Female (A)	0.23	0.34	0.57
Total	0.62	0.38	1.00

Panel B: Comparable Relative Frequencies

x	y $\bar{B}$	**B**	**Total**
$\bar{A}$	0.45	0.05	0.5
A	0.20	0.30	0.5
Total	0.65	0.35	1.0

Panel C: Distribution of the TRF and the CERF According to the TVR

TVR	TRF	CERF
0	0.0	0.05
0	0.0	0.20
1	0.5	0.30
1	0.5	0.45

Note to Panel A: This example was analyzed by Sakamoto and others (1986, p.121) by employing the Akaike statistic.
Note to Panel C: (1) $Kr(g) = 1.78$; (2) $Rc = 0.22$; (3) $Cec =$ not valid.

Table 9

Panel A: Ascorbic Acid and the Common Cold

			Common cold, y	
Treatment x	No cold $\bar{B}$		Cold B	Total
Placebo $\bar{A}$	0.180		0.322	0.502
Ascorbic acid A	0.260		0.238	0.498
Total	0.440		0.560	1.000

Panel B: Comparable Relative Frequencies

		y	
x	$\bar{B}$	B	Total
$\bar{A}$	0.18	0.32	0.50
A	0.26	0.24	0.50
Total	0.44	0.56	1.00

Panel C: Distribution of the TRF and the CERF According to the TVR

TVR	TRF	CERF
0	0.0	0.18
0	0.0	0.24
1	0.5	0.26
1	0.5	0.32

Note to Panel A: This example was analyzed by Dykes and Meier (1975).
Note to Panel C: (1) $Kr(g) = 1.92$; (2) $Rc = 0.08$; (3) $Cec =$ not valid.

Table 10

Panel A: Inoculation and Attack

		y	
x	Attacked $\bar{B}$	Not Attacked B	Total
Inoculated ($\bar{A}$)	0.003	0.366	0.369
Not inoculated (A)	0.015	0.616	0.631
Total	0.018	0.982	1.000

Panel B: Comparable Relative Frequencies

		y	
x	$\bar{B}$	B	Total
$\bar{A}$	0.004	0.496	0.50
A	0.012	0.448	0.50
Total	0.016	0.984	1.00

Panel C: Distribution of the TRF and the CERF According to the TVR

TVR	TRF	CERF
0	0.0	0.004
0	0.0	0.488
1	0.5	0.012
1	0.5	0.496

Note to Panel A: This example was analyzed by R. A. Fisher (1954, p. 85) by employing the χ^2 test statistic.

Note to Panel C: (1) $Kr(g) =$ not valid; (2) $Rc =$ not valid; (3) $Cec =$ not valid.

REFERENCES

Basu, D., "Statistical Information and Likelihood," in *A Collection of Critical Essays*, J. K. Ghosh, editor (New York, New York: Springer-Verlag, 1988).

Dykes, M. and Meir, P., "Ascorbic Acid and the Common Cold: Evaluation of its Efficacy and Toxicity," *Journal of the American Medical Association* (1975), 231, pp. 1073–1079.

Everitt, B. S., *The Analysis of Contingency Tables* (London, England: Chapman and Hall, 1977).

Fisher, R. A., *Statistical Methods for Research Workers* (New York, New York: Hafner Publishing Company, Inc., 1954).

Little, R. J. A. , "Testing the Equality of Two Independent Binomial Proportions," *The American Statistician* (1989), Vol. 43, pp. 283–288.

Pauling, L., *How to Live Longer and Feel Better* (New York, New York: Avon Books, 1986).

Sakamoto, Y., Ishiguro, M., and Kitagawa, G., *Akaike Information Criterion Statistics* (Tokyo, Japan: KTK Scientific Publishers, 1986).

Shvyrkov, V. V., Persidsky, A., "Nec Deciper, Nec Decipi," *Quantity and Quality in Economic Research, Volume III* (Santa Rosa, California: G. Throwkoff Press, 1988), pp. 94–126.

Shvyrkov, V. V., *The Mystery of Conventional Statistics* (Santa Rosa, California: G. Throwkoff Press, 1997).

7

CONTRASTING APPROACHES TO SOCIO-ECONOMIC STATISTICS IN EAST AND WEST

Othmar W. Winkler
Georgetown University

I. INTRODUCTION

Although this paper was written before the fall of the Berlin Wall, the findings of this study are of far wider than of historic interest. This study investigates the contrast between statistics in the U.S. and East Germany, two countries with very different social systems. The issue came into focus when the author reviewed the latest edition of the East German textbook *"STATISTIK"* by A. Donda, as well as five other textbooks on management- and economic statistics from that country, while at the same time selecting a new American textbook for the business school course "Applied Statistics." Striking differences between socio-economic statistics in the East and in the West became apparent. Statistics in east-bloc and in western societies has to respond to different tasks, resulting in different methodologies, and more importantly, in different conceptions of what constitutes the foundation of statistics. Textbooks from the east-bloc in the U.S. and western textbooks in the east-bloc have been mutually inaccessible, accentuating the isolation in which these separate developments of statistics have taken place. This comparison allows fascinating insights into the strengths and weaknesses of our own approach to socio-economic statistics, and potentially should benefit both sides.

II. BASIC DIFFERENCES IN THE ROLE OF STATISTICS IN EAST AND WEST

"I would like to predict here and now, that within the next two or three years the Cold War game of "Mutually-Assured Destruction" will have wound down–replaced by the emerging game, already beginning, of "Mutually-Assured Development." My evidence in support of this position lies in the accelerating globalization now progressing in our technologies and economies, as well as the global diffusion of pollution and militarization."[1]

The impulse to write this paper grew out of the review of A. Donda's sixth revised edition of *STATISTIK*,[2] a textbook[3] on socio-economic statistics for the study of Economics and (Public) Administration (Wirtschaftswissenschaften) at East German universities. The surprisingly different approach to socio-economic statistics in the textbook under review appears to be generally accepted in East Germany, and obviously also in other east-bloc countries, as was confirmed by other textbooks[4] that also have become available to this author. It was only natural to contrast their approach to statistics

---

[1] Hazel Henderson, *Mutually Assured Development*, Plowshare Press, Center for Economic Conversion, 222C View Street, Mountain View, CA 94041, autumn 1987. This view was expressed by author Henderson during a speaking engagement in Mainland China in the Fall of 1987, a prophetic voice, long before glasnost.

[2] *STATISTIK*, Prof. Dr. Arno Donda, Prof. Dr. Eva Herrde, Prof. Dr. Otfried Kuhn and Prof. Dr. Richard Struck, Verlag Die Wirtschaft, 6. Überarbeitete Auflage, 6th revised edition, (East) Berlin 1986, Demioctavo, 275 p. Literaturverzeichnis (Literature) 2 p., Stichworteverzeichnis (Index) 4 p.

This book, written in German, has been approved for use at Universities and Higher Technical Schools of the Deutsche Demokratische Republik–DDR–(East Germany) by that country's Department of Higher Education (Ministerium Für Hoch- und Fachschulwesen. The four co-authors are professors at East-German universities. Dr. Arno Donda, the first co-author, was also the director of the Central Statistical Office of that country (equivalent to our Bureau of the Census).

The author of this paper got acquainted with this and other university level textbooks of socio-economic statistics through personal contacts at meetings of the International Statistical Institute.

[3] We have become very specialized: discussion of statistical textbooks is believed to be about "teaching," not about theory and methods. Such a limited view is to be deplored. Although difference in "teaching" properly speaking will be touched upon, the following discussion is mainly concerned with differences in the foundation of statistical theory, and with differences in statistical methods.

[4] Prof. Dr. sc. Gotthard Forbrig *Grundriss der Industrie Statistik I*, verlag die Wirtschaft Berlin, Berlin, DDR, 1965. Prof. Dr. sc. Gotthard Forbrig, Prof. Dr. sc. Rumen Janakieff, *Grundiss der Industriestastik II*, Verlag die Wirtschaft Berlin, Berlin, DDR, 1967. Prof. Dr. sc. Gotthard Forbrig, Prof. Dr. sc. Otmar Brosch, Prof. Dr. sc. Ursula Wolff, *Betriebsstatistik*, Verlag die Wirtschaft Berlin, Berlin, DDR, 1983. Prof. Dr. Arno Donda, Prof Dr. Eva Herrde, Prof. Dr. Otfried Kuhn, Prof. Dr. Richard Struck *Statistik*, 3rd edition. Verlag die Wirtschaft Berlin, Berlin, DDR, 1976. Prof. Dr. sc. Gotthard Forbrig, Prof. Dr. sc. Günter Goll, Prof. Dr. sc. Werner Kreitel, Prof. Dr. sc. Ernst Kupfernagel, Dr. sc. Klaus Mätzig, Dr. Werner Modemann, Prof. Dr. sc. Edwin Polaschewski, Prof. Dr. sc. Manfred Reich, Prof. Dr. sc. Gerhard

with our western, Anglo-American, approach. Although the textbook *STATISTIK* and the other East-German textbooks referred to in this paper are not generally available in the U.S., their comparison with American textbooks[5] is fascinating and reveals startling differences which are worth our attention. The East and the West have developed separately along different independent paths from different foundations that underlie our and their approach to socio-economic statistics. The thaw envisioned by the author of the above quote, which actually has happened sooner than expected, will surely also affect the teaching and the substance of Statistics. This comparison should provide new perspectives on how to make statistics more effective in our business schools and departments of economics, particularly those who are preparing their students for a global economy, looking beyond present borders.

Although the title of the book under review is *STATISTIK*, it was written from the very beginning–attested by its five earlier editions–as a textbook about *socio-economic statistics*.[6] The present version of this book, as the foreword to the sixth, revised edition explains,

---

Reinecke, Prof. Dr. sc. Eberhard Schubert, Dr. sc. Ursula Wolff, Lektor Dipl.-Wirtschaftler Rolf Baumgart *Rechnungsfürung und Statistik*, Verlag die Wirtschft Berlin, Berlin, DDR, 1984.

[5] The American textbooks under review are (in alphabetic order of first author): Wayne W. Daniel and James C. Terrell, *Business Statistics–Basic Concepts and Methodology*, 4th edition, Houghton Mifflin Co., Boston, 1986; Morris Hamburg, *Statistical Analysis for Decision Making*, 4th edition, Harcourt Brace, Jovanovich, Publishers and Academic Press, San Diego, 1987; Gerald Keller, B. Warrack, Heinz Bartel, *Statistics for Management and Economics–A Systematic Approach*, Wadsworth Publishing Co., Belmont, Cal., 1988; Heinz Kohler, *Statistics for Business and Economics*, 2nd edition, Scott Foresman & Co. Glenview, Ill., 1988; Edwin Mansfield, *Statistics for Business and Economics–Methods and Applications*, 3rd edition, W. W. Norton & Co., New York, 1987; William Mendenhall, James E. Reinmuth, *Statistics for Management and Economics*, 4th edition, Duxbury Press, Boston, Mass., 1987; John Neter, Wm Wasserman, G. A. Whitmore, *Applied Statistics*, 3rd edition, Allyn and Bacon, Inc., Boston, Mass., 1988.

[6] "... It is the task of *"STATISTIK"* to serve as a guide and reference work for those who study to become public administrators and economists (Staat- und Wirtschaftsfunktionaere) ... this book is concentrating on the problems which ... every public and economic functionary must know ..."
In the formation of specialists in statistical services ... this knowledge will have to be deepened further. In contrast to its predecessor ... (which was entitled) *"Allgemeine Statistik"* this book ... limits itself to questions which every public functionary must know ... as he cannot comply with his leadership (management) role without correct work with statistical information ..." (translated from the foreword to the first edition, Berlin, 1971), p. 9.

has further evolved from a treatise on socio-economic statistics into a textbook about Statistics, Cost and Management Accounting! *"Rechnungsführung und Statistik,"* abbreviated throughout the book as RUST.[7]

The thought of integrating statistics with accounting is alien to western statisticians. If any field comes to mind as overlapping with Business-, Management- and Economic Statistics so that a merger might be considered, it would be mathematics, particularly mathematical statistics, probability-, combinatorial- and differential calculus. It certainly would not be Accounting! In our economic system in which accounting has important private and public roles to play, and in which statistics has veered into probability sampling and decision making under risk, such an affinity between statistics and accounting is indeed difficult to perceive! It is less surprising, however, in an economic system in which all the means of production and material inputs are owned by the same owner–the people (the state). Such an affinity and closeness between statistics and accounting is also taken for granted in the other East German textbooks.

There are differences in the outer appearance of the textbooks from the East and the West. Besides the multicolored pie chart that

---

[7] "... the sixth edition of *STATISTIK* was further submitted to a thorough revision ... because accounting and statistics have proved their value in over two decades in the praxis of the DDR (Deutsche Demokratische Republik) and ... has evolved as a separate and unified scientific field ... integrating socialist statistics and socialist accounting/bookkeeping based on EDP ...."

This process is not yet concluded ... but this book is no longer an introduction for the subject area "statistics" but clearly has become an introduction to the integrated subject field *"Rechnungsführung und Statistik"*–abbreviated as "Rust"[(Cost- and material) Accounting and Statistics]. We intend to further extend this development so that in a few years we will be in a position to present a unified and consistent textbook which will be composed of the following: (a) The foundations of cost and management accounting and statistics; (b) Cost- and management Accounting and Statistics of the (various) domains of economics (e.g., of manufacturing, agriculture, commerce); (c) National Accounting and Statistics; (d) A Lexicon of RUST ... in this revision we used the new laws and ordinances about RUST (decreed in 1963 by state law GBl. I, Nr. 23) ... while also incorporating everything that has so far been successful ..." (translated from p. 11). A thorough discussion of this development is given in chapter 1.4 *Entwicklung der Betrieblichen Rechnungsfuerung und Statistik*, pp. 21–29, G. Forbrig et al. *Industriestatistik*. On pp. 589–590 is a historic listing of the 31 pertinent laws and ordinances establishing RUST, beginning with a law from March 20, 1962, (Verordnung über Massnahmen zur Einführung des Prinzips der Wirtschaftlichen Rechnungsführung in den Betrieben der volkseigenen Wirtschaft) with the most important ruling from May 12, 1966. This law was overhauled in 1975.

graces the white dust jacket of *STATISTIK*–not pictures of a normal curve often found on the outer cover of American textbooks–there is little else that is colorful in that book. The paper is of a lesser quality than we are accustomed in American textbooks. The print of text is clear but small, in single color, with margins that are not sufficient to write comments. The entire book contains only one sketch of the normal curve. Graphs are quite general, usually without scales. Testing of hypotheses is discussed on less than six pages, without the typical graphs of sampling distributions. The algebra of multiple regression is condensed on two pages. "Wahrscheinlichkeit" (probability) is mentioned for the first time on p. 137, halfway into the book, and is not treated as a separate chapter. The term "random variable," or an equivalent expression, does not appear in any of the East German books. Fluctuations in time series other than trend and seasonal-cyclical fluctuations apparently do not exist in east-bloc countries and are not even mentioned–are not called "random fluctuations," but are referred to as "remainder fluctuations," (Restursachen), those that are due to causes that are not included in the investigation, or "unexplained fluctuations." The expression "random fluctuation" is also shunned when discussing residuals in regression analysis.

The book–like the other East German textbooks–does not contain exercises and work problems for the student to do. There are, however, 6–10 simple one-line questions at the end of each chapter to be answered verbally.[8] More surprising is the complete absence of mathematical-statistical tables! Nor are answers given to the questions as is customary in American textbooks. Quite obviously, statistics in East Germany has developed differently from ours, in a society with different goals and an organization that is different. Even the

---

[8] In the foreword to the 3rd edition the complementary workbook with problems for the student to solve is announced "... This textbook ... is complemented by the *"Aufgabensammlung Statistik für Hoch- und Fachschulen."* ... especially prepared for *STATISTIK* ... to practice and strengthen the subject matter ..." Diplom-Wirtschaftler Klaus Eichhorn, Plauen, Dr. Uwe Knabe, Berlin, Dr. Jörg Lange, Magdeburg, Diplom-Wirtschaftler Wolfgang Martin, Gotha, Dr. Theo Schneider, Dresden, Dr. habil. Heinrich Schwarz, Berlin, Professor Dr. sc. Richard Struck, Berlin, Dr. habil. Hans Waschkau, Berlin, Dr. Ulrich Wilczek, Berlin, *AUFGABENSAMMLUNG STATISTIK FÜR HOCH UND FACHSCHULEN MIT AUSFÜHRLICHEN LÖSUNGSWEGEN*. No new workbook is indicated for the 6th revised edition.

academic cultures of the East and the West, with implicit expectations by teachers and students, appear to differ significantly.[9]

At the root of these differences are the quite different expectations as to the role that socio-economic statistics is expected to play in the East and the West. From the first page on, throughout the entire book *STATISTIK*, the importance of statistics is seen in its ability to *reflect* ("Widerspiegeln") the socio-economic reality like in a mirror as its primary and most important task. The results are to guide the socialist decision maker in a non-specific, general, way. There are no hints to formalized decision algorithms of the kind that are typically found in American textbooks in the chapter(s) on "Decision-making under Risk (or uncertainty)." The first four chapters, especially chapter 3, deal extensively with the role statistics plays in the reflection of socio-economic reality in human populations, industrial production, consumption, exports and imports.[10] This "reflecting" of reality in American textbooks is included as a small subset in the chapter on "Descriptive Statistics." But the communists' "reflecting" is much broader, and more central to their thinking than Descriptive Statistics is to ours.[11] In fact, this "Reflecting of socialist reality" is the theoretical foundation of the book *STATISTIK*, rather than our "statistical inference from sample to population." On the other hand, probability and inference which are central to our understanding of socio-economic statistics, is completely de-emphasized in their treatment. Probability–as already mentioned, the word "probability" appears for the first time on p. 137–is neither explained nor

---

[9] The author was informed that in east-bloc universities students rise from their seats in respectful silence when the professor enters and sit down when he signals for them to do so. Students do not ask questions. His teaching is accepted by students without argument. The professor's authority is never questioned.

[10] By the definition of a socialist (communist) economy there is no unemployment and consequently, there are no data on unemployment. That topic, therefore, has no place in a textbook on socialist statistics.

[11] To give an idea of the low esteem in which we hold statistical "description" of reality–descriptive statistics–a quote from a book catalogue in which the textbook *Statistics–Meaning and Method* by Lawrence L. Lapin was advertised
"... a modern introduction to statistics *designed for students ... in the* sciences, *social sciences, ... or engineering ...* The overriding aim of this textbook is to make statistics more interesting and relevant ... To this end, *the author emphasizes inferential statistics, keeping his treatment of descriptive statistics to a minimum ...*" (italics to highlight the relevant passages). Harcourt, Brace, Jovanovich, College Book Catalogue, 1975, pp. 116–117.

discussed in a separate chapter. Bayes or his theorem is not even mentioned. Sampling and inference is discussed in chapter five on only 21 pages (8.14% of the book), but not in the context of probability. The chapter on sampling conveys the impression that a 'good' sample must be representative of the population *rather than random*!

Contrasting with this non-treatment of probability, American (and to an extent, all western) business- and economic- statistics textbooks stress the inference from scientific-experimental evidence, and from random sample surveys. Illustrative examples usually are drawn from engineering, e.g., frequency distributions of symmetrically distributed measurement data on quality control such as lengths of bolts, and from psychology, e.g., distributions of employee test scores. Both represent phenomena in the natural sciences which require a thinking-mode that is not well suited for the aggregate data of the social sciences, business, and economics in particular.

III. REVIEWING TEXTBOOKS FROM EAST AND WEST

The East German textbook under review is Donda, Herrde, Kuhn and Struck's *STATISTIK*,[12] while other pertinent and available East-German textbooks are used as background material.[13]

Seven American textbooks represent the typical western structure of business- management- and economic statistics (see Appendices A–L).[14] They are those textbooks that passed the second screening of the twenty odd new textbooks for eventual adoption for the Fall 1988 Semester. These books are fairly typical in content and structure.

All East German textbooks bear an official seal of approval by that country's Department of Education, permitting their use for university level courses of study in preparation for positions of management and economic planning (Leitungs-und Planungstätigkeit). No comparable official approval is needed for use of American textbooks, be that the U.S. Department of Education, or a professional association such as the ASA.

Of the thirty-four book references indexed in the list of authors (Literaturverzeichnis) of *STATISTIK*, covering the period 1965–1980, all but three are in German, originating in East Germany. Three

---

[12] See footnote no. 2 for full quotation.

[13] See footnote no. 4 for a listing of the complete reference for these books.

[14] See footnote no. 5 for a listing of the seven American textbooks.

books by Russian authors are in Russian, five others by Russian authors have been translated into German.[15] No English language literature is referenced, nor, for that matter, literature in any other language such as French, Swedish, Italian, Dutch or West German.[16] This list of authors is confined to the literature from east-bloc countries to a far greater extent, than was the list of authors in the earlier, third edition of *STATISTIK* which contained a larger number of western authors. It is an indication of the increasing isolation of East German–and probably also of all east-bloc–statistics from the West, especially after the promulgation of a law which declared (economic) Statistics and (Cost- and Management-) Accounting to be one field.[17] Apparently there also exists a growing desire to go their separate, independent ways, developing their own methods that are better suited for their needs than the probability-based statistical method of the West.

A look at our own textbooks, however, reveals an analog situation in reverse: No other than English language literature is considered, and mostly American at that. There are no references to authors from east-bloc countries nor to contributions by French, Italian, Swedisch or West German statisticians.[18] Both sides tend to ignore thinking that goes on outside their own sphere of intellectual and political influence, as if the other side had nothing to contribute and did not even exist.

---

[15] Although B. D. Chatfield, an author with a typical English name, is referenced in two separate footnotes (on p. 227 and p. 231) to the chapter on time series, with a German book title published in Leipzig by an East German publisher, and Irving Fisher's "The making of Index Numbers" quoted in another footnote (on p. 236), neither Chatfield nor I. Fisher are mentioned in the list of authors.

[16] Even discussing "Regression" and ARIMA the authors do not mention the English roots of these methods.

[17] "... wurde 1963 in der DDR auf Beschluss der Partei der Arbeiterklasse das einheitliche System von Rechnungsführung und Statistik geschaffen ... Diese Vereinigung zweiter Informationssysteme ist Resulatat ... der ständig voranschreitenden Vergesellschaftungsprozesse in unserer ... sozialistischen Gesellschaft." Donda, p. 15.

"Spezielle Rechtvorschriften, inbesondere die Verordnung über Rechnungsführung und Statistik vom 11. Juli 1985, (GB1., Teil I Nr.23.) und dazu erlassene Anordnungen des Leiters der SZS (Staatliche Zentrale Für Statistik) ... regeln, wie in allen Betrieben (und Institutionen) mindestens die Erfassung und Nachweisführung zu erfolgen hat ... welche zahlenmässige Informationen in welcher Periodizität zu erfassen und ... aufzubereiten sind ...." (p. 28).

[18] The references to the historic contributions by Poisson, Chebychev, Kolmogorov-Smirnov, Laspeyre, and Paasche are the exceptions.

The East German custom to refer to co-authored books as written by an "Autorenkollektiv " (collective authorship) strikes us as peculiar. In the West the names of all co-authors are listed, occasionally specifying the contribution of each. If there are too many authors, at least the names of the principal co-authors are spelled out.[19]

Although the textbook *STATISTIK* deals with industrial and commercial activities, the term "business" or "economics" never occurs. Instead, another expression recurs frequently and appears to be important for statistics in the east-bloc: "rational" used as an adjective ("rational"), and "to rationalize" statistics, used as a verb ("rationalisieren"). These expressions take the place of 'economizing,' 'streamlining an operation,' or 'cutting the costs of an operation,' e.g., by computerizing an operation. Stressing "Rationalität" and "rationalisieren" in statistics must be important, as it seems to anchor it in marxist philosophy. Its meaning is the opposite of 'unscientific,' or 'irrational,' which has a strong negative connotation.

Surprising also is the absence of the word "statistician" which is replaced, wherever it should be used, by the sentence "... of or by those who are responsible for accounting and statistics (... der verantwortlichen für Rechnungsführung und Statistik" (RUST)). The authors obviously avoid that the economist or manager in charge of

---

[19] I am referring to regular co-authorship, not to books that contain essays by different authors, which have been selected and published under the name of one scholar as the editor of that work.

The expression "collective authorship" is reminiscent of 'collective farms' where everything belongs to all, but no one in particular receives the credit for the success of the enterprise, or is held responsible for its failure. Although collegiality and humility among scholars is praiseworthy, scholarship is a demanding endeavor, usually without a commensurate pecuniary reward. The personal recognition of authorship, then, remains as an important incentive. Reference to a textbook as written by an "Autorenkollektiv" does not give credit to an individual contributing scholar, but also fails to indicate how many authors are involved: *STATISTIK*, for example, has four co-authors, but *INDUSTRIE STATISTIK* has eleven!

There are other expressions which are strange to western readers, like "A collective of workers in a large industrial 'Kombinat' (meaning a group of workers in an industrial corporation or enterprise) ("... ein Kollektiv von Arbeitern im Kombinat ...")". Because statistics is prerequisite to socialist economic planning, there is frequent reference to "der Plan" (what is planned, 'ought to be', the future) vs. "Erfüllung" (what actually was achieved or resulted, the past performance), by short (quarterly) time intervals as well as by five year spans (fünf Jahresplan), by small groups of production units as well as by entire industries." Equivalent references would be to budgets (of a firm) and goals, targets or scenarios (of politico-geographic entities).

statistical operations be mistaken for a mathematical statistician or mathematician. Although some calculus is used and mathematical proficiency by the student is assumed, mathematical demonstrations and proofs are absent in the reviewed textbooks. The authors implicitly assume that mathematics is only auxiliary to socio-economic statistics,[20] and much less part of it than cost- and management accounting. The statisticians' principal role as score keeper of economic activities is clearly understood as shared with the task of bookkeepers and accountants! In western thinking, a good deal of that recording activity is not even considered 'statistics.' Despite this difference in understanding of this recording function of statistics, we are witnessing in the West a revival of concern about it. The renewed interest in non-sampling errors attests to this fact with its concern about the possible distortions that can occur during the process of recording socio-economic reality. Otherwise western statisticians are oblivious of the fact that statistics shares many concepts and responsibilities with cost- and management accounting.[21] The wedge that drove statistics and accounting apart in the West is probability! Because probability only plays a subsidiary role in the statistical system of the east-bloc, it was natural for them to perceive statistics and accounting as one common area.

Statisticians in the West seem to have found the substance of statistical theory–if statistics ever had such a substance as a subject matter field in its own right–in random sampling and probabilistic inference. Statisticians jealously guard it as the core of their profession, as *the* theory of statistics. Sampling, and the need as well as the possibility to draw inferences with probability theory, has become

---

[20] "... besteht die Aufgabe der verantworlichen Für RUST darin aus gesamtvolkswirtschlicher bzw. der Sicht des gesamten Verantwortungsbereichs zu den entscheidenden Wirtschafts-und sozialpolitischen Schwerpunkten (eigenverantwortliche) Analysen auszuarbeiten ...." Donda, et al., p. 67.

(... The task of those who are responsible for managerial accounting and statistics consists of preparing reliable analyses for the centers of economic and/or social-political actions, from the perspective of the entire economy or from the perspective of the corresponding managerial responsibility.)

[21] Othmar W.Winkler, "Statistics in Accounting other than Sampling," *Proceedings of the Business and Economic Statistics Section of ASA* Washington, D.C., 1976, pp. 654–659. Also "Secret Allies? (Accountants and statisticians come from different worlds but have a common methodology and mission. That is why they should share their knowledge.)" *Management Accounting*, June 1985, pp. 48–53.

the most important theoretical instrument. The theory–but not the praxis–of sampling and inference dominate our textbooks to the near total exclusion of concern for the statistical recording of facts in censuses, complete surveys, in registers and inventories. In the book *STATISTIK*, and in east-bloc statistics in general, the stress is on the internal reporting channels in corporations and business firms, and in government activities, supplying complete coverage, with sampling and inference as only an occasional necessity. The textbook really has nothing to say about probability, and little about sampling and inference. This does not necessarily mean that socio-economic statisticians of the east-bloc have no use for sampling.[22] Nonetheless, the textbook under review which was written for future economists and administrators, reveals the relative unimportance the authors attribute to sampling. Sampling and inference are never treated as the foundations of statistics.

Textbooks, by and large, summarize established principles and practices, and, although often ignoring controversies on the cutting edge of the field, usually discuss the controversies of the past. The East-German textbooks under review do not refer to any controversies, past or present.

IV. COMPARING THE LAYOUT OF TEXTBOOK CHAPTERS

With minor exceptions, American textbooks essentially organize the subject matter along similar lines, as can be seen in the chapter sequence of the selected textbooks (see Appendices A–L) despite occasional idiosyncratic departures. As an example, Index Numbers appear in Daniel-Terrell's book as part of the second chapter on descriptive statistics. That relocation was not a bad idea, as index numbers do not really fit into our present theoretical system of sampling and inference. Textbook writers, not knowing what to do with this remnant of an earlier era of statistical theorizing, usually relegate it to one of the last chapters that are disconnected from the rest of the book. American statisticians' hearts are not set on index numbers. Time Series Analysis, on the other hand, to which index numbers are related, has regained respectability in western statisti-

---

[22] Only one book on inference and sampling is listed which apparently was written for a specialized course on sampling: H. Schwarz, *Stichprobenverfahren*, Verlag die Wirtschaft, Berlin, 1975.

cal theory because, especially since Box and Jenkins, it is treated as a special application of sampling theory.

There is also agreement among East German textbooks as to their basic orientation—which is quite different from ours—due to their common socio-economic setting. Although the chapter structure in the East German textbook *STATISTIK* cannot really be matched with American textbooks due to its completely different approach to the subject, the resulting insight was worth the effort.

The original chapter sequence can be seen in the twenty-four tables in Appendices A–L. Because of their completely different structure textbooks from the East, Table 3.B, are not comparable to those from the west, Table 3.A. The content of all textbook chapters, therefore, has been regrouped into eleven classes, as shown in Tables 1, 3.A and 3.B. The pages of text—exclusive of pages with tables, work problems and references—were converted to percentages and juxtaposed in Table 1. By further condensing these eleven groups into seven classes, the discrepancies between East and West are highlighted even more strongly. Although there might be minor changes depending on differences of opinion on where to include a given subchapter of a textbook, the discrepancies in these tables will hardly be affected by these differences in judgement.

V. LENGTH OF CHAPTER AS INDICATOR OF ITS RELATIVE IMPORTANCE

The importance of a topic is reflected in the length of the chapter dedicated to it. If a chapter is important, there will be a greater abundance of available methods, and the subject will be expounded with greater care, on a larger number of pages.[23] The percentage of pages occupied by a topic—assuming that most chapters deal with one topic at a time—can be used as an additional, rough gauge of a textbook author's assessment of the importance of each topic. One may of course object to using the number of textbook pages to assess the importance of topics, particularly when many textbook authors strive to keep the chapters of approximately equal length (as can be

---

[23] Books of a different number of pages had to be expressed in percentages to make them comparable. The East German textbooks do not contain mathematical tables, work exercises or answers to these as part of the book. Therefore the percentages for each chapter were determined for text pages only, excluding pages with mathematical tables and work problems.

seen in the listings of Tables A.1 to L.1 in the Appendix). Some slight condensing of chapters allows us to see more clearly in what these differences between the East and the West consist. Table 1 clearly reveals these discrepancies between the East and the West; the detail for each textbook is given in the Appendix.

Despite the fact that the seven American textbooks differ from each other in a few respects, and the five East German textbooks differ even more among each other, the differences between the East and the West clearly come into profile when comparing the percentages of textbook space devoted in the East and the West to each of the eleven subject matter groupings. Table 1 is worth studying with care. These differences become even more prominent when one combines further the groupings on probability and inference, rows 2, 3 and 4 of Tables 3.A, 3.B and 1; cross section groupings, rows 6 and 7; and all time series groupings, rows 8 and 9. The percentages for these further combined groupings are presented in Table 2.

A glance at these tabulations confirms the contrary distribution of topics. There is a vast difference between the model underlying the East German business and economic statistics, and that underlying the American business and economic statistics. In the American view the organization of statistics is of no concern for its theory (less than 1% of text pages). In the East German view nearly one third of the pages of their textbooks are dedicated to this topic. This discrepancy hints at the fact that in the West the theory of statistics developed in the natural sciences, particularly biology, and has ever since remained closely linked and oriented toward the sciences. American statisticians ignore that the relationship of statistical data with socio-economic reality is quite different from the relationship that exists between the measurement data of scientists and their planned experiments. The East German statisticians, in contrast, are fully aware of the social (not socialist) origin of all economic data.

The near total absence of probability in East German textbooks becomes even more prominent if, in a different grouping in Table 1, the second group "probability theory" is combined with the third group "statistical inference," the fourth group "non-parametric methods,"

Table 1

	TOPIC (Regrouping of the Groups in Table 3.A and 3.B)	All American Textbooks Number of Pages as % of Totals in Table 3.A	All East German Textbooks Numbers of Pages as % of Totals in Table 3.B
1.	Organization of Statistics	0.67%	29.02%
2.	Probability theory, Bayes	12.64%	0.37%
3.	Sampling theory, Inference	33.01%	2.74%
4.	Non-Parametric Methods	10.28%	0.58%
5.	Sampling and Survey Praxis	3.97%	3.85%
6.	Cross Section Analysis, One D	9.64%	24.96%
7.	Cross Section Analysis, more D	10.71%	7.92%
8.	Longitudinal Anlysis: Time Series	7.61%	11.87%
9.	Index Numbers & "Faktorenanalyse"	2.85%	16.78%
10.	Quality Control Methods	1.14%	1.90%
11.	Decision Making under Risk	7.50%	0.00%
	Total Pages of Text in Book	100.02%	99.99%

Table 2

TOPIC (Further regrouping of the Groups in Table 1)	All American Textbooks Number of Pages as % of Totals in Table 3.A	All East German Textbooks Number of Pages as % of Totals in Table 3.B
1. Organization of Statistics	0.67%	29.02%
2. Probability theory, Bayes' Sampling Theory, Inference Non-Parametric Methods	55.92%	3.69%
3. Sampling and Surveys Praxis	3.97%	3.85%
4. Cross Section Analysis, One D Cross Section Analysis, more D	20.35%	32.88%
5. Longitudinal Anal. Time Series, Index Numbers & "Faktorenanalyse"	10.46%	28.65%
6. Quality Control Methods	1.14%	1.90%
7. Decision Making under Risk	7.50%	0.00%
Total Pages of Text in Book	100.00%	99.99%

Table 3.A

TOPIC (Book Chapters and Subchapters grouped according to Topic)	Daniel/ Terrell	Ham- burg	Keller/ Warrack/ Bartel	Kohler	Mans- field	Mend- enhall/ Rein- muth	Neter/ Wasser- man/ White- more	Total Pages on Topic
1. Organization of Statistics	6	0	9	0	0	0	22	37
2. Probability theory, Bayes'	116	108	102	148	42	57	128	701
3. Sampling theory, Inference	208	181	382	173	268	324	295	1831
4. Non-Parametric Methods	95	51	131	92	45	89	67	570
5. Sampling and Surveys Praxis	35	24	6	41	17	64	33	220
6. Cross Section Analysis, one D	91	46	125	87	58	54	74	535
7. Cross Section Analysis, more D	69	94	68	94	86	85	98	594
8. Longitudinal Analysis: Time Series	62	46	48	44	49	85	88	422
9. Index Numbers & "Faktorenanalyse"	7	26	22	38	30	10	25	158
10. Quality Control Methods	35	0	0	0	10	0	18	63
11. Decision Making under Risk	29	121	32	48	76	50	60	416
Total pages of text in book	753	697	925	765	681	818	908	5547

Table 3.B

TOPIC (Regrouped Chapters and Subchapters)	Donda/ Herrde/ Kuhn/ Struck 6th	Donda/ Herrde/ Kuhn/ Struck 5th	Forbrig/ Goll/ Polas- chewski	Büttner/ Lange/ Lange/ Stroh- bach	Forbrig/ Brosch/ Wolff/	Total Textbook Pages on Topic
1. Organization of Statistics	79	20	354	32	65	550
2. Probability Theory, Bayes'	0	0	0	0	7	7
3. Sampling Theory, Inference	21	26	0	0	5	52
4. Non-Parametric Methods	5	6	0	0	0	11
5. Sampling and Survey Praxis	2	55	0	16	0	73
6. Cross Section Analysis, one D	54	59	94	124	142	473
7. Cross Section Analysis, more D	31	32	15	50	22	150
8. Longitudinal Analysis, Time Series	28	37	18	35	107	225
9. Index Numbers & "Faktorenanalyse"	38	33	88	78	81	318
10. Quality Control Methods	0	0	0	0	36	36
11. Decision Making under Risk	0	0	0	0	0	0
Total Pages of Text in Book	258	268	569	335	465	1895

and the eleventh group "decision theory." Whereas American textbooks devote over half of their available space to probability and its applications (53.13%), the East German books devote barely 3% to it. As a consequence of this very different outlook on statistics nonparametric methods are largely missing. If one adds the pages devoted to non-parametric methods the percentage dedicated to probability further increases to 63.41%. The discrepancy between the West and the East rises further to 63% to 3%.

Authors in the East and the West seem agreed to write very little, under 4% that is, about statistical surveys. Even here the similar percentages mask real differences in content. Authors in the East treat all types of statistical surveys. Authors in the West restrict the discussion to the mathematics of random samples, excluding the economic- and population censuses, and large scale continuing socioeconomic sample surveys. In the East and the West the discussion of surveys is not considered to belong into statistical theory.

Group six, "Cross Section Analysis in one Dimension" occupies three times as much space in the East German books than in the American textbooks. The reason lies in themes that are treated in East German but not in American textbooks. There are, e.g., methods of linear interpolation of frequencies to regroup frequency classes that are of different widths and therefore cannot be directly compared. By American standards these and other methods are not even considered as belonging to statistics because statistical theory is equated with random processes and inferences from these. In fact, American statistical theory is limited to these.

Although when joining groups 6 and 7 into the grouping "Cross Section Analysis" the American textbooks (20.35%) fall behind the East German books (32.88%), the real difference consists in their content. The American books treat cross section analysis, frequency distributions, mostly with data of continuing variables, while the East German textbooks consider mostly qualitative (attribute) data.

An analogous picture emerges when aggregating group 8 "Longitudinal Analysis" with group 9, "Index Numbers." The 10.46% of American textbooks contrasts with the 28.65% of the East German textbooks, a proportion of 1:3.[24]

---

[24] This contrast is somewhat overstated because in group 9 the East German textbooks also include "Faktoren Analyse," which applies the index number tech-

VI. THE IMPORTANCE OF A TOPIC INDICATED BY ITS POSITION IN THE CHAPTER SEQUENCE

The sequence in which statistical topics are presented follows an inner logic, although it is not as convincing an argument as the amount of attention that is paid to each topic. But there is a lot one can learn by exploring the sequencing of these topics. It would stand to reason that basic, important topics are treated before all others, because the other topics build on them, and are contained in what I would call "core chapters." Following these, at the end, are miscellaneous topics that do not fit into this system, yet are believed to be of sufficient importance so as not to be omitted altogether.

It has been customary in the English speaking West to discuss "Descriptive Statistics," i.e., frequency distributions, at the beginning of textbooks. That chapter is limited to one-dimensional cross section analysis with data in ratio–scales, interval and occasionally, ordinal scales–like measurements in the sciences–also includes the attendant measures of central tendency, dispersion and asymmetry. The main reason for this priority given to frequency distributions seems to be rooted in the fact that acquaintance with frequency distributions is deemed to be the proper introduction to probabilities. Also, this kind of 'Descriptive Statistics' is considered important because socio-economic statisticians in the West, like their colleagues from the hard sciences, believe that 'reality' is confined to that which can be measured quantitatively and accurately. In fact, the Anglo-American statistical theory is heavily indebted to the natural sciences, particularly biology. Yet the majority of socio-economic data are categorical attributes of economic activities, and social facts which defy precise 'scientific' measurement. These data, such as type of occupation, kind of industry, type of product, ethnic categories, marital status, and innumerable other non-quantitative socio-economic characteristics are not included in the Western idea of "Descriptive Statistics." The overwhelming majority of socio-economic data is of this kind and remains altogether excluded from textbooks in business and economic statistics.[25] The statistical description of socio-economic

---

nique also to data which are not a time series. That use of index numbers seems unknown to American statisticians.

[25] Chi-square analysis and statistical inference from sample proportions and percentages does not analyze attribute data in analogy to the measures of frequency

reality per se is not part of western statistical theory, despite statements such as "Descriptive statistics is concerned with summarizing and describing a given set of data."[26]

This attitude is rooted in the manner in which the natural sciences pursue empirical investigation. Its practitioners deal with quantities that are the result of scientific experiments. All measurements, regardless of how carefully carried out, tend to deviate from their true value due to a variety of factors that affect the measurement process. The results of such measurements then deviate from their true value. Repeat measurements of the same object should bring to light the "true" value of the measured object through the shape of the distribution of these error-afflicted measurements. Western statisticians today still rely on this model of "scientific measurement," even though most data in business and economics are not obtained from experiments, are seldom taken more than once, and do not originate in measurements of a kind and of a precision that would make them comparable to those in the hard sciences. In short, to begin the discussion of socio-economic statistical theory with frequency distributions is due to this model of scientific measurement which has been imported from the "hard sciences." It is a model of "data" that is alien to the social sciences in which aggregate data of qualitative (attribute) characteristics far outnumber data expressed in metric scales. To begin statistical theory for business and economics with frequency distributions is a false start.[27] The teaching of Statistics in our field ought to begin by studying the structure of qualitative data.

The East German, and apparently the socialist approach to statistics, in contrast, is not patterned after this western model of 'scientific measurements.' Their textbooks make it clear in chapter after chapter, that the unique role of statistics consists in conveying the social and economic reality through mostly qualitative statistical data.

---

distribution measures. They only test hypotheses about a "population" assuming that the data at hand are sample data. Measures of association between attribute data are not discussed in business and economic statistics textbooks.

[26] Mansfield, Edwin, *Statistics for Business and Economics*, 3rd edition, 1987, W. W. Norton & Co., p. 3.

[27] This appears to be one of the reasons why students of business and economics often lose interest in the study of statistics very early in the course. Students seem to have a better intuitive grasp of the inappropriateness of our western statistical theory than many of their teachers who seem oblivious of these facts.

It is this role–not the concern with probability and inference–that justifies their interest in statistics. The word constantly used in the East German textbooks is "Widerspiegelung," that is, 'reflection' of reality. The authors use a powerful poetic image, comparing the role of statistics with the mirroring quality of a lake in which the surrounding countryside is faithfully reflected.

In American statistics, Frequency Distributions seem of greater importance than Time Series, which customarily are relegated to the end of the textbook. Frequency distributions, however, are cross section data in one dimension, and, like all cross section data, convey a static image of the dynamic social processes, frozen in time, as it were. Such cross section data allow an initial grasp of a socio-economic situation. The main interest, however, resides in statistics' ability to convey a longitudinal perception of the dynamics of the situation. The analysis of time series through condensing the relevant objects into groups of categories, by geographic districts and by appropriate time intervals is of greater interest. But authors of textbooks on business and economic statistics in the West tenaciously cling to the scientific-experimental model according to which frequency distributions are the appropriate topic with which to open the discussion of statistical theory.

VII. OBSERVATIONS REGARDING CHAPTER CONTENT

Next we look at the treatment itself that the author(s) give the topic inside the chapter. After discovering, e.g., that M. Hamburg discusses Index Numbers extensively early on, the first impression that the author attributes importance to the topic, must be tempered by his treatment of index numbers: He accepts them as a routine item, without hinting at problems beneath the surface.[28]

The East German textbooks show a different attitude: At every opportunity the importance of statistics is stressed, for economic planning at all levels, and for the continued control over the flow of materials from warehouse to work site, and from the ready product to the ultimate consumer. This implies a much heavier burden on the Central Statistical office than on equivalent statistical offices in

---

[28] Compare, e.g., O. Winkler, "A New Approach to Measuring Prices," *Proceedings of the Business and Economic Statistics Section of ASA*, San Francsico, 1987, pp. 608–613.

the west. There are numerous examples of "Anmeldung" (a person having to report his (her) arrival to the local police) and Abmeldung (reporting his (her) departure from a locality), delivery of raw material, tools etc. Every change in a person's life, every product delivery, results in another Primärdokument (a statistical source document). The storing of the millions of such statistical source documents creates substantial costs (p. 53) and an obsession with making these tasks "rationell" (cost effective, economical). The automatic capture and transmission of data by EDV (Electronic Daten Verarbeitung–the western EDP) is discussed in detail.

American textbooks prefer marketing and finance examples. The book *STATISTIK* draws its examples from production in heavy industry. The arithmetic- and other means in American textbooks cannot be imagined apart from frequency distributions. That hides the true nature of the arithmetic mean as a ratio. In the East German treatment the examples for x-bar recognize and reveal the mean as a ratio, e.g., of the material consumed per unit produced, units produced per worker, costs per unit produced, etc. The possibility to use x-bar also for means in frequency distributions is only mentioned. This exploratory analysis of economic activities with different ratios is referred to as FAKTOREN ANALYSE. $X - bar = \sum m_i / \sum n_i$ is explained as "*Erscheinung (m)*" divided by "*Erscheinung (n);*" in English, "*phenomenon m*" divided by "*phenomenon n.*" No American statistician would call m_i, the use of material in firm i, a phenomenon! The language in the book *STATISTICS*, and in all East German textbooks, is the language of philosophy, not of mathematics. It is hard to say if this use of language has roots in the philosophic background of German academic culture, or is part of the Marxist vocabulary–which both go back to a common root.

An interesting detail emerges in the chapter on forming groups, (Gruppenbildung) p. 89, as shown by the following translation: "... nor can bourgeois statistics do without grouping–it bases its choice of grouping characteristics and delimitation of groups on bourgeois economic theories. From this follows that bourgeois statistics ... is subordinated to the interests of monopoly *bourgeoisie*. The latter (ab)*uses* the potential inherent in *grouping to hide* or mitigate *the facts* that reveal the exploitation. Despite such shortcomings one can use the grouped data of bourgeois statistics ... usually after forming new groups, to analyze the mass phenomena of (their) society. Lenin has shown this convincingly in his studies in which he had to depend on bourgeois statistics (data) ...," p. 89.

Chapter three, by the way, deals with groups that are not directly comparable because of different class widths. By linear interpolation frequencies are regrouped and made comparable. This technique, part of cross sectional statistical analysis, is a unique feature, completely missing in our textbooks.

On p. 101 is the first mention of "random" or "chance" events. In connection with the discussion of the effects of the chosen base on percent changes in a series. The entire chapter three deals with "Widerspiegelung der Struktur Gesellschaftlicher Erscheinungen" (reflecting the structure of phenomena occurring in a society). This is about formation of groups. By our western criteria, that East German textbook *STATISTIK* does not deal with statistics in the first 111 pages. For us Statistical Theory begins and ends with random experiments, random samples, and inference.

It is surprising that Donda's book does not mention "non-parametric statistics," although there is a small and good subchapter in correlation and regression on Rankkorrelation. The method is demonstrated on an example of only seven enterprises with regard to two characteristics x and y. There is no indication which industry, when, or where, nor what the two regressed characteristics represented. In that parsimonious description of its data material the East German authors have done not much better than their western counterparts. The rank correlation coefficient rho is computed as 0.8304 but not explained what that numeric value tells us about those two characteristics in those seven enterprises. Sampling is not mentioned and the reader is left with the impression that this is a population of seven firms.

Another unexpected feature is the discussion of chi-square to explore the association between attributes (non-quantitative characteristics) as a subchapter of correlation and regression. While one would expect to be presented with a measure of the degree of such association between qualitative variables, chi-square does not provide such a measure of association. All it does, is test the Null-Hypothesis of "no interdependence," no influence of one on the other. It does not measure the intensity of such a relationship, if it existed. At best one can reject a Null-Hypothesis, in which case one still has no idea what and how intense the relationship may be. The example used were three occupational groups and three levels of sickness: 'none,' 'light,' and 'severe.' No hint as to what professions and what kind of sicknesses were involved, nor what constitutes light, and what a severe sickness. Nor was there any explanation of the Hypotheses that were implicit, null or otherwise, neither in this example nor in those discussed before it. The formula as well as the dot-notation used was the familiar:

$$chi - square = n * \sum [(n_{ij} - v_{ij})^2 / n_{i.} * n_{.j}]. \tag{1}$$

As to mathematical sophistication, the East German *Statistik* had more than we usually present. In regression it presented and computed the slopes β for a variety of trend lines: linear, exponential, logarithmic, parabolic and hyperbolic. The shortcomings were similar to those in our textbooks: Much "how to," not much "why," and no interpretation of the results. The discussion on the dangers of extrapolating the different curve types beyond the range in x of a given data set, or beyond t in time series, was impressive.

The East German books do not distinguish between simple and multiple correlation, linear and non-linear, parametric and non-parametric regressions. Linear correlation is treated as an afterthought. There are some unaccustomed formulations, such as r, the Pearson coefficient of correlation as "normierte Kovarianz" and $r = \sqrt{(b_1 * b_2)}$ where b_1 belongs to $y = a_1 + b_1 x$ and b_2 belongs to $x = a_2 + b_2 y$.

The East German textbooks do not discuss Analysis of Variance, and regression is presented without the convenient ANOVA concepts.

Fisher's confidence formula for r is given without mentioning Fisher, without any table of the value for t, without explaining degrees of freedom, or the true meaning of its result.[29]

On the other hand, in American textbooks there is no mention, let alone description of any census or any of the numerous continuing data gathering efforts of government agencies. There is not one word

---

[29] A. Donda, p. 194, the "Prüefgrösse t" $t = r * sqr(n - 2)/sqr(n - r^2)$ is explained as: "whenever the value computed from r and n exceeds the tabular value for the random maximum value of t, given a desired degree of probability for the assurance of this information, then b and r respectively are not due to random, but due to an existing regression between x and y. In the table the maximum random value for t is to be read from the value of $n - 2$ ...."

about how statistical data in business and economics are produced. Instead data are treated as if they were "measurements" resulting from controlled scientific experiments. Nothing is said about economic data aggregates, and what happens to individual pieces of statistical information in the aggregation process.

VIII. DIFFERENCES IN HOW TEACHING IS ACCOMPLISHED

The East German textbooks are nicely presented with a colorful dust cover, though nowhere near the lavish appearance of American textbooks. Their writing style is lean and clear, examples are mostly taken from heavy industry but give little detail regarding the where, when and what (e.g., which industry) of the numeric examples, although these seem to be real data. Students are advised not to bother with hand held calculators, but to solve problems with the PP-S (Program Packet-Statistik) on the Kombinat Robotron (a mainframe computer). The East German textbooks reflect an austere cultural setting, and place the burden of learning on the student. These textbooks are not as user-friendly as the lavish textbooks we take for granted in the U.S. American students would find this textbook difficult. Graphs are few and small, only in black and white. There is only one example per topic. Some necessary calculations are missing, only two or three steps and the final answer are worked out for the reader. There are no exercise examples at the end of each chapter. The same publisher has published a statistical workbook with work problems written by different authors. There is no indication which textbook these work problems are meant to accompany, and whether it is required. Another reference work, *Tafeln der Mathematischen Statistik* by Müller, Neumann, and Storm, is repeatedly referred to, but it is not clear whether this collection of mathematical tables is required for students.

In contrast, all American textbooks contain mathematical statistical tables and work problems, are printed on high-gloss paper, with a large number of color graphs, summaries of formulas, even appendices for computer languages (e.g., MINITAB, SAS, SPSS or BMDP). It is amazing what the competition on the American textbook market has done to the appearance of these textbooks. But let me quote here one dissenting voice deploring such unnecessary lavishness, which adds to the rising cost of higher learning: "Textbooks of

125

seven or eight hundred pages are common in Business Statistics. Such length seems inexcusable for one semester courses where a student is typically expected to have 45 hours of class and put in a further 90 hours of study. Rather than expect students to skim through 50 pages ... of weekly study, give them something which will force them to think about the material they are studying. *Textbooks should be dense in ideas, but short in length, and modest in coverage* ... to cover selected material briefly and well ... consisting of core concepts, filled out and reinforced by examples of their application."[30] The East German textbooks, especially Donda's *STATISTIK*, only 275 pages long, yet covering a wide range of topics, would fill this prescription.

American textbooks have too many work problems. Because of their excessive number, work problems often are not thoughtful or realistic, often failing to show what statistics can do in real life.

On the other hand, every chapter in Donda's book ends with between 7–9 "Kontrollfragen" brief review questions. From these I suspect that the "bark" of this book is worse than its "bite." American textbooks have problems arranged not only by subject area (e.g., finance, production, etc.) but also by level of difficulty. The questions in East German textbooks are all simple, to be answered verbally. Questions like "what tasks does the statistical measurement of correlation of interdependency have to solve?" "Please explain the choice of various types of regression by means of Elasticity figures!" or "How does one determine the coefficient of determination B (Bestimmtheitskoeffizient), and what does it reveal?" These are vague questions to be answered obviously in an oral examination, not problems to be computed during a written examination. It does give an idea of what (little) seems to be expected from the students. Perhaps the distinction there is sharper between "Vorlesung" (lecture) and "Laboratorium" (stat lab) than in the U.S.

As an advantage, the basic ideas of each chapter come through more clearly as the student does not drown in a sea of calculations, easily losing sight of the forest for the trees. For the reader it be-

---

[30] Oliver D. Anderson, Temple University, "Statistics Teaching in the USA: A Personal Perspective," in *International Statistical Education Newsletter*, a publication of the ISI, Vol. 8, No.1, Feb. 1988. Despite such laudable suggestions the author continues giving a problem of male and female heights to compute means, etc., again revealing his roots in the natural sciences, not the social sciences!

comes very clear that the purpose of statistics is to "Widerspiegeln" the reality of the social and economic processes which are studied in their structure (cross section analysis) and in their dynamics (longitudinal analysis). This does not become nearly as clear after having worked through one of the voluminous American textbooks. For probability is essentially of no use for analyzing economic and social situations. That for which we spend over 80% of our time teaching statistics is good only to understand randomization .... The work problems in our textbooks convey a false impression: too many deal with numbers that appear to be taken from actual situations. Under closer scrutiny, however, they turn out to be freely invented artificial constructions.[31]

IX. REASONS FOR THE DIFFERENCES BETWEEN EAST AND WEST

There is, above all, a deeper lying difference in the way East and West approach their social reality. The planning in socialist societies stands against the laissez faire in capitalist free market societies that are not centrally planned and, therefore, have an innate uncertainty for the individual entrepreneur. Planning is equalled with "causing" something to happen. Obviously the connection between cause and effect is more direct in Engel's thinking than in that of western thinkers. In the discussion of regression and correlation we read "Die Ursache x_3 übt demnach einen grösseren zahlenmässigen Einfluss auf den Elektroenergieverbrauch aus als x_1," (p. 202). In *STATISTIK* the independent variables x_k are treated as causes! A western author would be more cautious if he would try at all to interpret the situation. He may say that total energy consumption was 2 units (Of what?) per produced unit of product x_2 as against 1 unit per produced unit of x_1. The intercept of the regression line $a = 5$ would have to be put on hold as neither x_1 nor x_2 had a value near zero. If strict linearity and continuity were guaranteed, if neither x_1 nor x_2 units are produced in a time interval, then five units of electricity would be consumed. Such stringent interpretation of statistical regression

---

[31] See, e.g., problems 3.64, 3.65, p. 113, Mendenhall. Also, problem 6.73, p. 114, or 3.67, giving a normal approximation of a binomial problem using Tschebychev. Exercises like these get our students accustomed to rely on results of a mathematical model (here: binomial) as a substitute for reality.

evidence as "causes" may be traced back to Engel's interpretation of all History as causality.

Another difference between the East and the West, which resides in the philosophic foundations of these societies, is the approach to the collection of socio-economic data. "The capture and elaboration must take place with absolute reliability, on time ... and following strictly instructions that have the character of legal regulations ..." (p. 23).[32] In communist countries the state has an absolute Monopoly on socio-economic statistical investigations. It is, e.g., strictly forbidden to launch a statistical inquiry on your own, or to provide data to an investigation that has not been authorized by the council of ministers.[33]

"Kennziffern," that is statistical ratios, are not discussed in American textbooks. The chapter on "Kennziffern und Definitionen" von RUST reveals the rigidity of these coefficients and ratios that are prescribed by law (pp. 50–51). Although all civilized countries have a "statistical law" which, among other things, states the duty of every citizen to cooperate with statistical data collections, such laws have never been enforced in the U.S. The existence of such laws in Holland and Western Germany has not persuaded the population to respond more fully and willingly to the official censuses. Although ideal from a statistician's viewpoint, the East German anchoring of statistics in state laws and ordinances does reveal a different philosophy of the relative (un)importance of the interest of the individual for privacy and withholding of information, or being denied a request for information when this conflicts with the public interest.

The important social topic of unemployment is not included in business and economic statistics, neither in the East nor the West, although for quite different reasons. Socialist countries of the East Bloc officially have no unemployment. Every citizen is guaranteed

---

[32] "Die Erfassung und Verarbeitung muss absolut zuverlässing, termingmäss ... und strikt nach diesen Instruktionen, die den Charakter von gesetzlichen Vorschriften tragen, erfolgen ...," (p. 23).

[33] "Das zentralisierte und das fachliche Berichtswesen wird vom Ministerrat beschlossen. Kein Staatsorgan ist berechtigt irgendwelche zahlenmäessig Angaben von Betrieben oder Kombinaten ohne Zustimmung des Ministerrates zu erfragen. Den Betrieben und Kombinaten ist es verboten ungenehmigten Berichtsanforderungen zu entsprechen, sie sind in diesem Fall verpflichtet unverzüglich eine Dienststelle der SZS zu informieren" (p. 37).

a place of work. In western statistics courses for economists unemployment is considered "Labor Statistics" and is not mentioned because it does not fit into the mathematical theory of inference. From a theory-of-statistics point of view, data and methods dealing with unemployment are not even considered statistics. Such topics like unemployment do not seem to belong to statistics as understood in the west, and therefore are not mentioned in statistics courses to future business leaders and economists. By implication these appear to be of no concern for future business leaders, a serious matter from a practical as well as from an ethical point of view.

Socialist bloc countries seem immune to capitalist business cycles. Even the discussion of such business cycles is missing in the treatment of time series. Their concerns are trend and seasonal fluctuations. But statistics is needed on the national levels for planning. In the West statistics is needed for Decision Making under Uncertainty by the individual entrepreneur. Socio-Economic Statistics and its theory is a product of the society which it must serve and in which it evolves. It is not independent of the social organization of a society. It is not an objective science like physics, or like statistics in the natural sciences.

Continental European Statistical theory became isolated from the Anglo-American Statistical developments during the pre-war and war years. Eastern bloc countries continued to be isolated up to our days. The German (East and West) approach to statistics historically has preferred a conceptual-definition approach to statistics, over the Anglo-American mathematical approach. The lack of exercises in these textbooks, although a separate book on exercises was published by one of the co-authors, this unreadiness to apply the learned theory to problems, but instead, rather to philosophize about it in general terms, seems to be a European, and in particular, a German trait.

X. FUTURE DIRECTIONS OF SOCIO-ECONOMIC STATISTICS

The bulk of American textbooks deals with probability, inference and hypothesis testing. Most of our data are large aggregate figures, totals of produced, exported, imported goods and materials, of price aggregates, etc. Most of these socio-economic data are affected only to a minor extent by sample-related uncertainties, yet by large margins of non-sampling errors. Have we become aware of this disproportion?

Let me offer some conclusions that one might draw from this investigation. Statistics applied to business, management, finance, marketing and economics should limit the treatment of probability strictly to random situations, and to inferences from actual random samples. The testing of unnecessary or useless hypotheses is to be avoided. Instead, the 'Total Survey Design' should become the Theory of Socio-Economic Statistics, from the initial conception of what is to be investigated, designing and testing of the questionnaire, to the final analysis of the socio-economic situation that was statistically investigated. Full attention will have to be paid to the accurate perception of social facts, especially to non-sampling errors. When illustrating analytical methods only actual, recent data about society ought to be used. Their source, place and time of occurrence should always be identified. The demonstration of statistical methods with data from the natural sciences is to be avoided. Statistics must get off the "Natural Science Bandwagon," that is, only those methods should be used without which essential features of the social situation could not be perceived. Probabilistic methods should never be used whenever they are not warranted. They should always be avoided when they add nothing to an analysis—no academic "window dressing." Instead, actual Economic and Population Censuses and large scale sample surveys should be described and evaluated as an important part of teaching future business leaders. Business- and economic-, in fact all social statistics, should be taken out of the hands of mathematicians. By preparation and inclination they have only scant interest in the actual perception of social and economic reality which statistics is to serve.

Neither the East nor the West has escaped the very different social environment within which their statistical thinking evolved. Both sides should discover where they are falling short. Both will benefit from developing a broader-based statistical theory the aim of which must be the undistorted perception and transmission of their socio-economic realities. The American approach to statistics needs to be changed because sampling and inference are insufficient as the theoretical foundation of business and economic statistics. When a broader foundation for its statistical theory is developed it will become easier to perceive its socio-economic environment through another than the probabilistic perspective prevailing today in the West. Random sampling and statistical inference must be given a more limited place among the techniques of statistical inquiry. Then statisticians from East and West will better understand each other.

APPENDIX A

Table A.1

Wayne W. Daniel, James C. Terrell, *BUSINESS STATISTICS*, 4th edition, Houghton Mifflin Co., 1986.

	Chapter	No. of pages	% of Text Pages
1.	Role of Statistics in Decision Making	6	0.80%
2.	Organizing and Summarizing Data	46	6.11%
3.	Some Elementary Probability Concepts	34	4.52%
4.	Some Important Probability Distributions	48	6.37%
5.	Some Important Sampling Distributions	34	4.52%
6.	Statistical Inference I: Estimation	60	7.97%
7.	Statistical Inference II: Hypothesis Testing	70	9.30%
8.	Analysis of Variance	69	9.16%
9.	Simple Linear Regression and Correlation	57	7.57%
10.	Multiple Regression and Correlation	73	9.69%
11.	The Chi-Square Distribution	55	7.30%
12.	Non-Parametric Statistics	40	5.31%
13.	Time Series Analysis and Forecasting	62	8.23%
14.	Elementary Survey Sampling	35	4.65%
15.	Statistical Decision Theory	29	3.85%
16.	Some Statistical Applications in Quality Control	35	4.65%
	Total Number of Text Pages	753	100.00%
	Preface	3	
	Appendix I: Statistical Tables	63	
	Appendix II: A Hypothetical Population	21	
	Appendix III: Ranking of 808 Different Corporations	17	
	Appendix IV: Summation Notation	3	
	Answers to Odd-Numbered Exercises	17	
	Index	5	
	Total Number of Pages in the Book	882	

Table A.2

Wayne W. Daniel, James C. Terrell, *BUSINESS STATISTICS*, 4th edition, Houghton Mifflin Co., 1986.

	Topic (Chapters and Subchapters Regrouped)	No. of Pages	% of Text Pages
1.	National and International Organization of Socio-Economic Statistical Agencies: The Basic Nature of Data	6	0.80%
2.	Probability Concepts and Theory, Random Variables, Bayes' Theorem	116	15.41%
3.	Parametric Sampling Theory, Sampling Distributions and Statistical Inference, Anova	208	27.62%
4.	Nonparametric Theory and Methods, Chi-Square	95	12.62%
5.	The Praxis of Census, Complete Surveys, and Sampling	35	4.65%
6.	Cross Section Analysis in One Dimension by Classes of Categorical, Ratio, Interval and Ordinal Data	91	12.08%
7.	Cross Section Analysis in Two or More Dimensions: Cross-tabulations, Measures of Regression and Association	69	9.16%
8.	Longitudinal Analysis: Time Series and Forecasting	62	8.23%
9.	Index Numbers (incl. "Faktoren Analyse")	7	0.93%
10.	Quality Control Methods	35	4.65%
11.	Decision Making under Risk and Uncertainty	29	3.85%
	Total Number of Text Pages	753	100.00%

APPENDIX B

Table B.1

Morris Hamburg, *STATISTICAL ANALYSIS FOR DECISION MAKING*, Harcourt Brace Jovanovich, Publishers, 4th edition, San Diego, 1987.

	Chapter	No. of Pages	% of Text Pages
1.	Frequency Distribution and Summary Measures	46	6.60%
2.	Introduction to Probability	40	5.74%
3.	Discr. Random variables and Probability Distributions	68	9.76%
4.	Statistical Investigation and Sampling	24	3.44%
5.	Sampling Distributions	38	5.45%
6.	Estimation	32	4.59%
7.	Hypothesis Testing	54	7.75%
8.	Chi-Square Tests and Analysis of Variance	60	8.61%
9.	Regression Analysis and Correlation Analysis	50	7.17%
10.	Multiple Regression and Correlation Analysis	66	9.47%
11.	Time Series	46	6.60%
12.	Index Numbers	26	3.73%
13.	Nonparametric Statistics	26	3.73%
14.	Decision Making using Prior Information	44	6.31%
15.	Decision Making with Posterior Probabilities	20	2.87%
16.	Devising Optimal Strategies prior to Sampling	38	5.45%
17.	Comparisons of Classical and Bayesian Statistics	19	2.73%
	Total Number of Text Pages	697	100.00%
	Preface	4	
	Appendix A: Statistical Tables	30	
	Appendix B: Symbols, Subscripts, Summation	4	
	Appendix C: Properties of Expected Values and Variances	4	
	Appendix D: Shortcut Formulas for equal Class Intervals	3	
	Appendix E: Data Bank for Computer Exercises	3	
	Total Number of Pages in the Book	745	

Table B.2

Morris Hamburg, *STATISTICAL ANALYSIS FOR DECISION MAKING*, Harcourt Brace Jovanovich, 4th edition, 1987.

	Topic (Chapters and Subchapters Regrouped)	No. of pages	% of Text Pages
1.	National and International Organization of Socio-Economic Statistical Agencies: The Basic Nature of Data	0	0.00%
2.	Probability Concepts and Theory, Random Variables, Bayes' Theorem	108	15.49%
3.	Parametric Sampling Theory, Sampling Distributions and Statistical Inference, Anova	181	25.97%
4.	Nonparametric Theory and Methods, Chi-Square	51	7.32%
5.	The Praxis of Census, Complete Surveys and Sampling	24	3.44%
6.	Cross Section Analysis in One Dimension by Classes of Categorical, Ratio, Interval and Ordinal Data	46	6.60%
7.	Cross Section Analysis in Two or More Dimensions: Cross-tabulations, Measures of Regression and Association	94	13.49%
8.	Longitudinal Analysis: Time Series and Forecasting	46	6.60%
9.	Index Numbers (incl. "Faktoren Analyse")	26	3.73%
10.	Quality Control Methods	0	0.00%
11.	Decision Making under Risk and Uncertainty	121	17.36%
	Total Number of Text Pages	697	100.00%

APPENDIX C

Table C.1

Gerald Keller, Brian Warrack, Henry Bartel, *STATISTICS FOR MANAGE-MENT AND ECONOMICS–A SYSTEMATIC APPROACH*, Wadsworth Publishing Co., Belmont, CA, 1988.

	Chapter	No. of Pages	% of Text Pages
1.	Introduction to Statistics	9	0.97%
2.	Descriptive Statistics	74	8.00%
3.	Probability	43	4.65%
4.	Probability Distributions	59	6.38%
5.	Statistical Inference: Introduction	13	1.41%
6.	Sampling and Sampling Distributions	20	2.16%
7.	Inference about ... a Single Population: Interval Scale	57	6.16%
8.	Inference about ... a Single Population: Nominal Scale	16	1.73%
9.	Inference about ... two Populations: Interval Scale	59	6.37%
10.	Inference about ... two Populations: Nominal Scale	18	1.95%
11.	Statistical Inference: A Review of Chs. 7 through 10	44	4.76%
12.	Analysis of Variance	55	5.95%
13.	Chi-Square Tests	42	4.54%
14.	Non Parametric Statistics	66	7.14%
15.	Simple Linear Regression	72	7.78%
16.	Multiple Regression	62	6.70%
17.	Multiple Regression Models	39	4.22%
18.	Statistical Inference: Conclusion	75	8.11%
19.	Time Series and Forecasting	48	5.19%
20.	Index Numbers	22	2.38%
21.	Decision Analysis	32	3.46%
	Total Number of Text Pages	925	100.00%
	(Table of) Content	10	
	Preface	4	
	Appendix A: Answers to Selected Even-Numbered Exercises	10	
	Appendix B: (Mathematical Statistical) Tables	34	
	Index	10	
	Total Number of Pages in Book	993	

Table C.2

G. Keller, B. Warrack, H. Bartel, *STATISTICS FOR MANAGEMENT AND ECONOMICS–A SYSTEMATIC APPROACH*, 1988.

	Topic (Chapters and Subchapters Regrouped)	No. of Pages	% of Text Pages
1.	National and International Organization of Socio-Economic Statistical Agencies: The Basic Nature of Data	9	0.97%
2.	Probability Concepts and Theory, Random Variables, Bayes' Theorem	102	11.03%
3.	Parametric Sampling Theory, Sampling Distributions and Statistical Inference, Anova	382	41.30%
4.	Nonparametric Theory and Methods, Chi-Square	131	14.16%
5.	The Praxis of Census, Complete Surveys, and Sampling	6	0.65%
6.	Cross Section Analysis in One Dimension by Classes of Categorical, Ratio, Interval and Ordinal Data	125	13.51%
7.	Cross Section Analysis in Two or More Dimensions: Cross-tabulations, Measures of Regression and Association	68	7.35%
8.	Longitudinal Analysis: Time Series and Forecasting	48	5.19%
9.	Index Numbers (incl. "Faktoren Analyse")	22	2.38%
10.	Quality Control Methods	0	0.00%
11.	Decision Making under Risk and Uncertainty	32	3.46%
	Total Number of Text Pages	925	100.00%

APPENDIX D

Table D.1

Heinz Kohler, *STATISTICS FOR BUSINESS AND ECONOMICS*, 2nd edition, Scott, Foresman & Co., Glenview, Illinois, 1988.

	Chapter	No. of Pages	% of Text Pages
1.	The Nature of Statistics	5	0.65%
2.	Collection of Data: Surveys and Experiments	41	5.36%
3.	The Presentation of Data: Tables and Graphs	41	5.36%
4.	The Presentation of Data: Summary Measures	44	5.75%
5.	Analytical Theory of Probability	54	7.06%
6.	Discrete Probability Distributions	49	6.41%
7.	Continuous Probability Distributions	45	5.88%
8.	Sampling Distributions and Estimation	53	6.93%
9.	Hypothesis Testing: Classical Techniques	59	7.71%
10.	Hypothesis Testing: The Chi-Square Technique	45	5.88%
11.	Hypothesis Testing: Nonparametric Techniques	47	6.14%
12.	Analysis of Variance	35	4.58%
13.	Simple Regression and Correlation	57	7.45%
14.	Multiple Regression and Correlation	60	7.84%
15.	Time Series and Forecasting	44	5.75%
16.	Index Numbers	38	4.97%
17.	Decision Theory	48	6.27%
	Total Number of Text Pages	765	99.99%

Preface	5
Contents	16
Appendix Tables T1–T38	38
Glossary G1–G19	19
Answer Section A1–A85	85
Acknowledgements	2
Subject Index	9
Glossary of Symbols (inside back cover)	2
Applications by Discipline (inside front cover)	2
Total Number of Pages in the Book	943

Table D.2

Heinz Kohler, *STATISTICS FOR BUSINESS AND ECONOMICS*, 2nd edition, Scott, Foresman & Co., Glenview, Illinois, 1988.

	Topic (Chapters and Subchapters Regrouped)	No. of Pages	% of Text Pages
1.	National and International Organization of Socio-Economic Statistical Agencies: The Basic Nature of Data	0	0.00%
2.	Probability Concepts and Theory, Random Variables, Bayes' Theorem	148	19.35%
3.	Parametric Sampling Theory, Sampling Distributions and Statistical Inference, Anova	173	22.61%
4.	Nonparametric Theory and Methods, Chi-Square	92	12.03%
5.	The Praxis of Census, Complete Surveys, and Sampling	41	5.36%
6.	Cross Section Analysis in One Dimension by Classes of Categorical, Ratio, Interval and Ordinal Data	87	11.37%
7.	Cross Section Analysis in Two or More Dimensions: Cross-tabulations, Measures of Regression and Association	94	12.29%
8.	Longitudinal Analysis: Time Series and Forecasting	44	5.75%
9.	Index Numbers (incl. "Faktoren Analyse")	38	4.97%
10.	Quality Control Methods	0	0.00%
11.	Decision Making under Risk and Uncertainty	48	6.27%
	Total Number of Text Pages	765	100.00%

APPENDIX E

Table E.1

Edwin Mansfield, *STATISTICS FOR BUSINESS AND ECONOMICS-METHODS AND APPLICATIONS*, 3rd edition, W. W. Norton & Co., New York and London, 1987.

	Chapter	No. of Pages	% of Text Pages
1.	Introduction to Statistics (Frequency Distribution, p. 16)	30	4.41%
2.	Summary and Description of Data	40	5.87%
3.	Probability	40	5.87%
4.	Probability Distributions, Expected Values Binom. Dist.	43	6.31%
5.	The Normal and Poisson Distributions	38	5.58%
6.	Sample Designs and Sample Distributions	43	6.31%
7.	Statistical Estimation	44	6.46%
8.	Hypothesis Testing	58	8.52%
9.	Chi-Square Tests and Nonparametric Techniques	43	6.31%
10.	Experimental Design and Analysis of Variance	43	6.31%
11.	Regression and Correlation Techniques	54	7.93%
12.	Multiple Regression and Correlation	52	7.64%
13.	Introduction to Time Series (incl. Forecasting)	49	7.20%
14.	Index Numbers	30	4.41%
15.	Decision Theory: Prior and Posterior Analysis	34	4.99%
16.	Decision Theory: Preposterior and Sequential Analysis	40	5.87%
	Total Number of Text Pages	681	99.99%
	Glossary of Symbols (inside book covers)	3	
	(Table of) Contents	8	
	Preface	6	
	Appendix (Mathematical Statistical Tables)	31	
	Answers to Odd-Numbered Exercises	86	
	Index	10	
	Total Number of Pages in the Book	825	

Table E.2

Edwin Mansfield, *STATISTICS FOR BUSINESS AND ECONOMICS–METHODS AND APPLICATIONS*, 3rd edition, New York, 1987.

	Topic (Chapters and Subchapters Regrouped)	No. of Pages	% of Text Pages
1.	National and International Organization of Socio-Economic Statistical Agencies: The Basic Nature of Data	0	0.00%
2.	Probability Concepts and Theory, Random Variables, Bayes' Theorem	42	6.17%
3.	Parametric Sampling Theory, Sampling Distributions and Statistical Inference, Anova	268	39.35%
4.	Nonparametric Theory and Methods, Chi-Square	45	6.61%
5.	The Praxis of Census, Complete Surveys, and Sampling	17	2.50%
6.	Cross Section Analysis in One Dimension by Classes of Categorical, Ratio, Interval and Ordinal Data	58	8.52%
7.	Cross Section Analysis in Two or More Dimensions: Cross-tabulations, Measures of Regression and Association	86	12.63%
8.	Longitudinal Analysis: Time Series and Forecasting	49	7.20%
9.	Index Numbers (incl. "Faktoren Analyse")	30	4.41%
10.	Quality Control Methods	10	1.47%
11.	Decision Making under Risk and Uncertainty	76	11.16%
	Total Number of Text Pages	681	100.02%

APPENDIX F

Table F.1

William Mendenhall, James E. Reinmuth, *STATISTICS FOR MANAGEMENT AND ECONOMICS*, 4th edition, Duxbury Press, Boston, Mass., 1982.

	Chapter	No. of Pages	% of Text Pages
1.	What is Statistics?	9	1.10%
2.	Describing Sets of Measurements	54	6.60%
3.	Probability	57	6.97%
4.	Random Variables and Probability Distributions	32	3.91%
5.	Three Useful Probability Distributions	51	6.23%
6.	The Normal Probability Distribution	39	4.77%
7.	Large-Sample Statistical Inference	71	8.68%
8.	Inference from Small Samples	49	5.99%
9.	Decision Analysis	50	6.11%
10.	Linear Regression and Correlation	47	5.75%
11.	Multiple Regression	71	8.68%
12.	The Analysis of Variance	49	5.99%
13.	Elements of Time Series Analysis	40	4.89%
14.	Forecasting Models	55	6.72%
15.	Survey Sampling	55	6.72%
16.	Analysis of Enumerative Data (Chi-Square)	32	3.91%
17.	Nonparametric Statistics	57	6.97%
	Total Number of Text Pages	818	100.00%
	Preface	3	
	Literature Cited	5	
	(Table of) Contents	5	
	Appendix Tables	27	
	Glossary	10	
	Answers to Exercises	26	
	Index	9	
	Total Number of Pages in the Book	903	

Table F.2

William Mendenhall, James E. Reinmuth, *STATISTICS FOR MAN-AGEMENT AND ECONOMICS*, 4th edition, Boston, Mass., 1982.

	Topic (Chapters and Subchapters Regrouped)	No. of Pages	% of Text Pages
1.	National and International Organization of Socio-Economic Statistical Agencies: The Basic Nature of Data	0	0.00%
2.	Probability Concepts and Theory, Random Variables, Bayes' Theorem	57	6.97%
3.	Parametric Sampling Theory, Sampling Distributions and Statistical Inference, Anova	324	39.61%
4.	Nonparametric Theory and Methods, Chi-Square	89	10.88%
5.	The Praxis of Census, Complete Surveys, and Sampling	64	7.82%
6.	Cross Section Analysis in One Dimension by Classes of Categorical, Ratio, Interval and Ordinal Data	54	6.60%
7.	Cross Section Analysis in Two or More Dimensions: Cross-tabulations, Measures of Regression and Association	85	10.39%
8.	Longitudinal Analysis: Time Series and Forecasting	85	10.39%
9.	Index Numbers (incl. "Faktoren Analyse")	10	1.22%
10.	Quality Control Methods	0	0.00%
11.	Decision Making under Risk and Uncertainty	50	6.11%
	Total Number of Text Pages	818	99.99%

APPENDIX G

Table G.1

John Neter, William Wasserman, G. A. Whitmore, *APPLIED STATISTICS*, 3rd edition, Allyn & Bacon, Inc., Boston, Mass., 1988.

	Chapter	No. of Pages	% of Text Pages
1.	Data Acquisition	18	1.98%
2.	Data Analysis I: Classification and Dist. Patterns	34	3.74%
3.	Data Analysis II: Summary Measures	44	4.85%
4.	Basic Probability Concepts	43	4.73%
5.	Random Variables	39	4.30%
6.	Common Discrete Probability Distributions	24	2.64%
7.	Common Continuous Probability Distributions	22	2.42%
8.	Statistical Sampling	20	2.20%
9.	Sampling Distribution of x-bar	20	2.20%
10.	Estimation of Population Mean	37	4.07%
11.	Tests for Population Mean	57	6.28%
12.	Inference for Population Proportions	31	3.41%
13.	Comparisons of Two Populations and other Inferences	41	4.52%
14.	Quality Control and other Applications of Sampling	39	4.30%
15.	Nonparametric Procedures	44	4.85%
16.	Goodness of Fit	23	2.53%
17.	Multinomial Populations	31	3.41%
18.	Simple Linear Regression	38	4.19%
19.	Inferences in Simple Linear Regression	36	3.96%
20.	Multiple Regression	60	6.61%
21.	Analysis of Variance	34	3.74%
22.	Bayesian Decision Making I: No Sample Information	36	3.96%
23.	Bayesian Decision Making II: Sample Information	24	2.64%
24.	Time Series Analysis Forecasting I: Classical Method	44	4.85%
25.	Time Series and Forecasting II: Exponential Smoothing and Regression Methods	44	4.85%
26.	Price and Quantity Indexes	25	2.75%
	Total Number of Text Pages	908	99.98%
	Appendix A: Mathematical Review	9	
	Appendix B: Chi-Square, t and F Distributions	11	
	Appendix C: (Mathematical Statistical) Tables	19	
	Appendix D: Data Sets	11	
	Answers to Selected Problems	20	
	Index, Table of Contents	17	
	Preface, Introduction, Tables in Book Covers	13	
	Total Number of Pages in the Book	1008	

Table G.2

J. Neter, Wm. Wasserman, G. Whitmore, *APPLIED STATISTICS*, 3rd edition, Allyn & Bacon, Boston, Mass., 1988.

	Topic (Chapters and Subchapters Regrouped)	No. of Pages	% of Text Pages
1.	National and International Organization of Socio-Economic Statistical Agencies: The Basic Nature of Data	22	2.42%
2.	Probability Concepts and Theory, Random Variables, Bayes' Theorem	128	14.10%
3.	Parametric Sampling Theory, Sampling Distributions and Statistical Inference, Anova	295	32.49%
4.	Nonparametric Theory and Methods, Chi-Square	67	7.38%
5.	The Praxis of Census, Complete Surveys, and Sampling	33	3.63%
6.	Cross Section Analysis in One Dimension by Classes of Categorical, Ratio, Interval and Ordinal Data	74	8.15%
7.	Cross Section Analysis in Two or More Dimensions: Cross-tabulations, Measures of Regression and Association	98	10.79%
8.	Longitudinal Analysis: Time Series and Forecasting	88	9.69%
9.	Index Numbers (incl. "Faktoren Analyse")	25	2.75%
10.	Quality Control Methods	18	1.98%
11.	Decision Making under Risk and Uncertainty	60	6.61%
	Total Number of Text Pages	908	99.99%

APPENDIX H

Table H.1

Prof. Dr. sc. Arno Donda, Prof. Dr. sc. Eva Herrde, Prof. Dr. sc. Otfried Kuhn, Prof. Dr. sc. Richard Struck, *STATISTIK*, 6th revised edition, Verlag die Wirtschaft, Berlin, DDR (East Germany), 1986.

	Chapter	No. of Pages	% of Text Pages
1.	Rechnungsführung und Statistik in der DDR (Cost and Management Accounting, and Statistics in East Germany)	20	7.75%
2.	Die Technologie von Rechnungsführung und Statistik (Techniques of Statistical Reporting)	56	21.71%
3.	Widerspiegelung der Struktur Gesellschaftlicher Erscheinungen (Reflecting the *Structure* of Social Phenomena)	23	8.91%
4.	Widerspiegelung des Niveaus Gesellschaficher Erscheinungen (Reflecting the *Levels* of Social Phenomena)	36	13.95%
5.	Representative Untersuchung Gesellschaftlicher Erscheinungen (Representative Surveys of Social Phenomena)	21	8.14%
6.	Widerspiegelung des Zusammenhanges zwischen den Erscheinungen (Reflecting the Association between Phenomena)	36	13.95%
7.	Die Widerspiegelung der Entwicklung (Reflecting the Dynamic Development over Time)	66	25.58%
	Total Number of Text Pages	258	99.98%
	Vorwort	3	
	Literature Verzeichnis	2	
	Stichwortverzeichnis	4	
	Inhaltsverzeichnis	4	
	Total Number of Pages in the Book	271	

Table H.2

Prof. Dr. sc. A. Donda et al., *STATISTIK*, 6th revised edition, Verlag die Wirtschaft, Berlin, (East Germany) 1986.		
Topic (Chapters and Subchapters Regrouped)	No. of Pages	% of Text Pages
1. National and International Organization of Socio-Economic Statistical Agencies: The Basic Nature of Data	79	30.62%
2. Probability Concepts and Theory, Random Variables, Bayes' Theorem	0	0.00%
3. Parametric Sampling Theory, Sampling Distributions and Statistical Inference, Anova	21	8.14%
4. Nonparametric Theory and Methods, Chi-Square	5	1.94%
5. The Praxis of Census, Complete Surveys, and Sampling	2	0.78%
6. Cross Section Analysis in One Dimension by Classes of Categorical, Ratio, Interval and Ordinal Data	54	20.93%
7. Cross Section Analysis in Two or More Dimensions: Cross-tabulations, Measures of Regression and Association	31	12.02%
8. Longitudinal Analysis: Time Series and Forecasting	28	10.85%
9. Index Numbers (incl. "Faktoren Analyse")	38	14.73%
10 Quality Control Methods	0	0.00%
11. Decision Making under Risk and Uncertainty	0	0.00%
Total Number of Text Pages	258	100.01%

APPENDIX I

Table I.1

Prof. Dr. Arno Donda, Prof. Dr. Eva Herrde, Prof. Dr. Otfried Kuhn, Prof. Dr. Richard Struck, *STATISTIK*, 5th edition (reprint of 4th edition), Verlag die Wirtschaft, Berlin, (East Germany) 1981.

	Chapter	No. of Pages	% of Text Pages
1.	Die Statistik in der Sozialistischen Gesellschaft (Statistics in socialist society)	20	7.46%
2.	Der Ablauf der Statistischen Arbeit (The sequence of steps in statistical work)	55	20.52%
3.	Die Widerspiegelung des Niveaus gesellschaftlicher Erscheinungen (Reflecting the level of social phenomena)	59	22.01%
4.	Die Widerspiegelung des Zusammenhangs zwischen den Erscheinungen (Reflecting between social phenomena)	28	10.45%
5.	Die Widerspiegelung der Entwicklung gesellschaftlicher Erscheinungen (Reflecting the development over time of social phenomena)	70	26.12%
6.	Die repräsentative Untersuchung gesellschaftlicher Erscheinungen (The representative sample survey of social phenomena)	36	13.43%
	Total Number of Text pages	268	99.99%
	Vorwort	2	
	Vorwort zur 5. Auflage	2	
	Inhaltsverzeichnis (Table of Content)	4	
	Abbildungsverzeichnis (List of figures)	2	
	Literaturverzeichnis (Literature)	3	
	Stichworteverzeichnis (Index)	3	
	Formelverzeichnis (Summary of Formulas)	23	
	Total Number of Pages in the Book	307	

Table I.2

A. Donda, Herrde, Kuhn, Struck, *STATISTIK*, 5th edition, Berlin, (East Germany) 1981.

	Topic (Chapters and Subchapters Regrouped)	No. of Pages	% of Text Pages
1.	National and International Organization of Socio-Economic Statistical Agencies: The Basic Nature of Data	20	7.46%
2.	Probability Concepts and Theory, Random Variables, Bayes' Theorem	0	0.00%
3.	Parametric Sampling Theory, Sampling Distributions and Statistical Inference, Anova	26	9.70%
4.	Nonparametric Theory and Methods, Chi-Square	6	2.24%
5.	The Praxis of Census, Complete Surveys, and Sampling	55	20.52%
6.	Cross Section Analysis in One Dimension by Classes of Categorical, Ratio, Interval and Ordinal Data	59	22.01%
7.	Cross Section Analysis in Two or More Dimensions: Cross-tabulations, Measures of Regression and Association	32	11.94%
8.	Longitudinal Analysis: Time Series and Forecasting	37	13.81%
9.	Index Numbers (incl. "Faktoren Analyse")	33	12.31%
10.	Quality Control Methods	0	0.00%
11.	Decision Making under Risk and Uncertainty	0	0.00%
	Total Number of Text Pages	268	99.99%

APPENDIX J

Table J.1

Prof. Dr. sc. Gotthard Forbrig, Prof. Dr. sc. Günter Goll, Prof. Dr. sc. Werner Kreitel, Prof. Dr. sc. Ernst Kupfernagel, Dr. sc. Klaus Mätzig, Dr. Werner Modemann, Prof. Dr. sc. Edwin Polaschewski, Prof. Dr. sc. Manfred Reich, Prof. Dr. sc. Gerhard Reinecke, Prof. Dr. sc. Eberhard Schubert, Dr. sc. Ursula Wolff, Lektor Dipl.-Wirtschaftler Rolf Baumgart, *RECHNUNGSFÜHRUNG UND STATISTIK IN DER INDUSTRIE-LEHRBUCH* (ACCOUNTING AND STATISTICS IN THE [MANUFACTURING] INDUSTRY–A TEXTBOOK), Verlang die Wirtschaft, Berlin, (East Germany) 1978.

Chapter	No. of Pages	% of Text Pages
1. Inhalt, Aufgaben, Stellung and Entwicklung der betrieblichen Rechnungsführung und Statistik (Content, tasks, position, and development of cost- and management accounting, and statistics)	15	2.64%
2. Aufbau und Leitung von Rechnungsführung und Statistik (Organization and performance of cost and management accounting, and statistics)	53	9.31%
3. Leistungsverrechnung (Productivity computation)	50	8.79%
4. Grundmittel und Investitionsrechnung (Computation of working capital and investments)	59	10.37%
5. Material und Warenrechnung (Determining quantity and value of input and output)	49	8.61%
6. Arbeitskräfterechnung (Determining labor input)	72	12.65%
7. Kostenrechnung (Determining the cost of production)	116	20.39%
8. Finanzrechnung (Determining the cost of financing)	61	10.72%
9. Nutzenrechnung (Determining rentability)	30	5.27%
10. Gesamtrechnung (Accounting for all activities)	64	11.25%
Total Number of Text pages	569	100.00%
Inhaltsverzeichnis (Table of contents)	8	
Vorwort	2	
Literaturverzeichnis (Literature)	7	
Sachwortregister (Index)	6	
Total Number of Pages in the Book	592	

Dr. G. Forbrig, Dr. G. Goll, Dr. E. Polaschewski, ed., *RECH-NUNGSFÜHRUNG UND STATISTIK IN DER INDUSTRIE–LEHRBUCH*, Verlag die Wirtschaft, Berlin, (East Germany) 1978.

	Topic (Chapters and Subchapters Regrouped)	No. of Pages	% of Text Pages
1.	National and International Organization of Socio-Economic Statistical Agencies: The Basic Nature of Data	354	62.21%
2.	Probability Concepts and Theory, Random Variables, Bayes' Theorem	0	0.00%
3.	Parametric Sampling Theory, Sampling Distributions and Statistical Inference, Anova	0	0.00%
4.	Nonparametric Theory and Methods, Chi-Square	0	0.00%
5.	The Praxis of Census, Complete Surveys, and Sampling	0	0.00%
6.	Cross Section Analysis in One Dimension by Classes of Categorical, Ratio, Interval and Ordinal Data	94	16.52%
7.	Cross Section Analysis in Two or More Dimensions: Cross-tabulations, Measures of Regression and Association	15	2.64%
8.	Longitudinal Analysis: Time Series and Forecasting	18	3.16%
9.	Index Numbers (incl. "Faktoren Analyse")	88	15.47%
10.	Quality Control Methods	0	0.00%
11.	Decision Making under Risk and Uncertainty	0	0.00%
	Total Number of Text Pages	569	100.00%

APPENDIX K

Table K.1

Prof. Dr. Helmut Büttner, Prof. Dr. sc. Heinz Lange, Prof. Dr. sc. Ursula Lange, Prof. Dr. Erich Strohbach, *WIRTSCHAFTSSTATISTIK* (ECONOMIC STATISTICS), Verlag die Wirtschaft, Berlin, (East Germany) 1978.

Chapter	No. of Pages	% of Text Pages
1. Aufgaben, Gegenstand und Methode der Wirtschaftsstatistik (Tasks, subject and method of economic statistics)	13	3.88%
2. Die Klassifikation der Volkswirtschaft (The classification of the economy)	16	4.78%
3. Bevölkerungs und Arbeitskräftestatistik (Demographic and labor force statistics)	41	12.24%
4. Die Statistik der Produktionsmittel (Statistics of the means of production)	35	10.45%
5. Die Statistik der Ergebnisse der Materiellen Produktion (Statistics of the results of physical production)	51	15.22%
6. Die Statistik der Produktion Materieller Erzeugnisse und Leistungen (Statistics of the production of goods and services)	29	8.66%
7. Die Statistik des Nationaleinkommens (National income statistics)	53	15.82%
8. Die Statistik der Konsumption (Consumption statistics)	58	17.31%
9. Die Volkswirtschaftlichen Berichtsbilanzen (The [macroeconomic] accounts of national income)	39	11.64%
Total Number of Text pages	335	100.00%
Inhaltverzeichnis (Table of Contents)	6	
Vorwort	3	
Literaturverzeichnis (Literature)	6	
Total Number of Pages in the Book	350	

H. Büttner, H. Lange, U. Lange, E. Strohbach, *WIRTSCHAFTSSTATISTIK*, Verlag die Wirtschaft, Berlin, (East Germany) 1978.

	Topic (Chapters and Subchapters Regrouped)	No. of Pages	% of Text Pages
1.	National and International Organization of Socio-Economic Statistical Agencies: The Basic Nature of Data	32	9.55%
2.	Probability Concepts and Theory, Random Variables, Bayes' Theorem	0	0.00%
3.	Parametric Sampling Theory, Sampling Distributions and Statistical Inference, Anova	0	0.00%
4.	Nonparametric Theory and Methods, Chi-Square	0	0.00%
5.	The Praxis of Census, Complete Surveys, and Sampling	16	4.78%
6.	Cross Section Analysis in One Dimension by Classes of Categorical, Ratio, Interval and Ordinal Data	124	37.01%
7.	Cross Section Analysis in Two or More Dimensions: Cross-tabulations, Measures of Regression and Association	50	14.93%
8.	Longitudinal Analysis: Time Series and Forecasting	35	10.40%
9.	Index Numbers (incl. "Faktoren Analyse")	78	23.28%
10.	Quality Control Methods	0	0.00%
11.	Decision Making under Risk and Uncertainty	0	0.00%
	Total Number of Text Pages	335	100.00%

APPENDIX L

Table L.1

Prof. Dr. sc. Gotthard Forbrig, Prof. Dr. sc. Otmar Brosch, Prof. Dr. sc. Ursula Wolff, *BETRIEBSSTATISTIK* (MANAGEMENT STATISTICS), Verlag die Wirtschaft, Berlin, 1983.

	Chapter	No. of Pages	% of Text Pages
1.	Inhalt und Aufgabe der Betriebsstatistik (Content and task of management statistics)	10	2.15%
2.	Statistik der Produktion und des Absatzes (Statistics of produced and dispatched output)	65	13.98%
3.	Die Qualitätsstatistik (Statistical quality control)	36	7.74%
4.	Statistik der Grundmittel und der Investitition (Statistics of working capital and investment)	70	15.05%
5.	Statistik des Materials (Statistics of materials and work in process)	57	12.26%
6.	Arbeitskräfte und Lohnstatistik (Statistics of workforce and wages)	66	14.19%
7.	Statistik der Arbeits und Lebensbedingungen (Statistics of quality of life in work and leisure)	16	3.44%
8.	Statistik des Wissenschaftlich-Technischen Fortschritts (Statistics of scientific-technological progress)	44	9.46%
9.	Statistik der Selbstkosten (Statistics of the cost structure)	37	7.96%
10.	Kemplexe Betriebsstatistik (Complex analysis of the production process)	64	13.76%
	Total Number of Text pages	465	99.99%
	Inhaltverzeichnis (Table of Contents)	6	
	Vorwort	2	
	Sachwortverzeichnis (Index)	4	
	Literaturverzeichnis (Books, Monographs, Journal Articles, Laws and Regulations)	6	
	Total Number of Pages in the Book	483	

Table L.2

G. Forbrig, O. Brosch, U. Wolff, *BETRIEBSSTATISTIK*, Verlag die Wirtschaft, Berlin, 1983.

	Topic (Chapters and Subchapters Regrouped)	No. of Pages	% of Text Pages
1.	National and International Organization of Socio-Economic Statistical Agencies: The Basic Nature of Data	65	13.98%
2.	Probability Concepts and Theory, Random Variables, Bayes' Theorem	7	1.51%
3.	Parametric Sampling Theory, Sampling Distributions and Statistical Inference, Anova	5	1.08%
4.	Nonparametric Theory and Methods, Chi-Square	0	0.00%
5.	The Praxis of Census, Complete Surveys, and Sampling	0	0.00%
6.	Cross Section Analysis in One Dimension by Classes of Categorical, Ratio, Interval and Ordinal Data	142	30.54%
7.	Cross Section Analysis in Two or More Dimensions: Cross-tabulations, Measures of Regression and Association	22	4.73%
8.	Longitudinal Analysis: Time Series and Forecasting	107	23.01%
9.	Index Numbers (incl. "Faktoren Analyse")	81	17.42%
10.	Quality Control Methods	36	7.74%
11.	Decision Making under Risk and Uncertainty	0	0.00%
	Total Number of Text Pages	465	100.00%

ECONOMETRICS:
THE WAY THE COOK CHOOSES!

Renuka Jain
Worcester State College
Robin Rowley
McGill University

I. INTRODUCTION

Fifty years have passed since Keynes was asked to review a book prepared by Tinbergen for the League of Nations. Keynes saw "a mass of unintelligible figurings" in the econometric study without "the slightest explanation or justification of the underlying logic" (Letter to Kahn of August 23, 1938). The book was found "grievously disappointing." Keynes' published review of "Professor Tinbergen's Method" (1939) reflects his severe disappointment and it expresses serious doubts concerning the application of multiple correlation techniques to complex economic problems. Tinbergen (1940a, b) responded with a clarification of his approach and illustrated the further use of econometrics in business-cycle research. But he left many of Keynes' objections unanswered. Letters from the two principals and from Harrod (clarifying Keynes' position) have been reprinted in Moggridge (1973). Now some ambiguities and poorly-expressed portions of Keynes' review can be put aside and the principal criticisms of econometrics can be reassessed from a more modern perspective that recognizes some of the subsequent changes in methodology.

Significant interest in the Keynes-Tinbergen exchange has been revived as part of the new critical approach to econometrics. See, for example, major comments by Bateman (1987), Bodkin, Klein and Marwah (1988), Hendry (1980), Klant (1985), Lawson (1985), Patinkin (1976, 1982, 1984), Pesaran and Smith (1985), Rowley (1988), and Stone (1978), which reveal some challenges to the orthodoxy of econometrics in the Cowles-Commission tradition that developed from Tinbergen's pioneering efforts. The disagreement between

Keynes and Tinbergen generated further responses, e.g., Koopmans (1941) and Haavelmo (1943, 1944), supporting multiple correlation or regression models and extending these models to systems of equations with economy-wide coverage. These responses contained discussions of persistent logical issues that still adversely affect econometrics. However, such discussions became unfashionable when the methodology of the Cowles Commission came to dominate the empirical research of economists during the 1950s.

Leamer (1985) described the subsequent methodological default in the following terms: "The slippery issues of causal inference have been kept in the econometric closet for over thirty years since Marschak (1953), Koopmans (1953) and Simon (1953) wrote about them. Those who rummaged in the closet in the intervening years no doubt quickly concluded that these were problems better left alone lest they devour our energies with little to show for the effort." Now attempts to redefine exogeneity, to develop practical tests of causality, to question the occurrence of structural autonomy, and to acknowledge the sequential nature of most modeling provide ample grounds for looking once more at the specific criticisms by Keynes. The inaugural lecture of Hendry (1980) and the views expressed by Bodkin, Klein and Marwah (1988), henceforth identified as BKM, provide a convenient focus and stimulus for the comments that follow. However, the themes explored by Jain (1985) and Rowley and Jain (1984) indicate prior consideration of these related matters.

II. GENERAL NEGLECT

For Keynes the central issue of econometric methodology was the "logic of applying the method of multiple correlation to unanalyzed economic material, which we know to be non-homogeneous through time" (Letter to Tyler of August 23, 1938). However, this issue is seldom identified when his contribution to econometrics is discussed. Instead stress is generally given to some aspects of his *General Theory*. For example, the *Handbook of Econometrics* edited by Griliches and Intriligator (1983, 1984) contains only one reference to Keynes: "Macroeconometric modeling also began in the 1930s by Tinbergen (1935, 1939) and was given additional impetus by the development of National Income Accounts in the United States and other countries and by Keynes' theoretical work." Contributors of surveys for

156

the *Handbook* offer no assessment of Keynes' views on econometric methodology.

Despite the apparent linking with macroeconometric models, integration of Keynes' theoretical constructs (as he expressed them) into empirical models proved difficult. Some economists claim an inability to locate the constructs in large econometric models, while others deny the possibility of expressing Keynes' theory in any econometric form. Certainly macroeconometric models are inconsistent with Keynes' own treatment of probability, his views on induction, and many of his comments in the exchange with Tinbergen.

III. RE-EXPRESSION OF SPECIFIC ISSUES

Bodkin, Klein and Marwah (1988) argue that some specific criticisms by Keynes are "in general, reasonably taken" while others "seem reasonable in themselves and appear to have stood the test of time." In similar vein, Patinkin (1982, 1984) points out the criticisms could not be dismissed "for some of them became basic concerns of the econometric literature." He excludes the misplaced criticism by Keynes of non-cyclical linear specifications and confesses to "find it somewhat depressing to see how many of them are, in practice, still of relevance today." These comments and similar ones by Hendry are surprising when one considers the contents of most econometric textbooks. Inspection of twelve prominent textbooks by Christ (1966), Dhrymes (1970), Goldberger (1964), Johnston (1963, 1972), Judge et al. (1980, 1982), Kmenta (1986), Klein (1974), Maddala (1977), Malinvaud (1970), Rowley (1973), and Theil (1971) reveals that none mention the dispute between Keynes and Tinbergen and none cite the basic references in the *Economic Journal*. Given this background, it seems appropriate to take a contrary view; namely, that Keynes' criticisms have been diluted, forgotten or misstated rather than absorbed into prevalent orthodoxy.

BKM suggest that Keynes' criticisms "could be interpreted as" pointing to single-equation bias, omitted-variable bias, problems of measurement in explanatory variables, misspecification of mathematical functions (due to a preoccupation with linearity), and structural change. Similarly, Patinkin reinterprets some criticisms as involving specification bias and simultaneous equation bias. These newer terms are indeed "incorporated into econometrics textbooks today,"

157

but the reinterpretation introduces a fundamental change in focus. The new language converts the basic focus of concern from structural autonomy, non-homogeneity and specification to technical issues of estimation by stressing bias.

The full extent of this change is difficult to understand unless we recall the adverse views of Keynes on frequentist aspects of probability. Now the term 'bias' is generally identified with the difference between the expected value of an estimator and the corresponding population parameter or structural constant. Keynes did not accept the validity of expected value in economics, where such a value is defined as the center of a completely-specified probability density function. He could never accept the usual constraints on non-homogeneous behavior that are necessary for ergodicity and he would have wasted little time on the theoretical assumption that time-averages over available economic data converge to corresponding population elements. Clearly he would have been profoundly disturbed by the edifice of asymptotic distribution theory that has grown, since his death, to support macroeconometric modeling in the Cowles-Commission tradition. Thus the notions of asymptotic bias and consistency in the statistical sense are quite incompatible with his views of the economic environment.

IV. STRUCTURAL INSTABILITY

When Keynes discusses structural change or instability, he always has in mind erratic phenomena that are markedly different from those that are invoked when we use Chow tests, Goldfeld-Quandt procedures, and recursive-residual checks or when we introduce models with switching regimes. Moreover, his concern here is with specification rather than with estimation and the use of formal diagnostic checks. He reacted to the persistent structural stability implicitly assumed for much of Tinbergen's modeling: "The coefficients arrived at are apparently assumed to be constant for 10 years or for a longer period. Yet, surely we know they are not constant. There is no reason at all why they should not be different every year." (Letter to Tyler of August 23, 1938). Earlier, he argues that since economics deals with elements such as motives, expectations and psychological uncertainties, one "has to be constantly on guard against treating the material as constant and homogeneous" in contrast with familiar situations occurring in the natural sciences (Letter to Harrod of July 16, 1938). Further, in the published review, he is unequivocal when he insists the "main *prima facie* objection to the application of the method of multiple correlation to complex economic problems lies in the apparent lack of any adequate degree of uniformity in the environment."

Such comments are reinforced in the "inductive transition" to prediction. Keynes assesses extrapolation from a situation in which a researcher has a free hand to choose coefficients and time lag and, hence, can "always cook a formula to fit moderately well a limited range of past facts" but has little likelihood of a good post-sample approximation (Letter to Tyler). He also points to the three problems of relying on data that are available rather than on data that are appropriate, dealing with non-numerical influences that are not constant in their impact, and identifying potential differences in the choice of models among researchers. All of these features might be linked to predictive inadequacies and within-sample instability.

In communicating with Tinbergen, Keynes made some practical suggestions. For example, he appears to recommend split-sample methods and pseudo-replication to check for instability: "The first step ... is to break up the period under examination into a series of sub-periods, with a view to discovering whether the results of applying our method to the various sub-periods taken separately are reasonable uniform. If they are, then we have some ground for projecting our results in the future" (Keynes' 1939). "Suppose you have statistics covering a period of 20 years, what is required, it seems to me, is to divide these into convenient sections, say, of five years, and calculate a proper equation for each period separately, and then consider what concordance appears between the different results. Until this is done, a formula applying to the whole of the twenty years can have very little significance" (Letter to Tinbergen of September 20, 1938). Such advice is surprisingly modern. If acted upon, the advice can involve the repeated use of Chow tests but it is more appropriately viewed as an aspect of interior data analysis, exploratory rather than confirmatory econometrics. Thus it appears closer to the techniques described by Belsley, Kuh and Welsch (1980) and Cook and Weisberg (1982) than to those found in the textbooks listed above. Here Keynes' advice is consistent with Hendry's assertion that the "three golden rules of econometrics are test, test and test."

V. TESTING

Keynes' review also reveals his concern for the interpretation of statistical tests. The feasibility of such tests rejecting economic theories is affected by the conditional softness of common testing procedures. At best, "only those theories can be shown to be incorrect which, in the view of the economist who advances them, accept as applicable the various conditions" that are essential for the validity of statistical testing procedures. Much of his review clarifies these conditions (including both homogeneity and stability) and seeks to assess their potential acceptability in the economic context.

Tinbergen's account is incomplete for he "leaves unanswered many questions which the economist is bound to ask before he can feel comfortable as to the conditions which the economic material has to satisfy, if the proposed method is to be properly applicable." In this assertion, Keynes markedly fails to foresee how readily economists would ignore the conditional nature of statistical inference for many years. His non-technical list of auxiliary conditions is supplemented in Tinbergen's reply by the recognition of necessary conditions for unbiased estimation—the relevant explanatory variables must be included, omitted variables in equation errors must not lead to correlation with the variables included explicitly, the appropriate mathematical form of the relationship among variables must be given—but applicability was not a pressing issue for more than three decades!

A modern re-statement of Keynes' stresses on conditions for modeling and inference is provided by Smith (1982): "[An] econometric model provides a mapping from specifications into conclusions about preferences, technology, and institutions. In so far as the conclusions are sensitive to the specifications, we are left with scientific propositions that are open-ended with respect to the environment, institutions, and agent behavior." Against this background, Smith provides an awkward scenario that would have confirmed Keynes' skepticism to the extent that it represents common practice among economists thirty years after the exchange between Keynes and Tinbergen: "Based on introspection, some casual observations of some process, and a contextual interpretation of the self-interest postulate, a model is specified and then 'tested' by estimation using the only body of field data that exists. The results turn out to be ambiguous or call for 'improvements' ... and now one is tempted to modify the model in ways suggested by these results to improve the fit with 'reasonable expectations'."

Both Keynes and Tinbergen identified the sequential character of testing that is noticeably absent from econometric textbooks until Judge et al. (1980). The attendant problem of pre-test bias, recognized by Bancroft in the 1940s and later associated with conditional regression, remains outside many academic courses in econometrics, another area of significant neglect.

Hendry's (1980) emphatic view of statistical testing emerged as a major shift in econometric research. His approach, associated with the need to establish some routine procedures that enhance the possibility of progress in the accumulation of empirical evidence by economists, also notes this need to check conditionality. As a guide to sensible behavior in research, Hendry insists that research strategies should test auxiliary conditions. However, the multiplicity of such conditions overwhelms the fragile tests that are considered by him. Such fragility leaves his approach quite susceptible to Keynes' criticism that the outcome of a research effort involving exploration (and sequential testing) might reflect "the way the cook chooses."

The order in which tests are undertaken and their hidden flaws may make the Hendry-style research strategies 'path dependent.' In particular, the robustness of inference and conclusions to different orderings of single tests, to changes in the 'special' assumptions that permit the few instances of joint tests to be undertaken (for example, normality and nesting of hypotheses), to the preoccupations of individual researchers with 'fashionable' methods (likelihood ratios, conventional levels of critical regions) and particular software packages, and to different sampling intervals is a major area of ignorance that enhances the potential for path-dependence. Hendry's stress of testing as the major component in 'criticism' of econometric modeling is well-taken but our lack of knowledge concerning how to modify testing criteria for integration within sequential procedures is a crucial obstacle to the success of his testing methodology.

The impact of auxiliary conditions on the interpretation of testing is only briefly considered by BKM. They comment on earlier discussions by Pesaran and Smith (1985) and link them with a critique that "no coherent model, macroeconometric or otherwise, can capture the essential message of Keynes [due to] the important role of uncertainty, the uniqueness of particular historical episodes" and some aspects of indeterminacy. Clearly it is easy to locate such factors in Keynes' criticism but the account by BKM gives inadequate attention to the auxiliary hypotheses that are unavoidable in testing. Perhaps Bodkin, Klein and Marwah, like other econometricians, are complacent, too comfortable with the neglect of conditional qualifications in macroeconometric modeling especially in the estimation and testing of large models, where pragmatism and 'tender loving care' are common features.

The softness of model specification and the replacement of qualifications by sequential experimentation in large models are clearly noted by Howrey, Klein and McCarthy (1974) in their account of common adjustments: "*A priori* information is not rich enough to provide us with complete specification .... The precise nature of the lag structures, nonlinearities, the degree of aggregation, and the selection of exogenous variables are not fixed *a priori*. They can only be ascertained by experimental study of particular samples." This experimental aspect contrasts with the conventional textbook treatment of single-step statistical theories of large models. The disparities among the postulates of the orthodox methods, the framework of Hendry, and the experimental approach are profound. None adequately deal with the criticisms of Keynes.

VI. THE PRIMACY OF PROBABILITY
AND COMPREHENSIVENESS

In response to Keynes, Haavelmo (1943) makes two initial claims. He suggests that "there is no harm in considering economic variables as stochastic variables having certain distribution properties" and "only through the introduction of such notions are we able to formulate hypotheses that have a meaning in relation to facts." These suggestions are markedly at odds with Keynes' own perspective and somewhat more restrictive than the views expressed by Tinbergen. They lead to the identification of testing with the now familiar Neyman-Pearson framework of drawing samples from a complete probability distribution instead of the informal notions of Keynes and Tinbergen. Hendry's methods, of the present time, retain the framework of samples and probabilistic populations from Haavelmo without the traditional 'axiom of correct specification.'

Haavelmo's view of testable hypotheses is straightforward. He asserts: "The observable variables involved have a joint probability law which belongs to a specified class of probability laws. If the hypothesis is true, we can make certain probability statements about the type of samples ... it will produce."

Keynes' doubts concerning the possible non-existence of complete probability distributions for economic phenomena is replaced here by Haavelmo's presumption of its existence. Moreover, the tester is assumed to have a specific class of distributions in mind for the observable variables. This is a substantial requirement. It extends the potential impact of auxiliary conditions on research to a new height. Further, it raises the difficulty of specifying distributions consistent with non-homogeneity and other features of economic behavior, and introduces a procedure affected by the possibility of incorrect choices (now entrenched in the concepts of significance levels, p-values and power). Such new elements reinforce the implicit criterion contained in Keynes' letter to Tyler. "Would someone else ... faced with the same problem and using the same method and the same statistics, but without having seen these calculation, necessarily bring out the same result? ... [How] far are the results mechanically and uniquely obtainable from the data, and how far do they depend on *the way the cook chooses* to go to work?" This is precisely one of the potential problems we have raised concerning Hendry's proposals for a testing research program. In exploring hypotheses and testing, Haavelmo (1944) provides the basis for subsequent macroeconometric methodology. He asserts that estimation problems in economics "come down to one and the same thing, namely, to study the properties of the joint probability distribution of the random (observable) variables in a stochastic equation system" so that it is "clear that the joint probability law of all the observable random variables in an economic system is the only general basis for estimating the unknown parameters of the system." This perspective is completely at odds with Keynes' views.

In his review, Keynes mistakenly suggests that specification must be comprehensive in a different sense: "Am I right in thinking that the method of multiple correlation analysis essentially depends on the economist having furnished, not merely a list of the significant causes, which is correct as far as it goes, but a complete list?" Haavelmo's (1944) framework also contains a comprehensive issue for it requires the stochastic interrelationships among all explanatory variables and these errors to be specified for the whole system prior to estimation. Thus, for example, the familiar transformation from the structural form of a simultaneous-equations model to its reduced form requires the prior partition of explanatory variables into endogenous and pre-determined classes according to their correlation with equation errors. Further, identification within the simultaneous-equations model involves the concept of a system being complete in a statistical sense, which again presumes this partition of variables. In the estimation of single equations within a system, advocacy of two stage least squares, limited information maximum likelihood and instrumental variables estimators too is associated with the classification of variables. Keynes' confusion with the listing of variables in a model is thus supplanted in the simultaneous-equations model framework by the hazards of specifying stochastic properties for all of these variables. These hazards are the basis for the attacks by Sims (1977), Sargent (1979) and others on causal notions in the simultaneous-equations models.

VII. GETTING ON WITH THE JOB

Keynes (1939) indicates Tinbergen's book "has been a nightmare to live with" and describes the archetypal feature of an econometrician as "much more interested in getting on with the job than in spending time in deciding the job is worth getting on with." He would have been appalled by the subsequent form taken by macroeconometrics. In particular, he would have dismissed the excessive reliability on probability distributions, stationarity, homogeneity and the Neyman-Pearson testing framework. He would also have been distressed by the neglect of logical issues until the rational expectations viewpoint provoked attempts to defend or refine the Cowles-Commission orthodoxy of econometric methodology. He would have recognized the partial retraction of Haavelmo (1958), scorned the comment that it "can be asserted without too much fear of controversy today that intuitive estimates ... are even more likely to be misleading than the econometric estimates" (BKM), and found small comfort in the rebirth of skepticism. For the rest of us, there remains regret that we have waited too long for econometric methodology to come of age and address its logical bases.

The changes brought about by Hendry (1980), Leamer (1983), Sims (1982) and others in the last decade may lead to better econometric research. But they have obvious inadequacies. New acceptance of criticism, sequential models, and 'data mining' removed unworthy elements of the Cowles-Commission orthodoxy that would have appalled Keynes. Further change is essential. Perhaps, we need to take Keynes' comments seriously instead of forcing them into a restrictive focus on bias. Hendry and Leamer persuaded us to give more attention to specification and model criticism at the expense of estimation. Sims reminded us of the fallibility of economic theory as a guide to specification. Looking forward, the successful integration of Keynes' criticisms within econometrics seems to be bound up with software development. Hendry's most important contribution in this respect is to lead the search for convenient user-friendly software that will permit us to explore more 'recipes' so that, even if the way the cook chooses is important, the other cooks can replicate the trials of others and explore the sensitivity of outcome to different choices. Research reports will eventually describe the evolving processes of choice rather than a single outcome.

However, as revealed in regard to the troublesome issues noted by Hamouda and Rowley (1996a, b) and the recent commentaries they cite, there remain major hurdles to overcome before popular econometric models can fit the economic context envisaged by Keynes and provide a suitable framework for representing economic phenomena.

REFERENCES

Bateman, B. W., "Keynes' Changing Conception of Probability," *Economics and Philosophy* (1987), Vol. 3, pp. 97–120.

Belsley, D. A., E. Kuh and Welsch, R. E., *Regression Diagnostics* (New York, New York: John Wiley & Sons, 1980).

Bodkin, R. G., Klein, L. R., and Marwah, K., "Keynes and the Origins of Macroeconometric Modeling," chapter 2 in *Keynes and Public Policy After Fifty Years, Volume II, Theories and Method* (Hants, England: Edward Elgar Publishing Limited, 1988).

Cook, R. D., and Weisberg, S., *Residuals and Influence in Regression*

(London, England: Chapman and Hall, 1982).

Griliches, Z. and Intriligator, M. D., editors, *Handbook of Econometrics, Volumes I* and *II* (Amsterdam, Holland: North Holland, 1983 and 1984).

Haavelmo, T., "Statistical Testing of Business-Cycle Theories," *Review of Economics and Statistics* (1943), Vol. 25, No. 1, pp. 13–18.

Haavelmo, T., "The Probability Approach to Econometrics," *Econometrica* (1944), Vol. 12 (Supplement).

Haavelmo, T. "The Role of the Econometrician in the Advancement of Economic Theory," *Econometrica* (1958), Vol. 26, No. 3, pp. 351–357.

Hamouda, O. F., and Rowley, R., *Probability in Economics*, chapter 7 (London and New York: Routledge, 1996a).

Hamouda, O. F., and Rowley, R., "Ignorance and the Absence of Probabilities," chapter 8 in *Uncertainty in Economic Thought*, C. Schmidt, editor (Cheltenham, U.K.: Edward Elgar Publishing Limited, 1996b).

Hamouda, O. F., and Smithin, J. N., editors, *Keynes and Public Policy After Fifty Years, Volume II, Theories and Method* (Hants, England: Edward Elgar Publishing Limited, 1988).

Hendry, D. F., "Econometrics: Alchemy or Science?," *Economica* (1980) Vol. 47, pp. 387–406.

Howrey, E. P., Klein, L. R. and McCarthy, M. D., "Notes on Testing the Predictive Performance of Econometric Models," *International Economic Review* (1974), Vol. 15, pp. 366–383.

Jain, R., *Econometric Fluctuations, Structure and Measurement*, unpublished Ph.D. Dissertation, McGill University (1985).

Keynes, J. M., "Professor Tinbergen's Method," *The Economic Journal* (1939), Vol. 49, pp. 558–568.

Klant, J. J., "The Slippery Transition," in *Keynes' Economics: Methodological Issues*, T. Lawson and H. Pesaran, editors (Armonk, New York: M. E. Sharpe, 1985), pp. 80–98.

Koopmans, T., "The Logic of Econometric Business-Cycle Research," *Journal of Political Economy* (1941), Vol. 49, 2, pp. 157–181.

Lawson, T., "Keynes, Prediction and Econometrics," in *Keynes' Economics: Methodological Issues*, T. Lawson and H. Pesaran, editors (Armonk, New York: M. E. Sharpe, 1985), pp. 116–133.

Leamer, E. E., "Let's Take the Con Out of Econometrics," *American*

Economics Review (March 1983), Vol. 73, No. 1, pp. 31–44.

Leamer, E. E., "Vector Autoregressions for Causal Inference?," in *Understanding Monetary Regimes*, K. Brunner and A. H. Meltzer, editors (Amsterdam, Holland: North-Holland Press, 1985), pp. 255–304.

Moggridge, D., editor, *The Collected Writings of John Maynard Keynes Volume XIV, The General Theory and After, II. Defence and Development* (London, England: Macmillan Publishing Co., Inc., 1973), pp. 285–320.

Patinkin, D., "Keynes and Econometrics: On the Interaction Between the Macroeconomic Revolutions of the Interwar Period," *Econometrica* (November 1976), Vol. 44, 6, pp. 1091–1123.

Patinkin, D., *Anticipation of the General Theory and Other Essays on Keynes*, chapter 9 (Chicago, Illinois: University of Chicago Press, 1982).

Patinkin, D., "Keynes and Economics Today," *American Economic Review* (1984), Vol. 74, pp. 97–102.

Pesaran, H., and Smith, R., "Keynes on Econometrics," in *Keynes' Economics: Methodological Issues*, T. Lawson and H. Pesaran, editors (Armonk, New York: M. E. Sharpe, 1985), pp. 134–150.

Rowley, J. C. R., "The Keynes-Tinbergen Exchange in Retrospect," chapter 3 in *Keynes and Public Policy After Fifty Years, Volume II, Theories and Method*, O. F. Hamouda and J. N. Smithin, editors (Hants, England: Edward Elgar Publishing Limited, 1988.)

Rowley, J. C. R., and R. Jain, "The Demise of Structural Estimation?," *Proceedings of the Business and Economic Statistics Section* (1984), American Statistical Society.

Sargent, T. J., "Estimating Vector Autoregressions Using Methods Not Based on Explicit Economic Theories," *Quarterly Review* (1977), Vol. 3, No. 3, pp. 8–14.

Sargent, T. J. and C. A. Sims, "Business Cycle Modeling Without Pretending to Have Too Much A Priori Economic Theory," *Methods in Business Cycle Research: Proceedings of a Conference*, Federal Reserve Bank of Minneapolis (1997).

Sims, C. A., "Policy Analysis With Econometric Models," *Brookings Papers on Economic Analysis* (1982), No. 1, pp. 107–152.

Smith, V. L., "Microeconomic Systems as an Experimental Science," *American Economic Review* (1982), Vol. 72, pp. 923–55.

Stone, R., "Keynes, Political Arithmetic and Econometrics," *Proceedings of the British Academy* (1978), Vol. 64, pp. 55–92.

Tinbergen, J., "On a Method of Statistical Business-Cycle Research: A Reply," *Economic Journal* (March 1940a), Vol. 50, pp. 141–154 (with further "Comment" by Keynes, pp. 154–166.)

Tinbergen, J., "Econometric Business Cycle Research," *Review of Economic Studies* (1940b), Vol. 7, pp. 73–90.

Part III

Issues in Applied Economics and Finance

9

EMERGING EXPENDITURE PATTERNS AND MARKETING STRATEGIES FOR STATE LOTTERIES

Nick L. Nicholas
St. Thomas University

I. LOTTERY REVENUES AND EXPENDITURES

Recent data reveal profound differences among states in the contribution of lotteries to revenues and in profiles of lottery players. An understanding of these differences may permit lottery officials to improve performance and increase the viability of lotteries as an appropriate economic and social alternative to taxation in generating revenue for the states.

In an analysis of the social and economic impact of lotteries Kaplan (1984) supported his conclusion that lotteries are incapable of making significant contributions to state budgets with data indicating gross ticket sales in 1983 were $5 billion and net state revenues $2 billion, only about 3% of the $72.4 billion in revenues for states with active lotteries. He argued that lottery revenues, in general, accounted for only 2 to 3% of a state's budget and that doubling lottery revenues would yield only 5% of a state's revenue. Further, less than half the revenue generated by a lottery found its way into a state's treasury, with administrative costs, ticket agent commissions, and advertising taking 10 to 15% of the gross and prizes averaging another 40 to 45%.

Mikesell and Zorn (1986), while concluding that lotteries represent a relatively small source of state government revenues, present data revealing significant differences among states. Net revenues generated by state lotteries averaged 1.5% of own-source revenue in 1978 and 1.95% by 1984 but Pennsylvania raised more than 4.4%, Maryland 4.2%, New Jersey almost 3.8%, and Illinois 3.5%. While Kaplan concluded that raising the 1983 Pennsylvania state income tax by only one-quarter of a percent would have generated as much money for that state as total net lottery revenues, Mikesell and Zorn, examining 1984 data, found Maryland, New Jersey, and Pennsylvania lotteries netted about as much revenue as would an increase in the state sales tax of one percentage point.

However, in the period from 1980–1991 lottery sales grew spectacularly at an annual rate of 22.3 percent. Part of the growth may be attributed to an increase in the number of states offering lotteries from 14 in 1980 to 32 plus the District of Columbia in 1991. Even without the new lotteries the annual growth rate in sales was 16.8 percent and in no year did annual sales fall (Mikesell, 1994). By 1995, 37 states relied on lotteries to supplement revenue from taxes and Americans spent more than $34 billion on lottery games (Falk, 1995). Revenues generated by games introduced in the late 1980's, like lotto, attract higher income consumers and bring revenues to state coffers that are an addition to funds from earlier games.

As Christiansen and Abt (1985) point out, high state sales figures don't necessarily reflect efficiency since a large state would be expected to generate more sales than a small one. One measure of market penetration reflecting differences in size among markets is per capita sales but, assuming identical levels of lottery management performance among states, those states with higher per capita income might be expected to have higher per capita sales. To overcome this problem, Christiansen and Abt suggest relating lottery sales to personal income rather than population.

In fiscal 1985, of the top ten states in total dollar lottery sales, nine were also in the top ten in sales as a percent of personal income: Pennsylvania, New York, Illinois, Massachusetts, New Jersey, Michigan, Ohio, Maryland, and Connecticut. The same nine states were the highest in total dollar expenses but were also among the ten states ranked lowest in cents spent to generate a sales dollar. This indicates that monies were spent efficiently (Gaming and Wagering Business, 1987).

II. EMERGING MARKETING STRATEGIES

In examining the stability of revenue flow, Mikesell and Zorn found great variability. During the 1978–1984 period lottery net revenues grew at an average rate of 9.7%. However, thirteen of the seventeen states which operated lotteries experienced a decline in at least one year ranging from 0.8% in Massachusetts to 50% in Maine while increases ranged from 0.8% in Michigan to 214.3% in Ohio. They concluded that lottery revenue is affected by changing consumer preferences, introduction of new games, marketing efforts, competition from neighboring states' games and illegal games, and other factors outside the states' control (Mikesell and Zorn, 1986).

Lottery revenues continue to show volatility. In fiscal 1994, Louisiana's lottery sales plummeted by $140 million, a 28 percent drop, and California's 1994 Superlotto sales dropped more than 13 percent from the previous year (Labalme, 1994). But, in a study by Andrew C. and Carol Matheny Szakmary (1995), the relevance of this data has been questioned. Critics have implied that highly volatile lottery revenue has been studied on a stand alone basis rather than examining the impact additional lottery revenue has on the variability of total state revenue. Examining state government data from 1978 to 1992 issued by the U. S. Bureau of the Census the researchers concluded that lottery revenues do not destabilize total state revenues because the low correlation of lottery revenues with revenues from other sources offsets the high stand-alone risk of lottery funding.

Given great variability in the contribution lottery revenues make to meet states' needs for funds, greater attention should be paid to the role of marketing strategy in contributing to the success of the state lotteries. Have lottery officials been using the tools of marketing to achieve their revenue objectives? Recent examples shed some light on these issues.

Lotteries may be expected to go through the same life cycle as other products and services and, ultimately, the slow revenue growth of a mature industry. Given lotteries are subject to the same supply/demand laws as every other business in a free-market economy they must be run like businesses and those lotteries with the strongest marketing programs, the most innovative new products, the most dramatic advertising and promotion campaigns, will still continue to produce good results for the states involved.

Understanding marketing principles, some state lotteries have identified particular demographic and cultural market segments to pursue and created advertising campaigns for them. New York and the District of Columbia have run a percentage of advertising in Spanish. Connecticut, Washington, Pennsylvania, Ohio, Arizona, and the province of Ontario in Canada have designed advertisements to appeal to identifiable demographic and psychographic segments. For example, for one game the province of Ontario has identified the "heavy player," a blue collar male, thirty-five years or older, who does shift work and who brings home a paycheck in the middle to upper-middle income range. He tends to live in a medium-sized city and, once he gets home from work, he unwinds by reading the newspaper or watching TV. The Pennsylvania State Lottery has purchased radio time to reach an upscale audience while Arizona identified four market segments for one game which were approached with radio spots. The youth market, 18–25, was approached with the fun of lottery play; instant prizes were emphasized to the middle-age market, 25–45; the older market–45 and older–was appealed to with the $500,000 cash Grand Prize; finally, last minute Christmas shoppers were encouraged to buy a ticket as a "stocking stuffer" (*Public Gaming Magazine*, April 1984).

Demand may also be shaped through distribution strategy. Lottery agents may be the most important link between a lottery and its players. Agents are the "middlemen" in contact with players on a day-to-day basis. Lottery-to-players marketing programs, the effectiveness of point-of-purchase materials, and player awareness all hinge on the retailer doing his or her job. Strategic decisions concerning the placement of lottery sales agents and the content of their "sales presentations," i.e., their comments to the buying public, may influence not only the volume of sales but also who does the buying.

Horton (1994) has reported on recent enhancements to promotion strategy by state lotteries seeking promotional partners. Illinois and California have made arrangements with United Airlines to offer round-trip domestic tickets and tickets to World Cup Games as prizes. California seeks to build long term relationships with firms offering prizes as a form of promotion.

III. CONCLUSION

Commenting on the role of promotion in lotteries, John Bergin notes that President McCann Erikson has pointed out that lotteries have to contend with negative public attitudes based on misconceptions that lottery players are the "wrong kind of people." Addressing a conference of the National Association of State Lotteries (now called the North American Association of State Lotteries), Erikson stated: "I recommend, then, that you and your agencies lock arms as partners, and that together you get to know the consumer from haircut to toenails, that together you lift the quality of advertising and lift the public image of those who play" (Bergin, 1985).

Ultimately, the success of state lotteries with the public and the support they receive from legislators depends on their perceived image. Martin M. Punke (1985), a president of the National Association of State Lotteries, associates the image of the lottery with its perceived integrity and fairness and Robert Laird (1985), Deputy Director of Marketing for the Maryland State Lottery, has explained: "It is the image or perception of what an enterprise is, what its goals are, how it operates, whether or not it gives its market a fair shake, and other images that will ultimately convey either a positive or negative impression." Marketing strategy has an important role to play in projecting a positive image for the lottery. The ultimate message of marketing is the benefit an organization offers to the public. States may be proud to communicate to the public the tax relief and support of education, health programs, programs for the elderly, etc., supported by lottery revenues.

REFERENCES

Bergin, John, "Lotteries Can Benefit From Proven Advertising Techniques," *Public Gaming Magazine* (August 1985), Vol. 13, No. 4, pp. 59–60.

Christiansen, Eugene Martin and Abt, Vicki, "$6.75 B sales, $2.7 B Revenue Forecast in Non-Lottery States," *Gaming and Wagering Business* (August 1985), Vol. 6, No. 8, pp. 22–27.

Falk, William B., "Gambling, The New National Pastime," *Newsday* (December 3, 1995), Section A, p. 4.

Gaming and Wagering Business (February 1987), Vol. 8, No. 2, pp. 35–36.

Horton, Cleveland, "California Lotto Learns to Prize Promos," *Advertising Age* (May 16, 1994), Vol. 65, p. 16.

Kaplan, H. Roy, "The Social and Economic Impact of State Lotteries," *Annals of the American Academy of Political and Social Science* (July 1984), Vol. 474, pp. 91–106.

Labalme, Jenny, "It's a Sure Bet State Lottery Chiefs Are Talking

Marketing," *The Indianapolis Star* (September 23, 1994), Section B, p. 1.

Laird, Robert J., "How The Public Perceives A Lottery Is Key To Survival," *The Lottery Journal* (September 1985), Vol. 4, pp. 34–51.

Mikesell, John L., "State Lottery Sales and Economic Activity," *National Tax Journal* (March 1994), Vol. 47, No. 1, pp. 165–171.

Mikesell, John L. and Zorn, C. Kurt, "State Lotteries as Fiscal Savior or Fiscal Fraud: A Look at the Evidence," *Public Administration Review* (July/August 1986), Vol. 46, No. 4, pp. 311–320.

Public Gaming Magazine, "Marketing Lottery Games: Taking a Cool Approach With a Hot Product" (April 1984), Vol. 12, No. 4, pp. 25–26.

Punke, Martin M., "Lotteries' Success Based on Positive Change," *The Lottery Journal* (October 1985), Vol. 5, pp. 42.

Szakmary, Andrew C. and Szakmary, Carol Matheny, "State Lotteries as a Source of Revenue: A Re-Examination," *Southern Economic Journal* (April 1995), Vol. 61, No. 4, pp. 1167–1181.

10

THE DEVELOPMENT OF
AN INTERNATIONAL SERVICE
MARKET OPPORTUNITY INDEX

Richard Telofski
The Becker Research Company, Inc.
Joe Kim
Rider University

I. INTRODUCTION

The successful marketing of services internationally has assumed a greater importance over the past two decades for two reasons. The first reason is that the United States is a post-industrial society, one which depends largely upon the service industry for the achievement of economic goals. This dependence on services has increased over the past several decades. In 1970 service consumption accounted for 68% of U.S. GNP and increased to 72% by 1980 (see Table 2). These figures suggest that the American economy is fueled by service production/consumption, thus supporting the proposition that services have assumed a crucial role in American business. Second, during this same period, the United States emerged as a debtor nation. Total U.S. imports grew by 424% while total U.S. exports grew by only 369% (see Table 1). These figures suggest that during the 1970s American consumers' needs were met more effectively by foreign businesses than by domestic ones.

When both of these factors are considered it appears that American expertise in services could be used as a relative advantage in its world trade and a tool to combat the U.S. trade deficit. Successful service marketing requires a sound estimating of potential markets that need to be targeted. To facilitate this, service marketers will need an estimating model indicating potential service markets overseas.

The use of such a model would be of benefit, yet no such model exists. Furthermore, there is presently a paucity of literature for estimating market potential for services.

Table 1

Trade Balance

(All numbers are in billions of corresponding year's U.S. dollars.)

	1970	1980	Percent Change
Total U.S. Service and Products Exports	56.39	264.65	369%
Total U.S. Service and Products Imports	54.32	284.90	424%
Trade Surplus (Deficit)	2.06	-20.25	-1082%
Total World Service and Product Exports	266.50	1718.50	545%

Source: The United Nations Yearbook of National Account Statistics, 1981.

To address this lack of research in measuring foreign market potential this study attempts to establish a new model. This model will then be validated by applying it to sample countries. Through the research, it will become apparent that the model measures what it intends to measure.

II. PURPOSE OF STUDY

This study has two purposes. The first is to construct a model that can be used to estimate service market potential. This estimating model can be applied not only to an initial market entry, but to changing market conditions, as well. The second purpose is to test the model's validity in application. Once constructed, the estimating model will be applied to sample data in an effort to validate its use in international business.

III. JUSTIFICATION OF STUDY

As previously noted, U.S. share of services in GNP increased by 4% from 1970 to 1980. The export and import of some services (see Table 6 for service categories) also changed during this period. In 1970 the share of services in total U.S. imports was 27%. By 1980 this percentage had decreased to 14% (see Table 2). These figures indicate that the progress toward a service economy from 1970 to 1980 was being supported domestically and that American marketers regained markets formerly served by foreign participation. The increased domestic service demand reduced the U.S. incentives for exports. Table 2 supports this assumption, as indicated by the declining share of U.S. services as a total of U.S. exports, from 25% in 1970 to 17% in 1980. Also, U.S. market share of world exports fell from 5% to 3%. The decline does not necessarily implicate the United States' loss of trade leadership in services. On the contrary, at the conclusion of the research period (1970–1980) the United States led the world in service exports. In fact, the International Monetary Fund (IMF) estimated that the 1980 value of global service exports was $370 billion with the U.S. as the largest single share holder at about 10% (Aronson and Cowhey, 1984, p. 6).

Table 2
Ratio Analysis

	1970	1980	Change
$\dfrac{U.S.ServiceConsumption}{U.S.GNP}$	68%	72%	4%
$\dfrac{U.S.ServiceExports}{TotalU.S.Exports}$	25%	17%	-8%
$\dfrac{U.S.ServiceExports}{TotalWorldExports}$	5%	3%	-2%
$\dfrac{U.S.ServiceImports}{TotalU.S.Imports}$	27%	14%	-13%
$\dfrac{U.S.ServiceImports}{U.S.ServiceExports}$	102%	91%	-11%

Source: The United Nations Yearbook of National Account Statistics, 1981.

This study will show the international service marketer how a model might be deployed in estimating the changing potential for international service markets through the use of recent, readily available demand factors. Simple in structure and easy to apply, it provides a foundation for estimating service potential in world markets given that the subject is absent from the literature.

Indeed, one study which classified the types of international marketing research published from 1976 to 1982, shows that only 2 out of 112 studies were concerned with international research methodology (Albaum and Peterson, 1984, p. 161).

IV. METHOD OF STUDY

To establish foreign demand potential for U.S. services, the model incorporates the factors of population, GNP, and capital formation in the model. It has been argued that supply and its price and demand as measured by the population and income are the factors which would substantiate a service market (Daniels, 1982, p. 30; Keegan, 1995, p. 58; Pappas, 1996, p. 123). This study incorporates these factors to measure income as the percentage in GNP. The capital formation variable has been incorporated to reflect the nation's need for services to facilitate its industrialization.

Thus, the selection of these factors is based upon the theory that there exists a direct relationship between the nation's need for U.S. services and the country's population, income and capital formation.

To identify potential service markets, the study groups the sample as developing, industrial and post-industrial nations to reflect different stages of economic growth. Sample countries within each group were selected based upon the availability and reliability of data.

V. CONSTRUCTION OF THE ESTIMATED MODEL

The International Service Market Opportunity Index (ISMOI) incorporates a multiple factor index comprised of: the sample country's population, GNP, and capital formation. Both GNP and capital formation statistics were recorded in foreign currencies and then converted to U.S. dollars at the corresponding year's average exchange rate. Each factor was measured as a percentage of its American equivalent, as shown in the model. (While certain services may be affected differently by these factors, this study has not weighted these factors to deal with general services.) The ISMOI is given by the following equation:

$$ISMOI = \frac{(F_{pi}/US_{pi})(FGNP_i/USGNP_i)(F_{cfi}/US_{cfi})}{(F_{pn}/US_{pn})(FGNP_n/USGNP_n)(F_{cfn}/US_{cfn})}. \tag{1}$$

Where F is the target foreign country; US is the United States; and GNP is gross national product, in U.S. dollars. Further, the subscripts p, cf, are population and capital formation–in U.S. dollars, respectively; and subscripts i and n represent the target year and comparison base year, respectively.

Since the factors interact to affect demand, the relative changes between the sample country and the U.S. in selected factors during the target year (e.g., 1980) are compared to the changes in the base year (e.g., 1970). The relative changes for the target year are multiplied by each other because of their interactive effect. This product was then divided by the same computation for a comparison year to arrive at the ISMOI coefficient for the sample nations. (For the base year, this study used 1970 and for the target year this study used 1980. This research period has been randomly selected to test the validity of the model.)

As a function of the three demand factors, a higher index ($ISMOI$) number would indicate higher service market growth and therefore more market potential. The model therefore allows the international service marketer to index the countries according to their potential in evaluating global market opportunities. The sample countries were indexed using the model and then ranked.

A Spearman rank correlation was then performed on the projected ISMOI ranking and the actual ranking of foreign service consumption figures which were ranked according to their percentage change during the research period (see Table 7). These figures were recorded in foreign currencies and converted to U.S. dollars at the corresponding year's exchange rate and were comprised of the service categories of: utilities, construction services, wholesale/retail services (including hotel services), transportation (including storage and communication), business services (including financial services, insurance, real estate services, marketing, management consulting, etc.) personal services (including community and social services), medical care, and recreation (including education, entertainment and cultural services).

Spearman rank correlations were also performed between ISMOI rankings and ranked changes in foreign service trade, exports and imports. Correlations were also projected to measure the sensitivity between ISMOI rankings and individual service categories, as well.

VI. FINDINGS AND DISCUSSION

The research period was used as an experiment. The study data that have been processed by the ISMOI produced the following results (see Table 3).

For 1980, the ISMOI forecasts that the two greatest market potentials existed in South Korea and Mexico. When this forecast is compared to the ranking of foreign service consumption changes (see Table 4), it appears to indicate that although the ranks of South Korea and Mexico did not match exactly, all of the ranks are highly correlated. The model appears to be reliable in measuring the relationship between the ISMOI forecasted market ranking and that of actual changes in foreign service consumption figures.

The correlation between the ranking of the ISMOI (Table 3) and the ranking of Foreign Domestic Service Consumption (Table 4) produced a correlation coefficient of 0.92, and was significant at the 1 percent level.

This powerful relationship seems to indicate that South Korea may be the best potential market. There are other positive statistics supporting the finding. A twelve percent increase of GNP from 1983 to 1984 supports the forecasting ability of the ISMOI. South Korea's burgeoning industrialization may increase the need for external services for their imported capital equipment, such as scientific instruments, electronic test equipment, industrial controls, food processing equipment and the other trappings of a rapidly industrializing society. The statistics appear to support this assumption. This emergence of Korea as a potential service market lends credence to the theory of an international product life cycle which maintains that as less- developed countries (LDCs) become newly industrializing countries (NICs), their level of demand for goods and services will increase (Keegan, 1995, p. 309).

High correlation is apparent between the ISMOI and the ranking of changes in foreign service trade (Table 5), 0.81 for exports and 0.77 for imports, significant at the one percent level.

As stated above, the ISMOI reveals strong correlations between the predicted and actual ranking of national service consumption. More specifically, this strong correlation appears in most service categories–wholesale/retail services, transportation services, recreation services, construction services, medical services, and business services–as presented in Table 6. The ISMOI finds less sensitivity in the forecasting of personal services and utility markets. These findings are supported at the one percent significance level.

Table 3
International Service Market Opportunity Index

National Market	Entries* 1970	1980	ISMOI	Rank	Strata**
South Korea	0.1610	1.2410	7.70	1	D
Mexico	3.8910	22.9880	5.91	2	D
Singapore	0.0010	0.0050	5.77	3	D
Japan	0.4380	1.7910	4.08	4	PI
Finland	0.0440	0.1110	2.52	5	I
United Kingdom	0.0430	0.0996	2.31	6	I
Australia	0.0013	0.0030	2.30	7	I
West Germany	0.1490	0.2900	1.94	8	PI
Canada	9.1840	12.0070	1.31	9	PI
Israel	0.0060	0.0060	0.92	10	D

* 1970 entries represent the denominator of the model. 1980 entries represent the numerator. All component entries were multiplied by 10,000 for easier representation in the table.

** Economic development strata are indicated by D (developing), I (industrial), and PI (post-industrial).

Table 4
Foreign Domestic Service Consumption Change & Rank, Aggregated
(In billions of corresponding year's U.S. dollars.)

National Market	Sales 1970	1980	Change	Rank
South Korea	$ 4.17	$29.0	612%	1
Singapore	1.46	8.5	484%	2
Japan	138.30	713.0	414%	3
Mexico	22.20	111.1	398%	4
Finland	4.91	23.2	372%	5
West Germany	91.70	391.9	327%	6
Australia	25.70	96.9	276%	7
United Kingdom	80.88	301.1	272%	8
Canada	42.90	126.6	195%	9
Israel	2.70	7.6	181%	10

Table 5
Foreign Service Trade–Ranking The Changes

National Market	Exports Change	Rank	Imports Change	Rank
United Kingdom	328%	6	285%	6
Japan	547%	2	980%	2
S. Korea	985%	1	2545%	1
Australia	345%	5	406%	5
W. Germany	442%	4	566%	3
Israel	N/A	N/A	N/A	N/A
Mexico	N/A	N/A	N/A	N/A
Finland	464%	3	541%	4
Singapore	N/A	N/A	N/A	N/A
Canada	180%	7	192%	9

Table 6
Categorized Foreign Domestic Service Consumption:
Rate Of Change and Rank

	Util. Change	Rank	Constr. Change	Rank	Who/Ret. Change	Rank
S.K.	743%	1	949%	1	492%	1
Jap	672%	2	-33%	10	390%	3
Sing	449%	4	491%	3	413%	2
Mex	345%	5	533%	2	368%	5
U.K.	318%	6	326%	4	319%	6
Aus	233%	8	198%	7	219%	8
W.G.	N/A	N/A	290%	5	231%	7
Isr	184%	9	141%	9	165%	10
Fin	477%	3	264%	6	374%	4
Can	273%	7	186%	8	169%	9

Table 6

(continued)

Categorized Foreign Domestic Service Consumption:
Rate Of Change and Rank

	Bus. Change	Rank	Pers. Change	Rank	Med. Change	Rank
S.K.	706%	1	571%	3	978%	1
Jap	600%	2	604%	1	417%	4
Sing	586%	3	319%	8	393%	5
Mex	266%	9	441%	4	507%	2
U.K.	453%	4	431%	5	-79%	10
Aus	333%	7	342%	7	325%	6
W.G.	377%	6	582%	2	430%	3
Isr	292%	8	93%	10	199%	8
Fin	401%	5	417%	6	289%	7
Can	184%	10	227%	9	160%	9

Table 6

(continued)

Categorized Foreign Domestic Service Consumption:
Rate Of Change and Rank

	Transp. Change	Rank	Recre. Change	Rank
S.K.	465%	4	573%	1
Jap	468%	3	258%	7
Sing	590%	2	569%	2
Mex	606%	1	428%	4
U.K.	310%	7	162%	9
Aus	226%	8	322%	5
W.G.	318%	6	313%	6
Isr	106%	10	132%	10
Fin	354%	5	515%	3
Can	188%	9	221%	8

Table 7
Spearman Rank Correlations By Service Category

	Correlation Coefficient	Significant?
Utilities	0.52	No
Construction	0.69	Yes
Wholesale/Retail	0.92	Yes
Transportation	0.89	Yes
Finance	0.61	Yes
Personal	0.52	No
Medical	0.67	Yes
Recreation	0.79	Yes

Calculated from ISMOI rankings in Table 3 and service category rankings in Table 6.

VII. CONCLUSIONS

Due to the strong correlations between ISMOI national service market estimates, actual domestic service consumption and foreign service trade, the authors conclude that it would benefit international service marketers to employ the ISMOI in their preliminary foreign market studies. It may be assumed that the international service marketer could obtain the sales figures from service accounts and compute market potential through the greatest percentage increases in sales of services. However, marketers find it difficult to attain such information, particularly to estimate the foreign market potential for their individual services. The ISMOI model, with variables that are fewer and readily available, can provide a more expedient indicator of international service market potential. The model's efficiency and efficacy are accentuated by the fact that the ISMOI has been found to have high statistical correlation between its national service market ranking and aggregate national domestic service consumption. It ranks the countries according to their need of service consumption, thus enabling the marketers to estimate the market potential of their services.

REFERENCES

Albaum, Gerald and Peterson, Robert, "Empirical Research in International Marketing," *Journal of International Business Studies* (Spring /Summer 1984), Vol. 15, No.1, pp. 161–173.

Aronson, Jonathan and Cowhey, Peter, *Trade in Services: A Case for Open Markets* (Washington D.C.: American Enterprise Institute, 1984).

Daniels, Peter, *Service Industries: Growth and Location* (London, England: Cambridge University Press, 1982).

Keegan, Walter, *Global Marketing Management*, fifth edition (Englewood Cliffs, New Jersey: Prentice-Hall, 1995).

Pappas, James, Brigham, Eugene and Hirschey, Mark, *Managerial Economics*, eighth edition (New York, New York: The Dryden Press, 1996).

11

INDUSTRY INFLUENCES ON MARKET REACTION TO STOCK SPLIT ANNOUNCEMENTS

Nikos I. Floros
University of Athens

George P. Tsetsekos
Drexel University

I. INTRODUCTION

Stock splits by corporations are a common occurrence. It has been estimated that five to ten percent of all AMEX and NYSE firms split their stock in a typical year, Lakonishok and Lev (1987). Although stock splits are merely an arithmetic exercise, announcements of stock splits generate abnormal positive returns to shareholders. Several studies find a significant positive reaction to split announcements; see for example Reilly and Drzycimski (1981), Ohlson and Penman (1985), Grinblatt, Masulis and Titman (1984), Lakonishok and Lev (1987), Lamoureux and Poon (1987), and Brennan and Hughes (1991).

Although there is not a convincing explanation for the positive reaction, many researchers posit that stock split announcements signal information about future cash flows and expectations of higher dividends. Research by Grinblatt, Masulis and Titman (1984), McNichols and Dravid (1990) and Brennan and Copeland (1988) suggests that stock splits are viewed as positive signals of a firm's performance and valuation. However, the firm's performance is dependent upon the industry within which the firm operates and therefore announcements of stock splits may have different impact on security returns across industries. While previous research has considered the impact of managerial rationale, trading volume effects, price volatility, and informational effect on stock prices, there is no study that deals with the industry effect on the magnitude of abnormal returns realized at the announcement of stock splits. To the extent that stock splits have informational content about increased future cash flows and earnings, interpretation of this information by shareholders is dependent on the firm's prospects. Firms in industries experiencing competitive pressures, would have cash flows and financial characteristics reflect the particular conditions under which they operate. Among several studies, Bowen, Daley and Huber (1982) found that there is an association between capital structure decisions of a firm and its industry. Leverage measures of firms within an industry tend to converge over time to a mean. Martin and Henderson (1984) have also found an industry influence on the financial structure of a firm. Similarly, we anticipate finding differences across industries regarding the stock price reaction of firms announcing stock splits. Our results provide evidence that the stock price reaction to stock splits is sensitive to the firms industry classification

This paper is organized as follows. In part two we present the data and in part three the methodology. Part four discusses the results of our study and we present our conclusions in part five.

II. DATA

We identified 2,517 regular split announcements listed in *Moody's Dividend Record, Moody's Industrial Manual,* and *Moody's Public Utilities Manual* between 1963 and 1986. We selected six industries to examine: Pharmaceutical, Chemical, Petroleum, Food Processing, Retail and Utilities. Split announcements were categorized by industry. This resulted in 789 firms identified as belonging to one of these industries at the time of split announcement. The sample was further reduced to 231 firms through the elimination of firms listed in exchanges other than NYSE and AMEX; firms without CUSIP numbers; and firms with missing data from CRSP tapes. For each of the split announcements, we verified through *The Wall Street Journal* the exact date of the announcement. In addition, each firm was checked for contamination by searching *The Wall Street Index* for contemporaneous events which might have material effect on stock prices for the time -10 to +10 days around the announcement. We thus excluded from the sample firms with contemporaneous announcement of restructuring activity, dividend and earnings announcements, and bond rating changes. The final sample consists of 109 firms with a total of 213 announcements of regular stock splits that occurred between 1963 and 1986. Panel A of Table 1, provides information on the calendar distribution of the announcements and Panel B of the same table presents information on the frequency of multiple stock split announcements for the same period. There is an even distribution of firms announcing stock splits during the period. Also, Table 2 presents the distribution of announcements across industries, as well as the distribution of split factors. It appears that all 109 firms are evenly distributed across industries.

Table 1
Sample Characteristics: Panel A
Calendar Distribution of 213 Stock Split
Announcements by NYSE and AMEX Firms: 1963–1986

Year	Number of Announcements	Percentage of Total
1963	6	2.8
1964	8	3.8
1965	3	1.4
1966	4	1.9
1967	6	2.8
1968	8	3.8
1969	7	3.3
1970	3	1.4
1971	14	6.6
1972	9	4.2
1973	7	3.3
1974	2	0.9
1975	2	2.3
1976	8	3.8
1977	11	5.2
1978	6	2.8
1979	9	4.2
1980	12	5.6
1981	12	5.6
1982	5	2.3
1983	12	5.6
1984	9	4.2
1985	20	9.4
1986	27	12.7
TOTAL	213	100%

Table 1

(continued)

Sample Characteristics: Panel B

Frequency of Multiple Stock Split Announcements

of 109 NYSE and AMEX Firms: 1963–1986

Number of announce-ments of stock splits	Number of firms	Percentage of firms in sample
1	52	47.70
2	26	23.85
3	20	18.34
4	6	5.50
5	5	4.58
TOTAL	109	100%

Table 2

Selected Summary for 109 NYSE and AMEX

Firms Announcing Stock Splits: 1963–1986

Industry	Stock-split anmts.	% in sample	No. of firms	% of sample
Pharmaceutical	28	13.2	12	11.0
Chemical	19	8.9	12	11.0
Petroleum	41	19.9	24	22.0
Food Processing	52	24.4	21	19.2
Retail	54	25.3	23	21.2
Utility	19	8.9	17	15.6
TOTAL	213	100%	109	100%

Table 2
(continued)
Stock Split Distribution

Split factor	Number	Percentage
5 to 4	31	14.55
4 to 3	29	13.61
3 to 2	49	23.00
2 to 1	67	31.45
3 to 1	37	17.37
TOTAL	109	100%

III. METHODOLOGY

The impact of industry on the strength of excess returns at the announcement of stock splits is analyzed by applying an event study methodology. We perform the event-study analysis first for the total sample and then for all the industry subsamples. To determine if there are differences in stock price reaction, we then compared the excess returns obtained from each industry subsample and the excess returns of the total sample.

In all the event-studies performed, we applied the following procedures. For each security, i, the market model is used to calculate excess returns (XRs) for the day t as follows:

$$XR_{it} = R_{it} - (a_i + b_i R_{mt}), \tag{1}$$

where R_{it} and R_{mt} are the rate of return on security i and the rate of return on the CRSP equally weighted index on event day t. The coefficients of the regression are ordinary least squares estimates of the intercept and slope of the market regression model. The estimation period is from $t = 200$ to $t = 600$ relative to the initial announcement day $(t = 0)$.

For each firm, i, and each trading day, t, within the period $(t = -60$ to $t = +60)$, an average excess return for the portfolio of n securities is calculated as follows:

$$AXR_t = 1/n \sum_{t=-b}^{n} XR_{it}. \tag{2}$$

The significance of the $AXRs$ is evaluated using a t-statistic. Complete analysis of changes in the value of the portfolio requires the accumulation of the average excess returns over time. The cumulative excess returns, CXR, surrounding the period of time beginning $-b$ days before the security offering event day and ending e days after the event is defined as:

$$CXR_i = \sum_{t=-b}^{e} AXR_{it}. \tag{3}$$

We used daily excess returns for the period from sixty days before the event and sixty days after the event. The examination of the $CXRs$ before and after the announcement date is useful in providing information on the market reaction to split announcements across different industries.

IV. RESULTS

Table 3 presents results on the performance behavior of the daily average excess returns for each day in the period $t = -10$ to $t = +10$ for the total sample. The z-statistics indicates whether the calculated $AXRs$ reveal a significant reaction on any given day. The results of Table 3 reveal that there are positive excess returns obtained during the event days -1 and 0 of 0.162 percent and 1.053 percent respectively. The result for day 0 is statistically significant at the one percent level. For the two-day period (-1, 0) we find that the average excess returns are 1.215 percent and statistically significant at the one percent level. These results are consistent with previous studies which find a similar magnitude of abnormal returns on the event window.

Table 3 also portrays the percentage of positive announcements that occurred during the period and the results of a Wilcoxon sign test. The test rejects the null hypothesis that the portion of positive announcements in the respective sample is equal to 0.5. For the two-day period (-1, 0) the percentage of positive announcements is 55.9 percent and, based on the Wilcoxon test, this figure is statistically different than fifty percent.

Table 4 presents a comparison of the two-day abnormal returns for all the subsamples. Two-day returns are all positive for all industries, however with different magnitude and different level of significance.

194

Table 3
Average of Cumulative Returns of
213 Stock Split Announcements of NYSE
and AMEX Firms: 1963–1986

Event Day Return	Average Excess Return (%)	z-Statistic Return	Cumulative Excess	% Positive (p-value)	Wilcoxon sign test
-30	-0.143	-1.312	-0.072	42.7	0.036
-20	0.036	0.591	-0.110	44.6	0.305
-10	0.060	0.227	-0.072	50.2	0.334
-9	0.088	1.458	0.017	49.8	0.474
-8	0.045	0.926	0.061	50.7	0.283
-7	0.047	0.453	0.108	48.8	0.363
-6	-0.074	-0.707	0.034	46.5	0.122
-5	-0.016	-0.150	0.018	47.9	0.254
-4	-0.001	-0.624	0.018	46.5	0.297
-3	0.081	0.799	0.099	45.3	0.427
-2	0.233	2.896*	0.332	56.3	0.006
-1	0.162	1.941	0.494	52.1	0.351
0	1.053	11.273*	1.547	61.5	0.000
1	0.844	9.394*	2.391	63.8	0.000
2	0.218	2.915	2.610	54.0	0.033
3	-0.137	-0.978	2.473	42.3	0.015
4	-0.173	-2.141	2.300	39.0	0.002
5	-0.155	-1.532	2.145	42.7	0.022
6	-0.056	-0.239	2.089	47.4	0.174
7	-0.190	-1.672	1.899	45.8	0.061
8	-0.058	-1.105	1.841	47.9	0.121
9	-0.071	-0.361	1.770	41.0	0.042
10	-0.038	1.755	1.825	48.8	0.317
20	-0.060	-0.893	1.386	46.5	0.143
30	0.066	1.148	1.158	47.9	0.488

Average two-day abnormal return: 1.215%
(z-value) (9.344%)
Largest 2-day positive abnormal return: 9.70%
Largest 2-day negative abnormal return: -13.33%
*Significant at the 1% level.

Table 4
Two-Day Average Abnormal Returns For Subsamples of
231 Announcements of Stock Splits

Sample	Sample size	CXRs (z-value)	Percentage Positive	Wilcoxon sign test (p-value)
Total sample	213	1.215 (9.344)*	56.0	0.000
Retail	54	1.775 (5.140)*	55.2	0.0005
Food Processing	52	1.752 (6.771)*	60.2	0.0000
Chemicals	19	1.444 (4.898)*	57.4	0.0201
Petroleum	41	0.857 (3.318)*	59.7	0.0256
Pharmaceutical	28	0.139 (0.684)*	46.4	0.3493
Utilities	19	0.286 (0.816)	34.5	0.3295

*Significant at the 1% level.

Table 5
Internal Analysis of Cumulative Abnormal Returns of
NYSE and AMEX Firms Announcing Stock Splits: 1963–1986
Panel A: Cumulative Abnormal Returns for the Total Sample

Interval	CAAR	t-Statistics	Percentage Positive	Wilcoxon test (p-value)
day -30 to day -2	0.261	0.350	55.4	0.164
day -1 to day 0	1.215	5.871*	63.4	0.000
day +1 to day +30	-0.389	-0.546	51.6	0.269
day -5 to day 5	2.111	5.126*	68.1	0.000
day -2 to day 2	2.511	7.963*	72.8	0.000
day -1 to day +1	2.060	7.642*	69.0	0.000
day 0 to day 4	1.806	5.569*	65.7	0.000

Table 5
(continued)
Internal Analysis of Cumulative Abnormal Returns of
NYSE and AMEX Firms Announcing Stock Splits: 1963–1986
Panel B: Cumulative Abnormal Returns For All Industries

	Cumulative Abnormal Returns (t-statistics) Selective Intervals				
Industry	D[-1,0]	D[-5,5]	D[-2,2]	D[-1,1]	D[0,4]
Retail	1.775	3.812	3.507	2.849	2.254
	(3.725)*	(4.387)*	(5.480)*	(4.494)*	(3.664)*
Food Processing	1.752	3.089	3.109	2.602	2.437
	(4.882)*	(3.896)*	(5.671)*	(6.367)*	(4.004)*
Chemicals	1.444	1.713	2.450	2.362	2.881
	(1.347)	(1.369)	(1.830)	(3.056)*	(2.226)
Petroleum	0.857	-0.384	1.274	1.048	0.191
	(2.161)*	(-0.348)	(1.742)	(1.621)	(0.256)
Pharmaceutical	0.139	0.396	0.941	0.537	0.263
	(0.354)	(0.568)	(1.419)	(0.935)	(0.351)
Utilities	0.286	2.915	3.086	2.456	3.488
	(0.151)	(2.811)*	(2.580)*	(2.305)*	(2.907)*

*Significant at the 1% level.

The retail, food processing, and chemical industries exhibit abnormal returns which are above those obtained from the total sample. These results are significant at the one percent level. The petroleum, utility, and pharmaceutical experience abnormal returns which are below those of the total sample. Utilities and pharmaceuticals exhibited statistically insignificant results.

We then focused attention on the cumulative abnormal returns and performed interval analyses for all of the samples. The results of the interval analysis for the total sample and industry subsamples appear on Table 5. In Panel A of Table 5, it appears that for the total sample more and more positive, statistically significant returns occur the smaller the interval we consider. This suggests that most of the excess returns occurred around the event day (-1, 0). In Panel B of Table 5, we compare for the same time intervals cumulative returns among different industry samples and we present t-statistics for each interval. It appears that the food processing, retail, and chemical industries exhibit a similar pattern of cumulative returns to the total sample. The petroleum, pharmaceutical and utility industries have mostly insignificant cumulative returns.

V. CONCLUSIONS

Stock split announcements generate positive revaluation effects to shareholders. A randomly selected sample of 350 regular stock split announcements exhibits excess positive returns surrounding the announcement day. In terms of the magnitude and statistical significance the results obtained in this study are consistent with previous studies. However, when we segmented our sample, we find that the strength of the positive reaction depends upon the industry within which the firm operates. More specifically, the retail, chemicals and food processing industries exhibit abnormal returns which are above those of the total sample. In contrast the pharmaceutical, utilities and petroleum industries exhibit returns which are lower than those of the total sample. Although we have empirically verified an industry influence on the magnitude of excess returns, we have not developed a theory that explains the phenomenon.

REFERENCES

Brennan, M. J. and Copeland, T. E., "Stock Splits, Stock Prices, and Transaction Costs," *Journal of Financial Economics* (October 1988), Vol. 22, No. 1, pp. 83–101.

Brennan, M. J. and Hughes, P.J., "Stock Prices and the Supply of Information," *Journal of Finance* (December 1991), Vol. 46, No. 5, pp. 1665–1691.

Bowen, R., Daley, L.A., and Huber, C., "Leverage Measures and Industrial Classification: Review and Additional Evidence," *Financial Management* (Winter 1982), Vol. 11, No. 4, pp. 10–20.

Grinblatt, M.S., Masulis, R. W., and Titman, S., "The Valuation Effects of Stock Splits and Stock Dividends," *Journal of Financial Economics* (December 1984), Vol. 13, No. 4, pp. 461–490.

Lakonishok, J. and Lev, B., "Stock Splits and Stock Dividends: Why, Who, When," *Journal of Finance* (September 1987), Vol. 42, No. 4, pp. 913–932.

Lamourex, C. G. and Poon, P., "The Market Reaction to Stock Splits," *Journal of Finance* (December 1987), Vol. 42, No. 5, pp. 1347–1370.

Martin, J. and Henderson, G., "Industry Influences on Financial Structure," *Quarterly Journal of Business and Economics* (Autumn 1984), Vol. 10, No. 2, pp. 27–39.

McNichols, M. and Dravid, A., "Stock Dividends, Stock Splits, and Signaling," *Journal of Finance* (July 1990), Vol. 45, No. 3, pp. 857–879.

Moody's Dividend Record, various issues.

Moody's Industrial Manual, various issues.

Moody's Public Utilities Manual, various issues.

Ohlson, J. and Penman, S. A., "Volatility Increases Subsequent to Stock Splits," *Journal of Financial Economics* (June 1985), Vol. 14, No. 2, pp. 251–266.

Reilly, F. K. and Drzycimski, J.C., "Short Run Profits from Stock Splits," *Financial Management* (Summer 1981), Vol. 10, No. 2, pp. 64–74.

The Wall Street Journal, various issues, Dow Jones & Co., New York.

The Wall Street Journal Index, various issues, Dow Jones & Co., New York.

12

A LOGIT MODEL OF
SUCCESS OF TAKEOVER BIDS

Siamack Shojai
Manhattan College
Seth A. Kurland
The Prudential

I. INTRODUCTION

Since the late 1970s Corporate America has witnessed a rapid growth in the number of corporate mergers and acquisitions. The Tax Reform Act of 1986, and the sharp stock market plunge of 1987, resulted in a renewed and a more energetic interest in merger activities. Recent hostile interests in companies previously thought too big to be taken over, such as RJR/Nabisco, Kraft and Pillsbury, have spawned new interest in studying mergers and acquisitions.

Previous studies of mergers have addressed issues such as the impact of mergers on stockholders' wealth, the reasons behind takeovers, the profitability of mergers to suitors' shareholders, the methods of payments for target shares, the determinants of the bid premium, and the determinants of success of tender offers. See, for example, the studies by Asquith and Han (1982), Carleton et al. (1983), Giammarino and Heinkel (1986), Hansen (1986), Lessard and Sarhan (1988), Samuelson and Rosenthal (1986), Saul (1985), Sercu (1995), Bhushan (1996), and Schwert (1996).

Many previous studies have addressed the determinants of success of takeover attempts. Hoffmeister and Dyl (1981) and Walking (1985) have utilized an OLS, a discriminate, and a logit model of predicting the outcome of a tender offer. The success of a tender offer is dependent on variables such as the size of the bid premium, managerial opposition by the target firm, percentage of the target shares owned by the bidder, solicitation fees, and competing bids. Empirical results of previous research indicate a significant positive correlation between success of a tender offer and the variables mentioned above, with the exception of the size of the bid premium. Walking (1985) demonstrates that the bid premium can become significant if it is specified correctly. He concludes that the bid premiums measured prior to the SEC filing of an offer are insignificant but bid premiums based on prices prior to the earliest of either SEC filing or offer announcement are significant. He suggests that the anomaly in the findings of previous studies are due to specification errors.

This paper attempts to overcome the bid premium specification error controversy by utilizing a more direct approach which bypasses the need for a bid premium measurement. To avoid the measurement bias, we regress the probability of success of a takeover attempt directly on determinants of the bid premium. These include financial ratios of the target firm. This approach is advantageous to others for two reasons. First, it eliminates the need for a bid premium measurement and the associated bias. Second, it can point out those financial attributes which contribute to the success of a takeover attempt. Certainly this is a relatively less costly tool which can be utilized by the suitor as well as the target firm to facilitate or discourage the takeover attempt.

The next section presents the model and the methodology of the paper. This is followed by a discussion of the empirical results. The last section concludes the paper.

II. THE MODEL AND METHODOLOGY

A logit regression model is employed in order to investigate the factors which contribute to a company's being a successful takeover target. The dependent variable measures the success or failure of a takeover attempt. It assumes a value of either "one" for "successful bids" or "zero" for "unsuccessful bids." The probability of success or failure is regressed on nine explanatory financial variables of target firms. These include the current ratio (CR), the dividend payout ratio (PR), the price-earning ratio (PER), the market price-book value ratio (MBR), the total debt-asset ratio (DAR), the average earning growth (EG), the earnings variability (EV), the mean of the target's earnings (ME), and the earnings' growth variability (EGV).

The current ratio is used as a measure of a company's ability to meet its short-term obligations. A high current ratio may suggest that a target firm is able to handle the additional debt burden which is generally placed on the target firm. One would expect that a firm with a relatively high current ratio commands a higher bid premium, which in turn can contribute to the success of a takeover exercise.

The dividend payout ratio is viewed in a controversial manner. When a nongrowth firm retains a large percentage of its earnings it can damage the firm's market price. On the other hand, a more liberal dividend policy can improve its stock price and make it difficult, i.e., uneconomical, for a suitor to offer a high bid premium. Thus, we conclude that a high payout ratio affects the probability of success adversely.

The price-earning ratio is utilized by many analysts for valuation purposes. A relatively high P/E is usually an indication of an overvalued company which does not deserve a high bid premium and a low P/E ratio contributes more to the success of a takeover attempt. However, a high P/E ratio can be due to factors such as a company being engaged in long-term projects which produce no earnings immediately but generate substantial positive cash flows and high earnings in future years. It is natural to assume that many suitors are aware of the perils of dwelling on a target company's past performance and consider the P/E ratio in conjunction with a careful study of its long-term projects.

Acquisition often involve the selling off of some assets or divisions of the target firm. Therefore, the ratio of the market value of the common shares to the book value of a firm is included as an explanatory variable. The lower this ratio, the more attractive a target firm, thus leading to a higher premium and a higher probability of success.

It is generally believed that a highly leveraged firm is not a good takeover target. Firms with a low debt/asset ratio are very attractive because they can absorb more debt and service it after the acquisition. A low level of borrowing may also indicate that a firm relies on internally generated funds from its operation. Thus, takeover attempts seem to be more successful when the target firm has a low debt/asset ratio. In fact, many firms attempt to fight potential suitors by taking so-called "poison pills" which rearrange their capital structure and make them less attractive. It must be noted that only firms with a strong operation and a high operating income can have a high debt/asset ratio and still be successfully acquired. A strong operating income provides a solid base to service the existing as well as the prospective post acquisition debt. Finally, two measures of earnings and variation in earnings are included in the model. These include the mean of the earnings over the past five years, the average annual rate of growth of earnings during the previous five years, and their respective standard deviations. The former two variables are expected to be positively correlated with the probability of success, and the latter two variables are measures of risk of earnings which are expected to have a negative impact on the success of a takeover attempt. Because these measures of earnings and earnings variation are highly correlated, we attempt to avoid the problem of multicollinearity by retaining only those with a higher t-statistic.

The following equation summarizes the model:

$$S = f(CR, PR, PER, MBR, DAR, EG, EV, ME, EGV). \qquad (1)$$

Where S is the probability of success of a takeover bid, success = 1 and failure = 0); CR is the target's current ratio; PR represents the target's dividend payment ratio; PER is the target's market price/earnings ratio; MBR the target's market price/book value ratio; DAR the target's total debt/asset ratio; EG the target's average earnings growth; EV the target's earnings variability; ME the mean of the target's earnings; and EGV is the target's earnings growth variability.

III. THE EMPIRICAL RESULTS

The model described in the previous section was estimated utilizing a logit estimation technique. A random sample of forty firms which received bids during the 1986–1988 period was obtained from *The Wall Street Journal Index*. Three firms were excluded from the sample because of lack of adequate data concerning them. Annual data for the purpose of estimation was extracted from various issues of *Moody's Industrial Manual*, *Standard and Poor's*, and the *Value Line Investment Survey*.

Table 1 presents the estimation results. As expected, when the probability of success (failure) was regressed on all explanatory variables, the problem of multicollinearity was present and resulted in low t-statistics. However, when one of the correlated variables (EV) was dropped, the remaining t-statistics improved substantially. The various versions of the empirical results indicate that most of the explanatory variables are statistically significant at a ten percent significance level or better. All the significant variables except for the debt/asset ratio and price/earnings ratio have the expected sign.

Table 1
Estimation Results

Variant One	Coefficient	t-stat.
CR	0.9808	1.5196**
DAR	0.0129	0.6720
EG	2.967	1.681**
EGV	-2.039	-1.697*
MBR	-3.385	-1.824*
ME	0.834	1.826*
PE	0.112	1.427*
PR	-0.582	-2.004*

*Significant at a 5% level or better.
**Significant at a 10% level or better.

Table 1
(continued)
Estimation Results

Variant Two	Coefficient	t-stat.
C	-1.8127	-.7802
CR	1.2978	1.642*
DAR	0.0245	0.9699
EG	2.7812	1.5489**
EGV	-1.9024	-1.5424**
EV	-0.0369	-0.0462
MBR	-3.1762	-1.6706
ME	0.9451	1.7603*
PE	0.1190	1.4363**
PR	-0.5119	-1.5297**

C is a constant.
*Significant at a 5% level or better.
**Significant at a 10% level or better.

Table 2
Predicted and Actual Probabilities
of Being a Successful Target

Observation	Predicted (Variant 1)	Predicted (Variant 2)	Actual
1	0.536847	0.535002	1.000000
2	0.519560	0.524669	1.000000
3	0.751135	0.783875	1.000000
4	0.990349	0.994404	1.000000
5	0.297381	0.299850	0.000000
6	0.560773	0.552593	1.000000
7	0.438318	0.560363	0.000000
8	0.894832	0.907770	1.000000
9	0.464841	0.389740	1.000000
10	0.801678	0.884272	1.000000
11	0.428476	0.455567	1.000000
12	0.447341	0.448827	0.000000
13	0.575325	0.590311	1.000000
14	0.865551	0.874548	1.000000
15	0.645276	0.586969	0.000000
16	0.813982	0.768213	1.000000
17	0.080037	0.066328	0.000000
18	0.253440	0.288249	0.000000
19	0.273155	0.160281	0.000000
20	0.793441	0.765499	0.000000
21	0.681445	0.667346	0.000000
22	0.599869	0.501128	0.000000
23	0.125089	0.168192	0.000000
24	0.257630	0.202056	1.000000
25	0.567025	0.528088	0.000000
26	0.007495	0.007995	0.000000
27	0.288981	0.275126	0.000000
28	0.738535	0.848529	1.000000
29	0.258478	0.261704	0.000000
30	0.541630	0.487205	1.000000
31	0.573232	0.528536	0.000000
32	0.544091	0.599568	1.000000
33	0.574605	0.466120	1.000000
34	0.675059	0.736637	1.000000
35	0.806889	0.660054	1.000000
36	0.807046	0.766373	0.000000
37	0.870970	0.823373	1.000000

Table 3
Predicted and Actual Probabilities
of Becoming a Successful Target

Firm	Actual	Predicted Variant 1	Predicted Variant 2
1	0	.00	.00
2	0	.02	.02
3	0	.86	.89
4	0	.02	.02
5	0	.97	.97
6	0	.85	.77
7	0	.67	.68
8	0	.06	.09
9	0	.08	.09
10	0	.00	.00
11	0	.11	.13
12	0	.72	.82
13	0	.73	.72
14	0	.82	.86
15	0	.18	.20
16	0	.01	.01
17	0	.47	.35
18	0	.97	.98
19	0	.07	.07
20	1	.17	.16
21	0	.62	.63
22	0	.26	.23
23	0	.65	.62
24	0	.00	.00
25	0	.07	.07
26	1	.57	.65
27	0	.58	.72
28	0	.06	.09
29	0	.02	.03
30	0	.00	.93
31	0	.26	.29
32	0	.02	.03
33	0	.03	.05
34	1	.82	.79
35	1	.97	.97
36	0	.51	.61
37	0	.66	.67
38	0	.69	.73
39	0	.09	.13
40	0	.00	.00
41	0	.97	.95
42	0	.98	.97
43	1	.29	.30
44	0	.18	.19
45	0	.60	.51
46	1	.08	.15
47	0	.99	.99
48	0	.11	.12
49	0	.87	.87
50	0	.49	.52

In order to test the predictive power of the model, two attempts were made to predict the probability of success of a takeover attempt on the original thirty-seven firms. The actual and the predicted probabilities of becoming a successful target are reported in Table 2. The in-sample forecasts indicate that twenty-six out of thirty-seven firms have a high probability of success.

In addition to the in-sample forecast, an attempt was made to forecast the probability of a successful acquisition of fifty randomly selected firms. Table 3 reports the actual and the predicted probabilities of success. A one indicates a successful attempt and a zero means failure. Three out of six firms which were actually targets were correctly pointed out by the model. However, the model indicates that twenty-two firms out of fifty firms included in the random sample are good potential successful targets. In some cases, it seems that firms have the desired financial ratios, but the market has already rewarded them by making their common shares overvalued. For example, the model indicates that Circuit City Stores possesses the characteristics that are usually found attractive in a takeover candidate. Its current ratio is high, it has only thirty percent debt relative to total assets, and its earnings have been rising steadily. However, the market has already rewarded the firm and its shares sell for 200 times book value. This high reward (price) is enough to discourage any potential raider.

III. CONCLUSION

This paper has attempted to overcome the bid premium specification controversy by regressing the probability of success of a takeover bid on nine explanatory financial ratios of target firms. The estimation results of the logit model indicate that there is a significant positive correlation between the probability of a successful takeover and explanatory variables such as the rate of growth of earnings, the variation in earnings, the market price to book value ratio, and the dividend payout ratio at a five percent significance level or better. The empirical results also indicate that the current ratio and the price-earning ratio are significant explanatory variables at a ten percent significance level or better. However, the price-earning ratio does not have the expected sign.

The predictive power and the stability of the model was tested by in-sample and out-sample forecasts. The model predicts twenty-six out of thirty-seven successful takeovers. This is a ratio of over seventy percent. The out-sample forecast predicts three out of six successful attempts. It also points out another twenty-two good potential candidates.

The model can provide an inexpensive and relatively fast approach for screening good potential takeover targets. Researchers as well as financial analysts can utilize the model in their search of those firms which possess the desired financial attributes. The management of potential target firms can also utilize the methodology of this paper to identify those financial ratios which make their firms attractive to potential suitors. Once the crucial ratios have been identified, one may attempt to encourage a takeover bid by making those ratios even more attractive. On the other hand, a hostile takeover bid can be diffused by restructuring the firm's financial statements in a way which would make ratios such as the current ratio, the dividend payout ratio, and the market price to book value ratio less attractive. It must be mentioned, however, that no model can totally replace the good judgment of an analyst. The model can provide clues to a very sophisticated process which requires a lot of foresight and experience.

REFERENCES

Asquith, Brennan P., and Han, Kin E., "The Impact of Merger Bids on the Participating Firms' Security Holders," *Journal of Finance* (December 1982), pp. 1209–1228.

Bhushan, Ravi, "Acquisitions and the Information Environment of Firms," *Financial Review* (February 1996), pp. 105–125.

Carleton, W., and Guilkey, D., Harris R., and Stewart J., "An Empirical Analysis of the Role of the Medium of Exchange in Mergers," *Journal of Finance* (June 1983), pp. 813–826.

Giammarino, Ronald M., and Heinkel, Robert L., "A Model of Dynamic Takeover Behavior," *Journal of Finance* (June 1986), pp. 465–480.

Hansen, Robert G., "A Theory for the Choice of Exchange Medium in Mergers and Acquisitions," *Journal of Business* (June 1986), pp. 75–96.

Hoffmeister, J. and Dyl, E., "Predicting the Outcomes of Cash Tender Offers," *Financial Management* (Winter 1981), pp. 50–58.

Lessard, J.P., and Sarhan, M.H., "Merger Selection Strategy: A Multidimensional Perspective," *Akron Business and Economic Review* (Fall 1988), pp. 15–34.

Samuelson, William, and Rosenthal, Leonard, "Price Movements as Indicators of Tender Offer Success," *Journal of Finance* (June 1986), pp. 481–500.

Saul, Ralph J., "Hostile Takeovers: What Should be Done?" *Harvard Business Review* (September/October 1985), pp. 18–27.

Schwert, William G., "Markup Pricing in Mergers and Acquisitions," *Journal of Financial Economics* (June 1996), pp. 153–192.

Sercu, P., "On the Structure of Takeover Models, and Insider-Outsider Conflicts in Negotiated Takeovers," *Journal of Banking and Finance* (April 1995), pp. 11–44.

Walking, Ralph, "Predicting Tender Offer Success: A Logistical Analysis," *Journal of Financial and Quantitative Analysis* (Winter 1985), Vol. 20, No. 4, pp. 461–478.

13

AN ANALYSIS OF THE HOME MORTGAGE REFINANCING DECISION

Maury Randall
Rider University

Kuang-Chian Chen
Rider University

I. INTRODUCTION

The subject of refunding corporate debt is discussed in virtually all major financial management textbooks. In addition, numerous articles have been written describing various aspects of bond refunding.[1] On a related topic, however, analysis of home mortgage refinancing, relatively little has appeared. Some information is available from Sirmans (1985) who describes a number of the elements of the problem on a before tax basis. However, because of the brevity of the discussion, a number of important items are not examined. These items include the minimum time required to keep a new mortgage in order to justify refinancing, some issues related to the maturity of the refinanced mortgage, and the impact of taxes on home mortgage refinancing.[2]

In this paper we examine the home mortgage refinancing problem including the impact of taxes, updated with regulations adopted in 1986. We compute net present values and the number of years a new mortgage must be held to justify the refinancing decision. We also perform sensitivity analysis to examine how results are influenced by changes in key variables such as tax rates, interest rates, and the maturity of the new mortgage.

---

[1] For example, see A. Offer and R. Taggart, "Bond Refunding: A Clarifying Analysis," *Journal of Finance*, March 1977, pp. 21–30; R. Harris, "Refunding of Discounted Debt: An Adjusted Net Present Value Analysis," *Financial Management*, Winter 1980, pp. 7–12; A. Kilotay, "On the Structure and Valuation of Bond Refundings," *Financial Management*, Spring 1982, pp. 41–42.

[2] See C. F. Sirmans, *Real Estate Finance* (New York, New York: McGraw-Hill, 1985), pp. 201–203. Sirmans does provide additional information, such as effects of taxes, on the separate topic of income property refinancing.

II. GENERAL FRAMEWORK

The basic approach in analyzing home mortgage refinancing is the same as in bond refunding. An investment of funds is made at a point in time in order to reduce future cash outflows associated with borrowed funds. In home mortgage refinancing the initial investment covers items such as loan application fee, points, legal expenses, prepayment penalties (if any), and other transactions costs. Future benefits from this investment may include lower mortgage payments or the fact that the mortgage balance may be falling more rapidly if refinancing occurs. If the present value of the future benefits exceed the initial investment, refinancing is justified.

III. DIFFERENCES BETWEEN BOND REFUNDING AND HOME MORTGAGE REFINANCING

In bond refunding analysis it is usually assumed that the new set of bonds have a maturity equal to the remaining maturity of the original set of bonds outstanding. Moreover, it is usually assumed that interest savings on the new bonds over the original bonds will occur over the entire number of years that the new bonds will be outstanding. [3] While these assumptions are appropriate for bond refunding, they cannot be assumed for home mortgage refinancing. For example, an individual who refinances an original 30-year fixed-rate mortgage after interest rates dropped may replace it with a new 15-year mortgage. Moreover, most people do not stay in the same house long enough to completely pay off the new or the original mortgage. In fact, the yields on mortgage-backed securities, such as GNMA certificates, might be computed with an expected life of approximately ten years.[4]

The home mortgage case also involves a more complicated computation of the tax effects of interest expense. The interest deduction on bond interest is generally a constant each year. In a fully or partially amortized mortgage the portion of the fixed mortgage payment which represents interest declines each year. Thus, the tax shield also

---

[3] For example, see E. F. Brigham and L. Gapenski, *Financial Management: Theory and Practice* (Fort Worth, Texas: The Dryden Press, 1994), pp. 922–925.

[4] See L. Gitman and M. Joehnk, *Fundamentals of Investing* (New York, New York: HarperCollins, 1996), p. 346.

declines over time. Finally, the tax treatment of transactions costs is different in bond refunding and mortgage refinancing.

IV. ASSUMPTIONS AND RELEVANT VARIABLES

In our analysis we assume the amount borrowed for the new loan is the same as the balance on the existing loan. In this way we compare the benefits and costs of the refinanced loan against the existing mortgage. Among the variables which are used in the analysis are the original mortgage interest rate, the new mortgage interest rate, homeowner's tax rate, new closing costs, points on new mortgage, the number of years remaining on the old mortgage, the number of years the household will be paying off the new mortgage, the remaining balance on the old mortgage, and the opportunity costs of funds.

The following equation may be used to compute the net present value, NPV, in refinancing. This equation is relevant in the most common case in which the home is sold prior to maturity date of both new mortgage and original mortgage.

$$
\begin{aligned}
NPV = {} & (M_0 - M_N) PVA_{\frac{r}{12}(1-T),H} - T \sum_{t=1}^{H} \frac{(INT_{0,t+m} - INT_{N,t})}{[1 + \frac{r}{12}(1-T)]^t} \\
& + (BAL_{0,H+m} - BAL_{N,H})\Big[\frac{1}{1 + \frac{r}{12}(1-T)}\Big]^H \\
& + \frac{T(PTS)}{n_2} PVA_{\frac{r}{12}(1-T),H} \\
& + T\Big[PTS - (H)\frac{PTS}{n_2}\Big]\Big[\frac{1}{1 + \frac{r}{12}(1-T)}\Big]^H - TRC.
\end{aligned}
\tag{1}
$$

Where M_0 is the monthly payment on the original mortgage; $PVA_{\frac{r}{12}(1-T),H}$ relates the present value of an annuity of \$1 at an interest rate of $\frac{r}{12}(1-T)$ per month for H months; r is the before tax opportunity cost of funds to the homeowner for an investment lasting H months with same risk as the refinanced mortgage; T is the homeowner's tax rate; H is the "holding period," which is equal to number of months that payments are made on the new mortgage until the home is sold; $INT_{0,t+m}$ represents the interest payment on original mortgage $t + m$ months after that mortgage began; $INT_{N,t}$, in contrast, is the interest on the new mortgage t months after that mortgage began; m is the number of months between taking out original mortgage and subsequent refinancing; $BAL_{0,H+m}$ is the balance on the original mortgage, assuming no refinancing, $H + m$ months after it was taken out; $BAL_{N,H}$, in contrast, is the balance in the new mortgage H months after it was taken out; PTS relates the total value of points paid to refinance; and TRC is the total transactions costs associated with refinancing.

The first term in equation (1) is the expected present value of the savings on the monthly mortgage payments. It is computed for a period of H months, the expected holding period before sale of home. The after-tax opportunity cost of funds to the homeowner, $\frac{r}{12}(1 - T)$, is used in discounting cash flows. The value of this first term may be either positive or negative depending on the interest rates on the original and new mortgage, the initial time to maturity on the original mortgage, and the initial time to maturity on the new mortgage.

The second term in the equation is the present value of the lost tax benefits due to interest payments on the new mortgage being less than interest payments on the original mortgage. For each month the difference in interest payments under original and new mortgages is calculated starting at the time that the refinancing occurs. In computing interest payments on the original mortgage one must keep in mind that it was outstanding for m months prior to obtaining the new mortgage loan.

The third term computes the gain or loss due to the fact that the loan balance is not dropping at the same rate in both mortgages. For example if a 15-year mortgage replaces a mortgage with more than 15 years remaining, the balance on the new loan will drop more rapidly. If the new mortgage matures after the original mortgage would have matured, the value of the third term would be negative. To compute the mortgage balances t months after refinancing equations (2) and (3) are used.

$$BAL_{0,t+m} = M_0 PVA_{\frac{i_0}{12}, n_{rem}}. \qquad (2)$$

Where i_0 and n_{rem} are the interest rate on the original mortgage and the number of monthly payments remaining on original mortgage at time t, respectively.

$$BAL_{N,t} = M_N PVA_{\frac{i_N}{12}, n_{2-t}}. \qquad (3)$$

Where i_N gives the interest rate on the new mortgage; n_2 are the months to maturity on new mortgage at time of refinancing; and n_{2-t} are the remaining months on new mortgage at time t.

The fourth and fifth terms in equation (1) represent the present value of the tax savings due to the points paid on the refinanced mortgage. Points are amortized on a monthly basis and the balance of points outstanding at the end of the holding period is deducted as a lump sum. We have used monthly amortization of points although annual amortization is used in filing tax forms. This, however, has no significant effect on the results.

V. MINIMUM NUMBER OF YEARS TO JUSTIFY REFINANCING

Another very useful measure in assessing the merits of refinancing is the minimum number of months required in order to justify the transactions costs incurred in refinancing. This number is obtained by solving for the value of H, which results in NPV equal to zero. We denote this value as H^*. Given the uncertainty of the mortgage holding period, H^* provides information on the likelihood or risk that refinancing will be profitable.

VI. AN ILLUSTRATION

Assume an individual took out a $100,000 30-year fixed-rate mortgage in order to buy a home. The annual borrowing rate was $i_0 = 12\%$, and three years later the annual mortgage rate dropped to $i_N = 10\%$, for a 15-year mortgage. The homeowner is in a 30 percent tax bracket, has a before tax opportunity cost of funds of 9% per year, and expects to remain in the home for an additional 6 years. The homeowner does not believe interest rates will drop further and wishes to determine if there is a net gain in refinancing. We assume transactions costs will amount to $1,500 plus 3 points on the amount of the refinanced loan.[5] With the use of equation (1) we find NPV = $3,248 and H^* = 35 months.

VII. SENSITIVITY ANALYSIS

Starting with the assumptions in the above illustration, we can examine how results are sensitive to changes in key variables. First consider how changes in the homeowner's tax rate will effect the outcome. The findings are shown in Section I of Table 1.

---

[5] In some locations there may be prepayment penalties, but we assume none exist in our case.

Table 1
Sensitivity Analysis Using Basic Illustration*

I. Variation in Tax Rate

	T = 0	T = 15 %	T = 30 %
NPV	4,868	4,086	3,248
H*	31	33	35

II. Incentive to Refinance as Interest Rates Drop

Drop in Mortgage Rate (%)	0.5	1.0	1.5	2.0
H*	161	78	49	35

III. Effect of n_2 upon H* and NPV

	$n_2 = 15$	$n_2 = 20$	$n_2 = 25$	$n_2 = 25$
H*	35	35	36	36

H		NPV		
24	-1,063	-1,081	-1,091	-1,096
60	2,250	2,135	2,074	2,040
120	6,783	6,335	6,102	5,970

IV. Variation in m/n_1

m/n_1	0.1	0.2	0.3	0.4	0.5	0.6	0.7	0.8
m	36	72	108	144	180	216	252	288
NPV	3,251	3,082	2,844	2,505	2,019	1,324	329	-1,095
H*	35	36	37	38	40	44	57	0

* NPV in dollars, $H*$ in months.

As can be observed NPV drops substantially, from $4,868 to $3,248 as T increases from 0 to 30%. This occurs because of the reduced tax savings on interest expense associated with the lower interest rate of the new mortgage. This loss was partially offset by the lower discount rate, $r(1 - T)$, and tax savings on points. However, the reduced tax savings on interest is the dominant factor in our example. Associated with the decrease in NPV as T rises is an increase in the number of months required for NPV to equal zero. NPV, however, was more sensitive, dropping 33% compared to an increase in $H*$ of 13%.

The second set of results concerns how much of a decline in interest rates is required to provide an incentive to refinance. In Section 2 we show how $H*$ declines as the new mortgage rate drops below the original mortgage interest rate. All conditions described in our original example apply, except we now examine the impact of a decline in interest rates. With a drop in interest rates of only 1 percent, refinancing would be justified in 78 months. A 2.0 percent drop in rates provides an H^* of 35 months which previously appeared in Table 1. Thus, refinancing may be profitable for a number of people when interest rates drop as little as .5 to 1.0 percent.

A third item examined was the effect of varying n_2, the maturity of the new mortgage. If a household which is contemplating refinancing is not certain how long it plans to reside in its home, can the household reduce its risk through the selection of n_2? As can be observed in Section III of Table 1, H^* falls slightly with lower values of n_2. While the monthly mortgage payment becomes larger, this is offset by the greater value of tax savings on the interest payments and points on the new mortgage and the more rapid drop in the loan balance on the new mortgage.

Values of NPV were also calculated for $H = 24, 60$ and 120 months. These results are consistent with the H^* findings. NPV is larger for lower values of n_2 irregardless of whether $H \leq H^*$ or $H \geq H^*$. However, the effect is relatively small except for larger values of H, such as $H = 120$ months.

The fourth relationship examined in Table 1 concerns the effect of m, the number of months which have passed since the original mortgage was taken out. In Section IV we vary m/n_1, where n_1 is the initial maturity of the original mortgage. As m increases the original mortgage balance is dropping, but the transactions costs of refinancing do not drop by the same percentage due to the fixed component of those costs. In Section IV of Table 1 we observe NPV falling and H^* rising as m increases. At the lower values of m, changes in NPV and H^* are relatively small as m increases because of the relatively smaller decline in the original mortgage balance. As that balance drops more rapidly with larger m, NPV and H^* change more rapidly. As our example shows, however, refinancing may be worthwhile even if considerable time has elapsed since the original mortgage was obtained. After 21 years (252 months) a positive NPV was still feasible.

VIII. CONCLUSION

The principal objective of this paper was to present a model for analyzing the home mortgage refinancing decision updated to include 1986 tax regulations. All equations in the model can be incorporated into an interactive computer program for answering a variety of questions related to home mortgage refinancing. The program developed in our study was written in BASIC, but other computer programming languages could also have been used. With the BASIC program we then conducted a sensitivity analysis to illustrate the impact of changing several key variables. Clearly, the computer-based model can be used to perform a series of sensitivity analyses to examine other issues associated with home mortgage refinancing.

REFERENCES

Brigham, E. F., and Gapenski, L., *Financial Management: Theory and Practice* (Fort Worth, Texas: The Dryden Press, 1994), pp. 922–925.

Gitman, L. and Joehnk, M., *Fundamentals of Investing* (New York, New York: HarperCollins, 1996), p. 346.

Harris, R., "Refunding of Discounted Debt: An Adjusted Net Present Value Analysis," *Financial Management* (Winter 1980), Vol. 9, No. 4, pp. 7–12.

Kilotay, A., "On the Structure and Valuation of Bond Refundings," *Financial Management* (Spring 1982), Vol. 11, No. 1, pp. 41–42.

Offer, A. and Taggart, R., "Bond Refunding: A Clarifying Analysis," *Journal of Finance* (March 1977), pp. 21–30.

Sirmans, C. F., *Real Estate Finance* (New York, New York: McGraw-Hill, 1985).

14

THE IMPACT OF SFAS NO. 52
ON ANALYSTS' FORECAST ERRORS:
AN EMPIRICAL ANALYSIS

Augustine Arize
Texas A&M State University–Commerce
Gordian A. Ndubizu
Drexel University

I. INTRODUCTION

Statement of Financial Accounting Standard (SFAS) No. 52 required multinational corporations to exclude foreign currency translation gains/losses from the reported earnings, leading to decreased earnings volatility; Collin and Salatka (1993) and Griffin (1993). Such reduction in volatility is expected to improve analysts' forecast accuracy. The results of the current study are consistent with this expectation. Both the volatility of foreign currency translation gains/losses and analysts' forecast errors decreased after SFAS No. 52 was implemented. It appears that SFAS No. 52 helps achieve an important financial reporting objective: prediction of corporate performance.

Statement of Financial Accounting Standard (SFAS) No. 8 required multinational corporations (MNCs) to include foreign currency translation gains and losses in their reported earnings, leading to increased earnings volatility. Managers of these MNCs undertook costly hedging activities to overcome this adverse effect on earnings. They also pressured the Financial Accounting Standard Boards (FASB) to revise the accounting practice for foreign currency translation gains/losses.

In 1981 the FASB changed the accounting practices for foreign currency translation and eliminated the pressure on managers to hedge foreign currency translation gains/losses. This change to SFAS No. 52 is a movement from a volatile earnings to a less volatile earnings information environment. Volatility increases the uncertainty about future earnings, which in turn makes earnings prediction more difficult. SFAS No. 52 is expected to reduce earnings volatility and maximizes analysts' forecast accuracy.

Many studies have attempted to explain the impact of SFAS No. 52 on analysts' forecast accuracy, and have provided evidence on the statement's information content. Griffin and Castanias (1987) questioned analysts regarding their forecast revision behavior in response to SFAS No. 52, concluding that analysts revised their forecasts following the issuance and implementation of SFAS No. 52. Jaggi and Chhatwal (1990) find no significant difference in accuracy or variability of analysts' forecasts between the pre- and post-adoption periods of SFAS No. 52. These studies produced mixed results; depending on formulation of the analysis, they either demonstrate or dismiss a link between analysts' forecast accuracy and SFAS No. 52. Given these mixed results, an empirical assessment of the impact of SFAS No. 52 on analysts' forecast errors is warranted.

This study examines the impact of SFAS No. 52 on the accuracy of analysts' forecasts. The results show that analysts' forecast errors decrease significantly after the implementation of SFAS No. 52. Further analysis confirmed that earnings volatility decreases after the issuance of SFAS No. 52 as predicted. These results appear to suggest that SFAS No. 52 reduces earnings volatility, which in turn decreases analysts' forecast errors. The weight of foreign currency translation gains/losses volatility in explaining analysts' forecast errors is determined through cross-sectional regression analysis of the sample. The results of the cross-sectional analysis are consistent with the hypothesis that SFAS No. 52 improves analysts' forecast accuracy.

II. HYPOTHESIS

This study assumes that SFAS No. 52 reduced the volatility of foreign currency translation gains/losses included in the reported earnings, leading to decreased earnings volatility. Evidence from analyzing the pre- and post-SFAS No. 52 foreign currency translation gains/losses (FCT) supports our prediction. Specifically, the variability of FCT decreases from 7.97 in the pre-SFAS No. 52 to 3.36 in the post-period. This reduction in volatility is statistically significant at the 1% level ($Z = 4.69$).

To corroborate further the premise that SFAS No. 52 reduces

volatility, the controllers of the sampled firms were surveyed. The results reported in Appendix A, Table A.1, indicate that the exclusion of foreign currency translation gains/losses (*FCT*) from reported earnings as required in SFAS No. 52 reduces earnings volatility.

Assuming that SFAS No. 52 reduces earnings volatility and that such reduction improves analysts' forecast accuracy, the following hypothesis is formulated: H1: Analysts' forecast errors decrease after the implementation of SFAS No. 52.

III. METHODOLOGY

(A) Data and Sample

The primary data base consisted of 489 firms that disclosed quarterly foreign currency translation gains/losses included in net income on the Compustat Commercial quarterly tape. The existence of foreign currency translation data provides initial evidence of multinational activity for the sample firms. From this data base the sample was selected using the following criteria:

1. Quarterly net income, foreign currency translation gains/losses and net sales available on the quarterly Compustat tape or Compustat Commercial tape from 1976 to 1986.
2. Number of foreign countries in which each firm operates obtained from the Directory of American Firms Operating in Foreign Countries. This variable was used as a substitute measure of size. The result of this measure is consistent with net sales.
3. Quarterly security analysts' earnings-per-share predictions from the Value Line Investment Survey (VLIS) from 1976 to 1986. The VLIS forecasts are widely used by investors and researchers, see Brown (1983) and Jaggi (1978).

These selection criteria reduce the initial sample to 73 firms, mostly because of missing values on quarterly foreign currency translation gains/losses. Two-digit industry distributions of the sample are reported in Table 1, Panel A. Descriptive statistics on size (total assets), earnings per share (EPS), dividend per share (DPS), leverage (LEV) and dollar value of common stock per dollar of book assets (MVA) appear in Panel B of Table 1. These tables show that the pre- and post- SFAS No. 52 periods have roughly similar descriptive statistics and financial characteristics.

Evidence has shown that firm size is positively related to the amount of information, Atiase (1985) and Holthausen and Verrecchia (1988). Firms of similar size are expected to have roughly the same information environments. It appears from the descriptive evidence that the sample firms have roughly the same information environments in the pre- and post- SFAS No. 52 periods (size and MVA). The descriptive statistics also show equivalent production (EPS) and financing (leverage) environments in the test periods. Thus, an observed association between forecast errors and translation adjustments cannot be attributed to differences in information, production and financing environments.

Table 1

Descriptive Statistics and Sample
Industry Membership

Panel A: Total Sample (N = 73)

SIC	NO.	SIC	NO.	SIC	NO.	SIC	NO.	SIC	NO.
10	2	23	1	30	2	36	4	44	1
13	1	26	2	32	2	37	5	61	1
20	2	27	2	33	2	38	4	63	1
21	1	28	17	34	4	39	1	73	2
22	1	29	2	5	11	42	1	75	1

Panel B: Descriptive Statistics

Variable	1979	1980	1981	1982	1983
SIZE	2087	3655	2566	2705	2675
EPS	3.53	3.37	3.60	3.29	1.18
DPS	1.08	0.89	1.32	1.22	1.20
LEV	0.19	0.11	0.18	0.18	0.18
MVA	0.57	0.45	0.69	0.56	0.59

The Descriptive data were collected from the 1989 Compustat Industrial tape. The variables are defined as follows: SIZE = Total assets (item no. 6); EPS = Earnings per share (item no. 18 divided by item no. 25); DPS = Dividend per share (item no. 21 divided by item no. 25); LEV = Long term debt/total assets (item no. 9 divided by item no. 6); and MVA = Total market value of common stock/total assets (item no. 24 multiplied by item no. 25 divided by item no. 6).

(B) Cross-Sectional Models

A regression model was formulated to examine jointly the effect of foreign currency translation gains/losses (FCT) on analysts' forecast error in the pre- and post-SFAS No. 52 periods. The two periods are compared using a binary variable technique developed in Gujarati (1970). Using one single equation, the Gujarati approach allows the effect of FCT on analysts' forecast errors to be compared for the pre- and post-periods. The joint comparison maximizes the degree of freedom and thus provides a more powerful test statistic. This advantage is important because of the limited sample observations used in this study.[1]

For each firm, the dependent (e.g., forecast error–FAF) and independent (e.g., FCT) variables were separately computed for each period. The relationship between FAF and FCT in the pre- and post-SFAS No. 52 periods is compared using the Gujarati techniques. This technique fits the pre- and post-SFAS No. 52 observations together and estimates the following regression:

$$FAF_{ij} = a + bFCT_{ij} + zD_{ij} + eFCT_{ij}*D_{ij} + dSIZE_{ij} + U_{ij}. \quad (1)$$

For $i = 1, \ldots\ldots, n$, and where:

$$FAF_{ij} = \sum_{t=1}^{T} |\frac{A_t - P_t|A_{t-1}}{A_t}|.$$

Further, FAF_{ij} = analysts' forecast error metric for each firm at j period; A_t = actual quarterly earnings per share for each firm at time t; $P_t|A_{t-1}$ = analysts' forecast of time t quarterly earnings per share, conditional upon knowledge of time $t - 1's$ quarterly EPS.

---

[1] The advantages of using the Gujarati approach as opposed to estimating two independent regressions are documented in Gujarati (1978) as follows:

    a. Run only a single regression because individual regressions can easily be deduced from it.

    b. The single regression can be used to test a variety of hypotheses. Thus, if the differential slope coefficient e (in equation (1)) is statistically significant, we may reject the hypothesis that the pre- and post-SFAS No. 52 periods' coefficients of FCA are identical. This also indicates a significant association between analysts' forecast errors and foreign currency adjustment volatility in the post-SFAS No. 52 period.

    c. Pooling the pre- and post-SFAS No. 52 observations increases the degree of freedom and hence improves the relative precision of the estimated parameters.

FAF is computed for each firm for period j, $j =$ pre- (1976–1980), and post- (1983–1986) SFAS No. 52 periods. 1981 and 1982 data were eliminated to make the sample comparable across time because of differences in the adoption date of SFAS No. 52; | | = absolute value operators; $FCT_{ij} =$ | Standard deviation of CA_t / Mean CA_t |, i. e., the foreign currency translation gains/losses volatility for each firm at j period; $CA_t =$ quarterly foreign currency translation gains/losses included in the reported earnings for each firm at time period t; $D_{ij} = 0$ for the period before SFAS No. 52 (1976–1980) and 1 for the period after SFAS No. 52, which was issued in December 1981 (1983–1986); $SIZE_{ij} =$ mean of net sales for each firm at time period j. The number of foreign countries in which each firm operates was used as a substitute measure of size and the results are consistent with net sales. $z =$ the differential intercept; $e =$ the differential slope coefficient, indicating by how much the slope coefficient of a pre-SFAS No. 52 function differs from the slope coefficient of a post function; $U_{ij} =$ a white-noise associated with the model term; $a =$ constant term; and $n =$ number of firms.

Assuming that the $E(U_i) = 0$, the results of estimating equation (1) were used to derive the pre- and post-SFAS No. 52 periods' model. Since $D = 0$ for the period before SFAS No. 52, the pre- and post-models are derived, respectively, from equation (1) as follows:

$$E(FAF_i | D_i = 0) = a + bFCT_i + dSIZE_i + U_{1_i}. \tag{2}$$

$$E(FAF_i | D_i = 1) = (a + z) + (b + e)FCT_i + dSIZE_i + U_{2i}. \tag{3}$$

Where the intercept terms for the pre- and post-models are respectively a and $(a + z)$. Similarly, the coefficients of foreign currency translation volatility (FCT) are b for the pre- and $(b + e)$ for the post-SFAS No. 52 period model.

To evaluate changes in FCT coefficients, two statistics are important. First is the sign of the coefficients of b and $(b+e)$. This statistic indicates the direction of the change in FCT coefficient after SFAS No. 52. Second, a significant coefficient of the multiplicative time dummy $(FCT * D$ in equation 1) suggests a statistically significant change in the FCT coefficient after SFAS No. 52. These two statistics should be considered jointly in evaluating the results of estimating equation (1).

(C) Model Specification

Some of the variables this study uses require additional discussion. Following O'Brien (1988) an unscaled forecast error metric ($A_t - P|A_t - 1$) was tried in addition to the scaled error metric specified above. Once heteroscedasticity is corrected, both methods give essentially the same result.

Because this study's purpose is to evaluate the association between forecast accuracy and foreign currency translation gains/losses, evidence that firm size affects analysts' forecast errors is taken into account. Brown et al. (1987), Atiase (1985) and Cox (1987) found that large firms generally have more information than small firms. The flow of more timely information about larger firms allows security analysts to form predisclosure expectations which better approximate the actual information. On the other hand, the larger a multinational firm, the more complex is its information-reporting environment. This complexity makes analysts' forecasts more difficult. Thus, analysts' forecast accuracy depends on information availability as well as reporting complexity.

For this reason, the Lagrange multiplier test, Engle (1984), was applied to determine whether size is an important explanatory variable in equation (2). The results of this test indicate that size is an important explanatory variable.[2] Thus, size was included in equation (1) to avoid model misspecification. A similar analysis was performed on the other descriptive variables. The result shows that the variables are not important factors.

---

[2] An important principle in model building is the principle of parsimony or Ockham's razor. This principle suggests that other factors being equal, a simple model should be preferred to a complex model because (a) simple models are usually easier to explain and interpret, and (b) the estimation of each unnecessary parameter will increase the variance of the prediction error by a factor of $1/n$. To check whether the size was an important factor, equation (1) (excluding size) was estimated and the residuals from this equation were then regressed upon the expanded set of regressors as follows:

$$U = a + bFCT + cD + eFCT*D + dSIZE.$$

The Lagrange multiplier statistic is $n(\bar{R}^2)$, where n = number of observations and $\bar{R}^2$ is the coefficient of determination from the residual regression. $n(\bar{R}^2)$ is distributed as a chi-square with one degree of freedom. The critical value of 3.84 is less than the calculated $n(\bar{R}^2)$ values of 15.3.

Equation (1) was estimated using the weighted least-square procedure because both the Goldfeld and Quandt (1972) and White (1980) tests suggest the presence of heteroscedastic error terms. Following Bahmani-Oskooee (1987), the White test was re-applied after correcting for heteroscedasticity. The result indicates that the corrected models are well specified.

In addition to this test, the RESET (Regression Specification Error Test) procedure originally suggested by Ramsey (1969) and extended by Thursby (1981, 1985) was applied.[3] The advantage of RESET is that omitted variables, incorrect functional form, and non-independence of regressors are checked. The results of the RESET show that the models employed in this study are correctly specified.

IV. RESULTS

Table 2 provides the univariate statistics on forecast errors and volatility of foreign currency translation gains/losses included in the income statements. As reported in Table 2, analysts' forecast errors (FAF) and foreign currency translation gains/losses volatility (FCT) decreased significantly after the implementation of SFAS No. 52. The FAF is 0.6388 in the pre-SFAS No. 52 period and decreased to

Table 2

Univariate Results on Forecast Errors
in the Pre- and Post-SFAS No. 52

Variable	Pre-SFAS No. 52 (1976–1980)		Post-SFAS No. 52 (1983–1986)		Mann-Whitney 2-Sample Test	
	Mean	St. Dev.	Mean	St. Dev.	Z-Value	Prob.
FAF	0.6388	0.5857	0.4544	0.5367	-2.48	0.013***
FCT	7.9734	14.7509	3.3614	8.6178	-4.69	0.000***

*** Significant at the 1% level; Prob. refers to a one-tailed probability. The variables are defined as follows: FAF = Analysts' Forecast Errors and FCT = Foreign currency translation gains/losses volatility.

---

[3] See Ndubizu et al. (1989) for detailed discussion of the Regression Specification Error Test (RESET).

0.4544 in the post-period. This decrease in FAF is statistically significant at the 1% level. The Mann-Whitney 2-Sample Test has a Z-value of -2.48. Thus, the results support the hypothesis that SFAS No. 52 reduces analysts' forecast errors because of lower volatility associated with foreign currency translation gains/losses.

For additional insight into the impact of SFAS No. 52 on analysis' forecast accuracy, the general cross-sectional regression (equation 1) was fitted on the sample firms. Table 3 provides estimates of equation (1). The results show that the observed analysts' forecast errors are significantly related to the volatility of foreign currency translation gains/losses (FCT). However, the association between FAF and FCT differs in the pre- and post-SFAS No. 52 periods.

In the earlier period, FCT is positively associated with FAF. This implies that the volatility of foreign currency translation gains/losses increases analysts' forecast errors during SFAS No. 8. The results for the later period are distinctly different. The coefficient of FCT has a negative sign, indicating that the foreign currency translation volatility reduces analysts' forecast errors. Apparently, the reduction in FCT during SFAS No. 52 improved analysts' forecast accuracy. Thus, the results are quite consistent with the hypothesis that SFAS No. 52 reduces volatility, which in turn improves analysts' ability to forecast earnings per share.

Table 3
Cross-Sectional Results of the Impact of Foreign Currency Translation Gains/Losses on Analysts' Forecast Errors

General Model	Intercept	FCT	D	FCT*D	SIZE	$\bar{R}^2$
B-value	0.627	0.064	-0.224	-0.065	0.0003	0.40
t-ratio	(0.57)	(3.42)***	(-0.14)	(-3.31)***	(7.11)***	
Pre-Model						
B-value	0.627	0.064	—	—	0.0003	
Post-Model						
B-value	0.40	-0.001	—	—	0.0003	

***Significant at the 1% level. The pre- and post-SFAS No. 52 models were derived from the general model given in equation (1).

V. CONCLUSION

This study examines the impact of SFAS No. 52 on analysts' forecast accuracy. The results are consistent with the hypothesis that SFAS No. 52 reduces the volatility of foreign currency translation gains/losses included in income, which improves analysts' forecast accuracy. Both the analysts' forecast errors and the volatility of foreign currency translation gains/losses decrease after the implementation of SFAS No. 52.

The cross-sectional regression analysis shows distinctly different results for the pre- and post-SFAS No. 52 periods. For the later period, foreign currency translation volatility is negatively associated with analysts' forecast errors. This result indicates that the reduced foreign currency translation volatility appears to improve analysts' forecast accuracy. On the other hand, a positive coefficient of foreign currency translation volatility was observed in the pre-SFAS No. 52 period. Such results suggest that foreign currency translation volatility impedes analysts' forecast accuracy during SFAS No. 8. Thus the change to SFAS No. 52 is synonymous to a movement from a coarser to a finer information environment.

REFERENCES

Atiase, R., "Predisclosure Information, Firm Capitalization, and Security Price Behavior Around Earnings Announcements," *Journal of Accounting Research* (Spring 1985), pp. 21–36.

Bahmani-Oskooee, M., "Demand for International Reserves: Corrections for Serial Correlation and Heteroscedasticity," *Applied Economics* (1987), pp. 609–618.

Brown, L., "Accounting Changes and the Accuracy of Analysts' Earnings Forecasts," *Journal of Accounting Research* (Autumn 1983), pp. 432–443.

Brown, L., Richardson, G., and Schwager, S., "An Information Interpretation of Financial Analyst Superiority in Forecasting Earnings," *Journal of Accounting Research* (Spring 1987), Vol. 25, No. 1, pp. 49–67.

Collins, D. W. and Salatka, W., "Noisy Accounting Earnings Signals and Earnings Response Coefficients: The Case of Foreign Currency Accounting," *Contemporary Accounting Research* (Fall 1993), pp. 119–159.

Cox, T., "Earnings Variability, Firm Size, and the Information Content in Management Forecasts of Annual Earnings," *Journal of Accounting and Public Policy* (1987), pp. 139–153.

Engle, Robert F., "Wald, Likelihood Ratio and Lagrange Multiplier Tests in Econometrics," chapter 13 in *Handbook of Econometrics, Volume 2*, Z. Griliches and M. D. Intriligator, editors (Amsterdam, Holland: North Holland, 1983).

Goldfeld, S. M. and Quandt, R. E., *Nonlinear Methods in Econometrics*, (Amsterdam, Holland: North-Holland Publishing Co., 1972).

Griffin, P., "Discussion of Noisy Accounting Signals and Earnings of Response Coefficients: The Case of Foreign Currency Accounting," *Contemporary Accounting Research* (Fall 1993), pp. 167–169.

Griffin, P. and Castanias II, R., *Accounting for the Translation of Foreign Currencies: The Effects of Statement 52 on Equity Analysts* (Stanford, Connecticut: FASB, 1987).

Gujarati, D., "Use of Dummy Variables in Testing for Equality Between Sets of Coefficients in Linear Regressions: A Generalization," *The American Statistician* (December 1970), Vol. 24, No. 5, pp. 18–21.

Gujarati, D., *Basic Econometrics* (New York, New York: McGraw-Hill Book Company, 1978).

Jaggi, B., "Comparative Accuracy of Managements' Annual Earnings Forecasts," *Financial Management* (Winter 1978), Vol. 7, No. 4, pp. 24–32.

Jaggi, B. and Chhatwal, G., "Impact of SFAS No. 52 on the Accuracy of Analysts' Earnings Forecasts," *Advances in International Accounting* (1990), Vol. 3, pp. 139–154.

Holthausen R. and Verrecchia, R., "The Effect of Sequential Information Releases on the Variance of Price Changes in an Intertemporal Multi-Asset Market," *Journal of Accounting Research* (Spring 1988), Vol. 26, pp. 82–106.

Ndubizu, G., Arize, A., and Chandy, P. R., "The Market Model Specification and the Structural Stability of the Beta," *The International Journal of Finance* (1989), Vol. 2, pp. 1–14.

O'Brien, P., "Analysts' Forecasts as Earnings Expectations," *Journal of Accounting and Economics* (1988), pp. 53–83.

Ramsey, J. B., "The Test for Specification Errors in Classical Linear Least Squares Regression Analysis," *Journal of the Royal Statistical*

Society (1968 Ser. B), Vol. 31 (1969), pp. 350–371.

Thursby, J. G., "A Test for Strategy for Discriminating Between Autocorrelation and Misspecification in Regression Analysis," *Review of Economics and Statistics* (1981), Vol. 63, pp. 117–123.

Thursby, J. G., "The Relationship Among the Specification Tests of Hausman, Ramsey, and Chow," *Journal of American Statistical Association* (December 1985), Vol. 80, pp. 926–928.

White, H., "A Heteroscedasticity-Consistent Covariance Matrix Estimator and a Direct Test for Heteroscedasticity," *Econometrica* (1980), Vol. 48, No. 4, pp. 817–838.

APPENDIX A

Table A.1
SFAS NO. 52 and Management Flexibility:
Some Real World Evidence

NO.	Questions from Questionnaire	Percentage of Responses	
		YES	**NO**
A3	Did FASB No.52 reduce earnings volatility from your company?	63%*	37%
B1	Based on your practical, knowledge of FASB No.52 could firm use functional currency choice as a mechanism to reduce earnings volatility (manage earnings)?	63%*	37%
B2	Could the exclusion of translation adjustments from income statements (in some cases) reduce earnings volatility?	88%**	12%
B3	FASB No. 52 requires certain transaction adjustments to be excluded from income statements. Given this new requirement, could firm reduce earnings volatility through foreign currency translations?	88%**	12%
B4	Could firms reduce earnings volatility by properly maintaining dollar-denominated balances in foreign operations with a local functional currency?	63%*	37%
B5	Could firms change functional currency because of major changes in international business environment (e.g., exchange rates change)?	50%*	50%*

A first draft of the questionnaire was reviewed with a faculty member experienced in questionnaires to reduce the likelihood managers would misunderstand the questions. Then a revised draft was completed by the Controller or Vice President of Finance from the sample firms. Since no question was raised by the respondent, the questionnaire was mailed to Controllers or Vice President of Finance from the remaining thirty-five firms. A response rate of nineteen percent is achieved.

*Percentage above 50. **Percentage above 70.

Table A.2
Questionnaire Cover Letter

March 12, 1990

Mr.

Dear Mr.

I wrote to you five years ago when I was completing my doctoral dissertation regarding the effect of FASB No. 52–Foreign Currency Translation–on earnings volatility. Your company responded. Your responses and time are greatly appreciated.

To accurately analyze the data collected, your company has been selected from the respondent firms to provide some practical insight on the effect of FASB No. 52 on earnings volatility. A copy of the results of the study will be provided to you. Individual responses will be considered confidential, only the aggregate results will be made public.

Please have the appropriate person in your organization complete the enclosed questionnaire and mail it in the self-addressed stamped envelope provided. It should take only a few minutes to complete. Your cooperation and participation is needed, and will be appreciated greatly. Please return the questionnaire by April 30, 1990.

Sincerely yours,

Table A.3

Effect of FASB No. 52–Foreign Currency
Translation–on Earnings Volatility

(Please circle the most correct answer.)

A.

1. How did FASB No. 52 affect your company's earnings?
   1. Increase　　**2. Decrease**　　**3. No effect**

2. How did FASB No. 52 affect your company's earnings volatility?
   1. Increase　　**2. Decrease**　　**3. No effect**

3. Did FASB No. 52 reduce earnings volatility for your company?
   1. Yes　　**2. No**

4. Based on your practical knowledge of FASB No. 52, do you expect FASB No. 52 to reduce earnings volatility?
   1. Yes　　**2. No**

5. Please describe how firm could use FASB No. 52 to reduce earnings volatility:

B.

1. Based on your practical knowledge of FASB No. 52, could firm use functional currency choice as a mechanism to reduce earnings volatility (manage earnings)?
   1. Yes　　**2. No**

2. Could the exclusion of translation adjustments from income statements (in some cases) reduce earnings volatility?
   1. Yes　　**2. No**

3. FASB No. 52 requires certain transaction adjustments to be excluded from income statements. Given this new requirement, could firm reduce earnings volatility through foreign currency translations?
   1. Yes　　**2. No**

4. Could firms reduce earnings volatility by properly maintaining dollar denominated balances in foreign operations with a local functional currency?
   1. Yes　　**2. No**

5. Could firms change functional currency because of major changes in international business environment (e.g., exchange rates change)?
   1. Yes　　**2. No**

6. If a foreign operation with local functional currency has dollar-denominated balances, FASB No. 52 requires that the amount be remeasured in local functional currency, and resulting translation adjustment reported in functional currency income statement. However, translating local financial statements into U.S. dollars requires reporting the resulting adjustments in stockholders' equity, bypassing the income statement. Could firms use dollar-denominated balances to reduce earnings volatility?
   1. Yes　　**2. No**

15

ECONOMIC DETERMINANTS OF JUVENILE CRIME: A CASE STUDY OF NEW YORK CITY

Farahmand Rezvani
Montclair State University

Theologos Homer Bonitsis
New Jersey Institute of Technology

David T. Geithman
New Jersey Institute of Technology.

I. INTRODUCTION

An economic analysis of the causes of property crime begins with the basic idea that illegal or criminal behavior is a purposeful way in which individuals respond to their perceptions of economic opportunities. Thus, following Becker (1968, p. 176), we argue that at least some individuals engage in crime "not because their basic motivation differs from that of other persons, but because their benefits and costs differ." The analytical framework employs the theory of traditional household choice, which rests on the principle of constrained utility maximization and implies rational behavior on the part of decision makers in response to perceived market incentives. In other words, some people engage in property crime because they have reason to expect that by doing so they can better their economic condition. Examples of this theoretical and conceptual framework is present in the research of Andreoni (1995), Block and Heineke (1973), Ehrlich (1970, 1973, 1974), Fleisher (1963, 1966a, 1966b), Sjoquist (1973), and Weicher (1970).

The economic approach, which explains property crime by offering theoretical foundations for its existence based on individual rationality, can be contrasted both with a tradition in criminology which often sees crime as the product of an abnormal and irrational criminal mentality, e.g., Meyer (1968); and with a broad sociological perspective which tends to interpret crime as reflecting "the character of the entire society," Clark (1970, p. 17). The economic approach, however, has been most rigorously formulated and has developed and tested statistical models to analyze relationships between property crime and other explanatory variables. Perhaps the most serious criticism of the economic approach, and the underlying theory of household choice, in identifying the causes of property crime is that, although in principle it allows for both economic and noneconomic considerations, the theoretical structure thus far developed inadequately deals with noneconomic affairs, especially as these affect the origins of tastes and preferences entering the utility function, Bennett (1994).

We attempt to remedy, in part, the narrowness of the economic approach by incorporating into our model a new time allocation variable as a relevant factor for explaining juvenile property crime. Given a fixed total amount of time available, an individual must allocate time among those various activities that consume time. Previous economic models of crime have specified three time-consuming activities: time allocated to consumption; to legal market work; and to illegitimate or criminal activities. To these three we add a fourth time-consuming variable: time spent by the individual in schooling activities.

Moreover, Phillips et al. (1972, p. 491) conclude, based on nationwide arrest data, that property crime is "predominantly an urban, youthful male phenomenon." Accordingly, an empirical model of property crime determinants is developed and estimated for male offenders aged 16–19 years in New York City. The data span an eleven year period (1970–1980) and refer to four principle types of juvenile property crime: robbery, burglary, larceny, and motor vehicle theft.

II. THEORETICAL CONSIDERATIONS

The following analysis is restricted to property crime, thus concentrating on what Stigler denotes as "production offenses," Block and Heineke (1973, p. 315). Specifically, we consider a utility maximizing individual who is confronted with two types of income generating activities–one legitimate, the other illegitimate:

$$E(U) = (1 - p)U_1(Y_1, t_c) + pU_2(Y_2, t_c), \qquad (1)$$

where p is the probability of being arrested for a criminal offense,

Y_1 and Y_2 are the income levels of an individual when not arrested and when arrested, respectively, and t_c is a fixed amount of time allocated to consumption activity. Denoting T as the total amount of time available to an individual, and recalling that consumption time is fixed, then the remaining amount of time available for either work, t_w, or schooling, t_s, is also fixed and given as:

$$T - t_c = t_w + t_s = t_l + t_i + t_s, \tag{2}$$

where time spent at work may take the form of legal market work, t_l, or illegitimate activities, t_i . Assuming that wage rates for legal market work, W_l, and for illegitimate activities, W_i, are stable, then the individual's income levels when not arrested and when arrested, respectively, are:

$$Y_1 = W_l t_l + W_i t_i + R(t_s) \tag{3}$$

and

$$Y_2 = Y_1 - F = W_l t_l + W_i t_i - F + R(t_s), \tag{4}$$

where F is the capitalized value of punishment and R the capitalized value of the net return to schooling.

The individual maximizes his or her expected utility as given by equation (1) subject to the income constraints as related by equations (3) and (4). The resulting first-order conditions of this optimizing behavior are:[1]

$$-\frac{W_l - W_i}{W_l - W_i - f} = \frac{p \frac{\partial U}{\partial Y_2}}{(1-p)\frac{\partial U}{\partial Y_1}}, \tag{5}$$

where $f = \frac{\partial F}{\partial t_i}$ and $(W_i - W_l) \le f$, and:[2]

$$r = W_l, \tag{6}$$

---

[1] See Appendix A for a more complete formulation of this optimizing behavior.
[2] One of the assumptions of this analysis is that the second derivative of the capitalized value of punishment with respect to t_i, F'', is positive. In other words, the capitalized value of punishment increases at an increasing rate. The rationale for such an assumption is that, as an individual becomes involved in criminal activities, the probability of getting involved in more serious crime rises. For example, an individual might start his criminal activities with grand larceny and as time passes become involved with more serious crime like burglary or robbery.

where $r = \frac{\partial S}{\partial t_s}$, or the marginal return from time spent in schooling. The left-hand side of equation (5) gives the slope of the "opportunity boundary," or the rate one is able (or believes one is able) to substitute income from legitimate activities for income from illegitimate activities; whereas the right-hand side of this equation gives the slope of the individual's indifference curve, or the rate one desires to substitute income from legitimate activities for income from illegitimate activities. Similarly, equation (6) states the equilibrium value for time spent in schooling, r.

The above first-order conditions imply that the appropriate specification for an individual's crime rate equation is:

$$lnO = \alpha_0 + \alpha_1 lnW_i + \alpha_2 lnW_l + \alpha_3 lnf + \alpha_4 lnp + \alpha_5 lnr + \eta_1, \quad (7)$$

where O is the individual's crime rate per unit of time. It is expected that the coefficient of the variables for the wage rate from legitimate activities, α_2; the capitalized value of punishment, α_3; the probability of being arrested, α_4; and the marginal return from time spent in schooling, α_5, would all have negative signs; that is, an increase in the value of each variable would decrease the crime rate, other things equal. On the other hand, the expected sign of the coefficient of the variable for the wage rate from illegitimate activities, α_1, is positive; that is, an increase in the value of this wage rate would increase the crime rate, ceteris paribus.

Similarly, assuming time spent in schooling is a log linear function of the marginal return from time spent in schooling, r $(= w_l)$, we obtain the appropriate specification for an individual's equation for total schooling time:

$$lnS = \beta_0 + \beta_1 lnW_l + \beta_2 lnr + \eta_2. \quad (8)$$

The expected signs of the coefficients of the variables for the wage rate from legitimate activities, β_1, and the marginal return from time spent in schooling, β_2, are both positive; that is, an increase in the value of either variable would increase the individual's total time spent in schooling.

Solving equation (8) for r results in:

$$lnr = -\gamma_2 + \gamma_1 lnS - \gamma_3 lnW_l - \gamma_1 \eta_2, \quad (9)$$

where $\gamma_1 = \beta_2^{-1}$, $\gamma_2 = \beta_0\beta_2^{-1}$, and $\gamma_3 = \beta_1\beta_2^{-1}$. Substituting equation (9) into equation (7) yields:

$$lnO = \alpha_0 + \alpha_1 lnW_i + \alpha_2 lnW_l + \alpha_3 lnf + \alpha_4 lnp + \alpha_5\gamma_1 lnS$$

$$-\alpha_5\gamma_3 lnW_l - \alpha_5\gamma_1\eta_2\eta_1. \tag{10}$$

Since, a priori, $\alpha_5 < 0$ and $\gamma_1 > 0$, time spent in schooling would be negatively related to the individual's crime rate, as already stated. Moreover, lnS is positively related to η_2 because $\beta_2 > 0$; by implication, the $Cov(lnS, -\alpha_5\gamma_1\eta_2 + \eta_1) > 0$.[3] Therefore,

$$\beta^* = \beta + Cov(lnS, -\alpha_5\gamma_1\eta_2 + \eta_1). \tag{11}$$

β^* is the empirical estimate of the partial elasticity of the crime rate with respect to time spent in schooling, S, and β is the true partial elasticity of S. Unfortunately, with $\beta < 0$ and a positive covariance of S and the error term, simultaneous equation bias can be introduced that biases the impact of S towards zero. The important point for empirical testing is that the simultaneous equation bias can result in a statistically insignificant partial elasticity for the time spent in schooling variable when, in actual fact, the value of the parameter may be statistically significant; moreover, the simultaneous equation bias can result in an empirically incorrect sign for S.

---

[3] Proof: Letting $A = -\alpha_5\gamma_1$, which has a positive sign, then:

$$Cov(lnS, A\eta_2 + \eta_1) = E(lnS - \widehat{lnS})[(A\eta_2 + \eta_1) - (\widehat{A\eta_2 + \eta_1})].$$

$$= E[lnS(A\eta_2 + \eta_1) - lnS(\widehat{A\eta_2 + \eta_1})$$

$$-\widehat{lnS}(A\eta_2 + \eta_1) + \widehat{lnS}(\widehat{A\eta_2 + \eta_1})].$$

$$= E[lnS(A\eta_2 + \eta_1) - lnS(0) - \widehat{lnS}(A\eta_2 + \eta_1) + \widehat{lnS}(0)].$$

$$= ElnS(A\eta_2 + \eta_1) - \widehat{lnS}E(A\eta_2 + \eta_1).$$

$$= ElnS(A\eta_2 + \eta_1).$$

Since $E(lnS, \eta_1) = 0$, it follows that $E[lnS(A\eta_2 + \eta_1)] = AE(lnS, \eta_2)$. Further, since both A and $E(lnS, \eta_2)$ are positive, $Cov(lnS, A\eta_2 + \eta_1) > 0$. Parameters with wide-hats imply mean values.

III. AN EMPIRICAL MODEL OF CRIME DETERMINATION WITH SCHOOLING

The main question this paper addresses is the degree to which juvenile property crime is linked to various economic and socioeconomic circumstances and opportunities that systematically affect the potential costs and benefits of criminal behavior.

To obtain an empirical analog of the preceding theoretical model, we assume identical individuals so that, except for scale, the individual and aggregate crime functions will be the same. Therefore, the per capita number of crimes, or crime rate (O/N) is assumed to be a multiplicative function of the probability of being arrested (A/O), the wage rate from illegitimate economic activities (W_i), the wage rate from legitimate economic activities (W_l), time spent in schooling (S), and a vector of other economic and socioeconomic variables (B), viz.:

$$O/N = B^{\beta_0}(A/O)^{\beta_1} W_i^{\beta_2} W_l^{\beta_3} S^{\beta_4}. \tag{12}$$

Unfortunately, simple reported crime data are highly unreliable. Webber (1991) points out then New York City Police Commissioner Lee Brown argued that Uniform Crime Reports primarily measure the degree to which people in a city respect their police and criminal justice system rather than the actual degree of occurrence of crime. When more people believe that it matters if they actually report the commission of crimes, more crimes are reported, and vice versa (p. 125).

Even more troublesome for conducting an empirical analysis of crime determinants is the fact that with simple reported crime data, i.e., crimes reported to police, the ages and economic and socioeconomic characteristics of the criminals are unknown. Only after an arrest is made are the individual characteristics (including age) of the alleged criminals revealed. Therefore, age specific analysis of crime determinants requires that the crime rate equation be respecified as an arrest rate equation.[4] This respecification can be accomplished

---

[4] Actually, individual characteristics of alleged criminals could be gained from either arrest data or court data, which also are available (and which were used by Fleisher as a part of his analysis). Arrest data, however, are probably superior to court data because of such problems as plea bargaining in the disposition of crimes in the judicial system. According to a study of New York City by the Vera Institute of Criminal Justice (1977), few alleged offenders who reach court are

by multiplying both sides of the crime rate equation by A/O, with the result:

$$A/N = B^{\beta_0}(A/O)^{1+\beta_1}W_i^{\beta_2}W_l^{\beta_3}S^{\beta_4}. \tag{13}$$

In terms of the coefficients of the variables, the only difference between equation (12) and equation (13) occurs in the elasticity of A/O, the probability of being arrested. Theoretical considerations suggest a negative sign for the elasticity of A/O in the crime rate equation (i.e., as the probability of being arrested increases, other things equal, the crime rate would decrease); but the sign of the elasticity of A/O in the arrest rate equation is ambiguous.[5]

This section presents and discusses ordinary least-squares estimates of an empirical model of crime in New York City committed by 16–19 year old males for the period 1970 to 1980. The dependent variables are arrest rates for four different types of property crime: robbery, burglary, larceny, and motor vehicle theft. The study employs pooled cross sectional-time series data for the five boroughs of New York City (Bronx, Brooklyn, Manhattan, Queens, and Staten Island), resulting in 55 observations (5 times 11 years).[6] The arrest rate data were collected from unpublished records at New York City Police Headquarters prepared by the New York City Police Department for the Federal Bureau of Investigation's Uniform Crime Report.

Six hypotheses regarding the relationship between arrests and economic/socioeconomic characteristics are tested. The hypotheses,

---

prosecuted for their actual crime. In a sample of 369 felonies in New York City in 1973, for example, for robbery 30 percent of the defendants were immediately dismissed and, of the remaining defendants, all but two were allowed to plead guilty to reduced charges; for burglary 25 percent were dismissed and, of the remaining defendants, 94 percent had their charges reduced to misdemeanors or less. Thus, court records drastically under-report actual crime, which would lead to biased statistical results if the under-reporting is correlated with any of the explanatory variables in the analysis.

[5] Specifically, if the absolute value of β_1 (in the crime rate equation) were less than unity, then $1 + \beta_1$ (in the arrest rate equation) would be positive; but if the absolute value of β_1 were greater than unity, then $1 + \beta_1$ would be negative.

[6] Using cross sectional-time series data increases the number of observations over the alternative of using time series data only. Moreover, since cross sectional data for different years are pooled, this procedure incorporates variations in independent variables among the boroughs at a moment in time as well as over time. Thus, we mitigate the possibility of multicollinearity in the sample data that frequently arise in using only time series data, Jacobowitz et al. (1981).

briefly stated, are: (1) A higher civilian unemployment rate lowers the opportunity cost of criminal behavior. Thus, the unemployment rate will be positively associated with the arrest rate. (2) The level of real per capita income measures potential criminal earnings, or the wage rate from illegitimate activities. With the unemployment rate held constant in the analysis, a rise in real per capita income reflects an increase in the income of potential victims, the "swag effect," which increases the incentive for criminal activity. Thus, a positive relationship between the level of real per capita income and the arrest rate is expected. (3) The per capita level of Aid to Families of Dependent Children (AFDC) acts as a proxy for potential legitimate earnings, or the wage rate from legitimate activities. With the level of per capita income held constant in the analysis, a rise in AFDC payments increases the costs of criminal activity. Thus, a negative association between the per capita level of AFDC payments and the arrest rate is predicted. (4) A sociological variable, the divorce rate, is introduced as a proxy for lack of family structure and reduced parental supervision. A positive relationship between the divorce rate and the arrest rate is expected. (5) A demographic variable for race, the number of blacks per 10,000 of population, also is included. With black unemployment rates above white unemployment rates, a higher percentage of blacks per 10,000 of population will be associated with higher arrest rates because the opportunity cost for criminal behavior is less.[7] (6) The average daily school attendance rate serves as a proxy for time spent in schooling. A negative association between school attendance and the arrest rate is expected because more time spent in schooling raises the opportunity cost of criminal behavior, ceteris paribus.

---

[7] Census data analyzed by Danziger and Gottschalk (1987) for the same decade as the one covered by this study reveal several trends that support the particular hypotheses presented here. Specifically, the spatial concentration of the urban poor increased over this decade, especially for blacks. In the fifty largest U.S. cities Danziger and Gottschalk (1987, p. 214) state "the proportion of the urban poor living in poverty areas increased from 26.3 to 35.8 percent for blacks and from 8.0 to 13.7 percent for non-blacks."

The analysis of data produced by Danziger and Gottschalk is intended to support and amplify several hypotheses advanced by Wilson (1985, 1986). Wilson argues that the increased male earnings inequality, the reduced male labor force participation rates, and desegregation, which has enabled middle-income blacks to move out of segregated inner-city neighborhoods, are all contributory factors to the development of an "underclass" of black urban poor.

Unfortunately, the form in which the arrest rate equation is specified prevents testing for the expected inverse relationship between the probability of being arrested and the arrest rate. As noted above, in the crime rate equation if the absolute value of β_1 is less than unity, then in the arrest rate equation $1 + \beta_1$, the predicted sign of the coefficient for the probability of being arrested, would be positive; but if the absolute value of β_1 is greater than unity, then $1 + \beta_1$ would be negative. Thus, in the arrest rate equation the sign of the coefficient for the probability of being arrested is ambiguous.

The ordinary least squares double log estimations of the arrest rate functions are specified as follows:

$$AR_{ij} = \alpha_0 + \alpha_1 PROAR_{ij} + \alpha_2 TOTUN_i + \alpha_3 REALIN_i + \alpha_4 ASSISR_i$$

$$+\alpha_5 DIVRTE_i + \alpha_6 BLKR_i + \alpha_7 ATTENR_i + \alpha_8 TIME_i$$

$$+\alpha_9 D2 + \alpha_{10} D3 + \alpha_{11} D4 + \alpha_{12} D5 + \eta_{ij}. \qquad (14)$$

Where AR_{ij} = the number of arrests of males aged 16–19 per 10,000 population in the ith year for the jth type of crime; $PROAR_{ij}$ = the number of arrests per 10,000 complaints in the ith year for the jth type of crime; $TOTUN_i$ = the civilian unemployment rate for all ages in the ith year; $REALIN_i$ = the level of per capita income in the ith year; $ASSISR_i$ = the per capita level of Aid to Families with Dependent Children in the ith year; $DIVRTE_i$ = the number of divorces per 10,000 population in ith year; $BLKR_i$ = the number of blacks per 10,000 population in the ith year; $ATTENR_i$ = the average daily school attendance rate per 10,000 students registered in the ith year; $TIME_i$ = a time trend variable; $D2$ = a dummy variable indicating one for Brooklyn, zero otherwise; $D3$ = a dummy variable indicating one for Manhattan, zero otherwise; $D4$ = a dummy variable indicating one for Queens, zero otherwise; $D5$ = a dummy variable indicating one for Staten Island, zero otherwise; η_{ij} = normally, independently distributed stochastic disturbances; $\alpha_0, ..., \alpha_{12}$ are regression parameters; and where $i = 1, ..., 11$ and $j = 1, ..., 4$.

Appendix B indicates the various sources used for each of the variables in the study. Note that all variables are expressed in log forms except the dummy variables ($D2, D3, D4, D5$) used to differentiate the intercepts of the five boroughs of New York City and the time trend

243

variable $(TIME)$.[8] The time trend variable is used to eliminate possible systematic effects of other unmeasured variables on arrest rates over time (for example, increased police efficiency in making arrests per 10,000 reported crimes).

Estimated arrest rate functions for males 16–19 years of age in New York City for four types of property crime between 1970 and 1980 are shown in Table 1. Column (1) refers to robbery arrests, (2) to burglary arrests, (3) to larceny arrests, and (4) to motor vehicle theft arrests. In the equations where autocorrelation in the residuals was detected by the Durbin–Watson statistic, the parameters were re-estimated using the Cochrane–Orcutt technique. Finally, since all of the equations are estimated in the log linear form, the estimated coefficients represent the elasticities of the response of arrest rates to percentage changes in each of the independent variables, ceteris paribus.

The coefficients of multiple determination (R^2's) for the four arrest rate functions range from 0.62 to 0.87, with the larceny and robbery functions having the best fit and the motor vehicle theft function the least best fit. Thus, the empirical model captures from slightly less than two-thirds to more than four-fifths of the variation in New York City arrest rates for the eleven-year span of this study.

The specific empirical results can be briefly summarized as follows:

A major finding of this study is the consistent and highly statistically significant positive relationship between arrest rates and levels of real per capita income. The level of per capita income is used as a proxy for potential illegitimate earnings, or the wage rate from criminal activities; in other words, it measures the incentive for crime in terms of the incomes of the potential victims. The study shows that, with the unemployment rate and other variables held constant, increases in the level of real per capita income of the general population significantly increase juvenile arrest rates for all four types of crime.

---

[8] Because the present study performs pooled cross sectional time series analysis, the homogeneity of the data in terms of intercepts is questionable. In order to test the homogeneity of the data sample, regressions were run both without using dummy variables (i.e., under the assumption that all boroughs had the same intercepts) and with dummy variables for the different boroughs. The resulting F-values of the analysis of variance indicate that the intercepts of the five boroughs differ, and therefore the use of dummy variables is indicated for.

The second major finding of this study pertains to the probability of being arrested, with a hypothesized negative relationship between

Table 1
Estimated New York City Arrest Functions:
Males 16–19 Years Old

	ARR (1)	ARB (2)	ARL (3)	ARMV (4)
PROAR	-.30	.04	.31	.09
	(.8)	(.1)	(1.3)	(.4)
TOTUN	.24	.35	.17	-.09
	(.8)	(1.1)	(.4)	(.3)
ASSISR	.03	-.007	.02	-.01
	(.8)	(.1)	(.4)	(.2)
REALIN	3.70	4.50	5.00	4.00
	(3.3)*	(4.1)*	(3.4)*	(3.5)*
DIVRTE	-.55	-.65	-.89	-.10
	(.6)	(.8)	(.8)	(.1)
BLKR	.09	.43	-.74	.25
	(.1)	(.5)	(.7)	(.3)
ATTENR	3.10	3.10	4.50	3.20
	(1.5)	(1.6)	(1.5)	(1.5)
TIME	.19	.20	.37	.13
	(2.0)**	(2.2)**	(3.0)*	(1.3)
D2	.55	.47	1.00	.46
	(.8)	(.7)	(1.2)	(.6)
D3	.46	-.54	.87	-.21
	(.3)	(.3)	(.4)	(.1)
D4	-1.00	-1.00	-1.10	-.51
	(1.1)	(1.1)	(1.0)	(.6)
D5	-1.30	-.62	2.50	-.47
	(.9)	(.4)	(1.4)	(.3)
C	-52.70	-63.00	-74.00	-60.20
	(2.2)**	(2.8)*	(2.6)**	(2.5)**
R^2	.85	.75	.87	.62
$D - W$	2.00	2.00	1.89	.94
$F(12, 42)$	20.40	10.60	23.70	5.80

*Significant at 1% level.

**Significant at 5% level.

Absolute values of t–statistics are in parenthesis.

this probability and the crime and arrest rates. As we have seen, in the arrest rate function the sign of the coefficient or the elasticity of the probability of being arrested is ambiguous; therefore, the hypothesis cannot be tested using the arrest rate function. However, in the crime rate function the elasticity of the probability of being arrested is unambiguously negative, which permits testing the hypothesis. From the elasticity of the probability of being arrested as estimated in the arrest rate function $(1 + \beta_1)$, we derive the elasticity of the probability of being arrested in the crime rate function (letting $1 + \beta_1 = \beta^*$, then $\beta_1 = \beta^* - 1$). The results, shown in Table 2, reveal a consistent and highly statistically significant negative relationship between crime rates and the probability of being arrested for all four types of crimes considered here. These elasticities (computed at the means of the arrest probabilities and crime rates) often are quite substantial. They indicate, for example, that a 10 percent increase in the probability of being arrested for robbery would reduce the robbery rate by 13 percent; and that a 9.6 percent reduction in the burglary rate could be expected from a 10 percent increase in the probability of being arrested for burglary. Thus, the deterrent effect of an increased likelihood of punishment appears to be beyond reasonable doubt.[9]

Table 2

Elasticities of the Probability of Being Arrested: For Males 16-19 Years Old

Type of Crime	Elasticity	Absolute Value of t-statistic
Robbery	-1.30	3.6*
Burglary	-0.96	2.9*
Larceny	-0.69	3.0*
Motor Vehicle Theft	-0.91	4.3*

*Significant at 1% level.

[9] The strong deterrent effect found here between lower crime rates and higher arrest rates dovetails with earlier research by Ehrlich (1973) that shows a strong deterrent effect between lower crime rates and higher *criminal penalties*. However, more recent research by Andreoni (1995) undoes part of Ehrlich's deterrent effect by showing that increased criminal penalties also exert a significant negative effect on the probability of *conviction*. Thus, while higher criminal penalties *ceteris paribus* exert a deterrent effect on crime rates, the total effect of higher penalties is approximately zero when factoring in the reduced probability of conviction (pp. 479–481).

With regard to the association between arrest rates and the other independent variables in this study, the t-statistics generally lack statistical significance, probably due to the presence of multicollinearity and simultaneous equation bias. Although pooling of data in cross sectional-time series analysis as performed here can increase the degrees of freedom, it also may introduce multicollinearity into the sample data, particularly due to the inclusion of dummy variables differentiating the intercepts of the five boroughs.[10] Therefore, interpreting the partial effects of the individual variables on arrest rates is difficult, i.e., an insignificant t-statistic may not be sufficient to conclude that a particular variable is, in reality, unimportant in determining arrest rates.

The empirical results for the other independent variables are: (1) Although the t-statistics are not significant, increased unemployment seems to lead to more arrests for robbery, burglary, and larceny, but not for motor vehicle theft. Thus, the idea that unemployment lowers the opportunity cost of crime receives only modest empirical support.[11] Nonetheless, aggregate data of the type used here

---

[10] Indeed, the simple correlation matrix for the independent variables employed in this study indicates very high simple correlations between some of the dummy variables and other independent variables. $D3$, for example, has a simple correlation of 0.83 with $REALIN$ and also -0.83 with $ATTENR$. Other examples are -0.86 between $REALIN$ and $ATTENR$, 0.80 between $DIVRTE$ and $TOTUN$, and 0.61 between $TOTUN$ and $BLKR$. This evidence suggests that the problem of multicollinearity may be present.

To further explore the possibility of multicollinearity the statistically insignificant $DIVRTE$, $BLKR$ and $ATTENR$ variables were dropped and new regressions run without these variables. TIME gained even more statistical significance and, with only four exceptions, all the dummy variables differentiating the intercepts of the boroughs became statistically significant at the 1 percent level. The R^2's remained virtually unchanged. These results also suggest the existence of multicollinearity, meaning that $DIVRTE$, $BLKR$, $ATTENR$ and $TIME$ are so interrelated with the borough dummy variables that their statistical significance to arrest rates cannot be determined. The simple correlation matrix is available upon request from the authors.

[11] Unfortunately, the civilian unemployment rate used in this study is not age-specific because unemployment data for 16 to 19 years old individuals in New York City by borough are unavailable. Fluctuations in the overall civilian unemployment rate may largely fail to capture the effects of fluctuations in the teenage unemployment rate, which can run several times higher than the adult unemployment rate. Even if age-specific unemployment rates were available, however, the information would reflect neither the teenagers who have dropped out of the labor force due to discouragement nor the factor of job quality. The latter is an important consideration particularly for teenage unemployment because so many teenagers experience low quality jobs characterized by a high degree of

are perhaps less appropriate than individual or case study data for uncovering the true connection between crime and unemployment.[12] (2) The per capita level of AFDC payments, as a proxy for potential legitimate earnings, is expected to be negatively related to the arrest rate because higher AFDC payments increase the opportunity cost of criminal activity. This expectation receives some empirical support for burglary and motor vehicle arrests, but not for robbery and larceny arrests. None of the t-statistics are significant. (3) The number of blacks per 10,000 of population is hypothesized to be positively associated with arrest rates because blacks have lower average incomes (a greater incentive for crime) and higher unemployment rates (lower opportunity cost for crime). This hypothesis is empirically supported for robbery, burglary, and motor vehicle theft arrests, but not for larceny arrests. However, all relevant t-statistics are insignificant.[13] (4) A positive association between the divorce rate and arrest rates is expected, but the regressions reveal a negative (but not statistically significant) relationship. Finally, (5) a negative relationship is anticipated between the daily school attendance rate and arrest rates due to higher opportunity costs of crime, but the regressions show a positive (but not statistically significant) association. In the preceding theoretical discussion the likelihood of simultaneous equation bias for the time spent in schooling variable was discussed. In that discussion we noted that simultaneous equation bias could

---

employment insecurity, Rees (1986).

[12] Indeed, as Sviridoff and Thompson (1979) and Petersilla et al. (1972) suggest, the nature of this relationship may really depends on the type of crime, the type of individual, and the type of legitimate employment held by the potential criminal. Some criminals alternate between holding legitimate jobs and crime. Others blend the holdings of legitimate jobs and criminal activity. Still others require a legitimate job in order to commit crime, e.g., white-collar crime and employee theft. Finally, some criminals are committed solely to a life of crime. Those individuals in the first category can be expected to react strongly and positively to a rise in the unemployment rate. For those persons in the second and third groups, unemployment actually makes criminal activity more difficult; and for those individuals in the last group (committed criminals) the unemployment rate is virtually irrelevant to their behavior.

Rubinstein (1992) is also highly dubious about the crime-unemployment nexus, but his arguments against a positive relationship are based on much more aggregative data than hat used in the present study, namely national unemployment and crime rates.

[13] It is possible that the t-statistics lack significance because the effects of higher black unemployment rates are picked-up directly by the $TOTUN$ variables.

result in both an empirically measured lack of statistical significance and an empirically measured "wrong" sign for the coefficients of the variables even though, in fact, the values of the parameters may be statistically significant and of the "correct" sign.

IV. SUMMARY

Employing the theory of household choice we have postulated a constrained utility maximization model to explain juvenile property crime in which an individual allocates time among consumption, legal and illegal work activities, and schooling. Since property crime is, to a high degree, a youthful, urban male phenomenon, we develop and test an empirical model on a sample composed of all males aged 16–19 years arrested in New York City for robbery, burglary, larceny and motor vehicle theft between 1970 and 1980.

The empirical results lend support to the basic hypothesis that property crime is a rational way individuals respond to their perceptions of the costs and benefits of criminal behavior. We find high coefficients of multiple determination for all four arrest rate functions. The strongest statistical relationships pertain to the level of real per capita income in the community at large (a proxy for potential earnings from illegitimate activities, the incentive effect–a benefit); and to the probability of being arrested for committing one of the four crimes (the deterrent effect–a cost). Both increases in the level of community real per capita income and decreases in the probability of being arrested result in increases in the number of reported crimes.

Unfortunately, in other regards the empirical findings of this study suffer from the presence of multicollinearity and simultaneous equation bias. The results achieved thus far suggest the need for further work with more sophisticated data prior to the formulation of much-needed public policy reforms in the area of crime prevention and control.

REFERENCES

Andreoni, James, "Criminal Deterrence in the Reduced Form: A New Perspective on Ehrlich's Seminal Study," *Economic Inquiry* (July 1995), Vol. 33, pp. 476–483.

Becker, Gary S., "Crime and Punishment: An Economic Approach,"

Journal of Political Economy (March/April 1968), Vol. 76, No. 2, pp. 169–217.

Bennett, Amanda, "Economists Demonstrate That Neighbors, Not Wardens, Hold Keys to Cutting Crime," *The Wall Street Journal* (December 7, 1994), pp. B1.

Block, M.K. and Heineke, J. M., "A Labor Theoretic Analysis of the Criminal Choice," *American Economic Review* (June 1975), Vol. 65, No. 3, pp. 314–325.

Clark, Ramsey, *Crime in America: Observations on its Nature, Causes, Prevention and Control* (New York, New York: Simon and Schuster, 1970).

Danziger, S. and Gottschalk, P., "Earnings Inequality, the Spatial Concentration of Poverty, and the Underclass," *American Economic Review* (May 1987), Vol. 77, No. 2, pp. 211–215.

Ehrlich, Isaac, *Participation in Illegitimate Activities: An Economic Analysis*, Ph.D. thesis, Columbia University (1970).

Ehrlich, Isaac, "Participation in Illegitimate Activities: A Theoretical and Empirical Investigation," *Journal of Political Economy* (Many/June 1973), Vol. 81, No. 3, pp. 521–64.

Ehrlich, Isaac, "Participation in Illegitimate Activities: An Economic Analysis," in *Essays in the Economics of Crime and Punishment*, W. M. Landes and G. S. Becker, editors (New York, New York: Columbia University, 1974), pp. 68–134.

Fleisher, Belton, "The Effect of Unemployment on Juvenile Delinquency," *Journal of Political Economy* (December 1963), Vol. 71, No. 6, pp. 543–555.

Fleisher, Belton, "The Effect of Income on Delinquency," *American Economic Review* (March 1966a), Vol. 56, pp. 118–137.

Fleisher, Belton, *The Economics of Delinquency* (Chicago, Illinois: Quadrangle Books, 1966b).

Jacobowitz, S., et al., "Variation in Infant Mortality Rates Among Counties of the United States The Roles of Public Policies and Programs," *Demography* (November 1981), Vol. 18, No. 4, pp. 695–713.

Meyer, Joel, "Criminology and Police Science," *Journal of Criminal Law* (1968), Vol. 58.

Petersilla, J., et al., *Criminal Careers of Habitual Felons* (Santa Monica, California: The Rand Corporation, 1972).

Phillips, L., Votey Jr., H. L., and Maxwell, D., "Crime, Youth, and the Labor Market," *Journal of Political Economy* (May/June 1972), Vol. 80, No. 3, Part 1, pp. 491–504.

Rees, A., "An Essay on Youth Joblessness," *Journal of Economic Literature* (June 1986), Vol. 24, No. 2, pp. 613–628.

Rubinstein, David, "Don't Blame Crime on Joblessness," *The Wall Street Journal* (November 9, 1992), p. A10.

Sjoquist, D. L., "Property Crime and Economic Behavior Some Empirical Results," *American Economic Review* (June 1973), Vol. 63, No. 3, pp. 439–446.

Sviridoff, M. and Thompson, J. W., *Linkages Between Employment and Crime A Qualitative Study of Rikers Releases*, Working Paper (New York, New York: Vera Institute of Criminal Justice, 1979.)

Vera Institute of Criminal Justice, *Felony Arrests Their Prosecution and Disposition in New York City's Courts* (New York, New York: Vera Institute of Criminal Justice, 1977).

Webber, Alan M, "Crime and Management An Interview with New York City Police Commissioner Lee P. Brown," *Harvard Business Review* (May/June 1991), Vol. 69, pp. 111–126.

Weicher, J.C., "The Effect of Income on Delinquency Comment," *American Economic Review* (March 1970), Vol. 60, No. 1, pp. 249–256.

Wilson, William J., "Cycles of Deprivation and the Underclass Debate," *Social Science Review* (December 1985), Vol. 59, pp. 541–559.

Wilson, William J. "Social Policy and Minority Groups," Institute for Research on Poverty Conference Paper, University of Wisconsin at Madison (1986).

APPENDIX A

Extending the earlier analysis developed by Ehrlich (1973) by explicitly incorporating time for schooling as a relevant variable in juvenile crime determination, the individual maximizes an expected utility function given by:

$$E(U) = (1 - p)U_1(Y_1, t_c) + pU_2(Y_2, t_c), \qquad (A-1)$$

with respect to two income constraints:

$$Y_1 = W_l t_l + W_i t_i + R(t_s). \qquad (A-2)$$

$$Y_2 = W_l t_l + W_i t_i - F + R(t_s). \qquad (A-3)$$

251

Substituting equations (A-2) and (A-3) into (A-1) yields:

$$E(U) = (1 - p)U_1[W_l t_l + W_i t_i + R(t_s), t_c] \\ + pU_2[W_l t_l + W_i t_i - f + R(t_s), t_c]. \qquad (A-4)$$

To obtain the first-order conditions of individual utility maximization, we differentiate equation (A-4) with respect to time devoted to illegitimate activities and time devoted to schooling:

$$\frac{\partial E(U)}{\partial t_i} = (1 - p)U_1'(W_i - W_l) + pU_2'(W_i - f - W_l) = 0 \qquad (A-5)$$

and

$$\frac{\partial E(U)}{\partial t_s} = (1 - p)U_1'(r - W_l) + pU_2'(r - W_l) = 0 \qquad (A-6)$$

Where: $U_1' = \frac{\partial E(U)}{\partial Y_1}$ and $U_2' = \frac{\partial E(U)}{\partial Y_2}$.

From equations (A-5) and (A-6) we obtain the first-order conditions for utility maximization:

$$-\frac{W_l - W_i}{W_l - W_i - f} = \frac{pU_2'}{(1 - p)U_1'}, \qquad (A-7)$$

and

$$r = W_l \qquad (A-8)$$

Equation (A-8) gives the equilibrium value for time devoted to schooling, i.e., an individual would pursue schooling activities until the return on an additional unit of schooling time, r, equals the wage rate in legitimate market activities. However, the marginal return to schooling time is not only effected by time devoted to schooling but also by time devoted to illegitimate activities because the probability of carrying a criminal record will rise as illegitimate activities increase. Due to the employment impediments entailed by a criminal record, as the probability of carrying a criminal record increases the expectation of employment in legitimate activities declines, which, in turn, implies a lower marginal return to schooling time function.

APPENDIX B

AR:

New York City Police Department Headquarters, unpublished arrest records prepared for Federal Bureau of Investigation Uniform Crime Report.

TOTUN:

U.S. Department of Labor, unpublished data, and *Employment Review*, July 1976. Due to lack of data for teenage unemployment, the total civilian unemployment rate was used as a proxy for teenage unemployment.

REALIN:

City and County Data Book, 1977. Data for the years 1978 to 1980 were unavailable; therefore, real per capita income for these years was projected based on the trend of real per capita income.

ASSISR:

New York State, Department of Social Services, Monthly Reports.

DIVRTE:

U.S. Department of Health, Education and Welfare, Vital Statistics.

BLKR:

U.S. Bureau of the Census, Population Census of 1970 and 1980. The number of blacks in the population for the years between 1970 and 1980 are estimated based on census data for 1970 and 1980.

ATTENR:

New York State, Statistical Yearbook 1979/80.

For Product Safety Concerns and Information please contact our EU
representative GPSR@taylorandfrancis.com Taylor & Francis Verlag GmbH,
Kaufingerstraße 24, 80331 München, Germany

Printed and bound by CPI Group (UK) Ltd, Croydon, CR0 4YY
08/05/2025
01864439-0001